N

Spires of Form

A STUDY OF EMERSON'S
AESTHETIC THEORY

Striving to be man, the worm
Mounts through all the spires of form.

Nature

Spires of Form

A STUDY OF EMERSON'S

AESTHETIC THEORY

By Vivian C. Hopkins

HARVARD UNIVERSITY PRESS · CAMBRIDGE

1951

For My Mother and Father

PREFACE

It is in the truest sense of Emersonian self-reliance that I wish to acknowledge the assistance I have received from various quarters in carrying on this study. A generous fellowship grant from the American Association of University Women gave me the opportunity to spend a sabbatical year, 1948–49, in study of the Emerson manuscripts. To my advisors in the English department of the University of Michigan, who offered critical and helpful advice in the early form of this book as a thesis submitted for the degree of Doctor of Philosophy, I am deeply indebted: Professors Clarence D. Thorpe, Warner G. Rice, Joe Lee Davis, Norman Nelson, and Mentor L. Williams. Professor Warner G. Rice of the Library at the University of Michigan, and Mr. Robert H. Haynes of the Harvard College Library have freely extended to me the use of their collections in American Literature. To Professor Howard Mumford Jones and Professor Perry Miller of Harvard University I owe sincere thanks for their criticism of this work and for suggestions concerning use of the manuscript materials. Mr. Edward W. Forbes has generously granted me the permission of the Ralph Waldo Emerson Memorial Association to make use of the Emerson manuscripts in the Houghton Library at Harvard University, and the books in the Emerson library at Concord. Mrs. Raymond Emerson has given me friendly encouragement. To the Ralph Waldo Emerson Memorial Association grateful appreciation is due for their material assistance in publication. Mr. William H. Jackson and Miss Caroline Jakeman have assisted me with many courtesies, over a period of years, in my work with the manu-

scripts in the Houghton Library. Mr. David McKibbin has
laid open for me the art collection and records of early art
exhibitions at the Boston Athenaeum. President Wilbur K.
Jordan and Dean Bernice Brown Cronkhite have extended to
me the hospitality of Radcliffe College during 1948–49. To
the Houghton Mifflin Company I owe permission to quote
from the Centenary edition of Emerson's *Works* and from his
Journals; to the Columbia University Press, permission to
quote from the *Letters* of Emerson edited by Professor Ralph
L. Rusk. Finally, to my brothers, my colleagues at the New
York State College for Teachers, and other friends, I acknowledge my debt for their kindness and unfailing inspiration.

State University of New York
New York State College for Teachers
Albany, New York
March 6, 1950

Contents

Spires of Form

The Background of Emerson's Aesthetic Theory

This study presents Emerson's aesthetic theory in a new synthesis. It seeks to analyze Emerson's ideas concerning literary and artistic production, and to relate these ideas to his own philosophical concepts as well as to similar views of his predecessors and contemporaries.

If Emerson himself, at the height of his powers and in the leisure of his voyage to England in 1847, had formulated his theory of art and literature, the result would have been invaluable. Had he composed such an essay, it might have lacked structure — "Who has not looked into a metaphysical book," he once asked, "and what sensible man has ever looked twice?" — but it would have possessed an inclusiveness which comments on his theory have not revealed. Scholarly analyses to date, chiefly concerned with evaluating Emerson as a critic or with defining his theory of poetry, have illuminated his aesthetic at some points, but have failed to present the whole picture of his theory of art and literature. It is my belief that Emerson's varied and provocative critical statements admit of a treatment broader in scope and more systematic in organization than they have yet received. New materials in the manuscript lectures and manuscript journals, and in Professor Ralph L. Rusk's admirable edition of the *Letters* (New York, 1939) widen the range of the critical comment which appears in the published work, while the notations made by Emerson in the volumes of his library point up his relation to other thinkers. These rich and suggestive statements reveal a surprisingly consistent aesthetic point of view.

Convinced that Emerson's aesthetic may best be considered in the same light as his observation of nature, as a *process*, with a vital impulse of its own, constantly renewed by fresh impulses of creative or receptive spirit, I propose to present Emerson's theory as a cycle of three phases, integrally connected with each other. The first phase is the creative process; the second, the completed work of art; the third, the reception of art by the observer. The interpretation of his critical theory as a cycle seems particularly fitting in view of his own hope that the "broken arcs" of his observations would be resolved by time into a complete circle.

Of these three phases, the first, represented by the creative process, has the prime importance of supplying the dynamism which sets the aesthetic cycle on its way, a power which Emerson interprets as kindred to God's. The work of art, though least necessary from the mystical point of view which dominates the whole process, brings Emerson's theory down to earth; and it is in speculation about the work of art that the unpublished materials show a variety and penetration not revealed by his statements in the published work alone. The third phase, aesthetic experience, which has been most neglected by Emerson's critics, provides an analysis of the psychological elements involved in enjoying art, which is unusual for Emerson's time.

This circular interpretation does not, however, indicate mere repetition, or a fruitless turning back of aesthetic enjoyment upon itself. From Plotinus Emerson derives the conception which governs his view of art as of nature, that spirit is energy projected from intellect, constantly flowing through matter and rendering it more alive; and implicit in this Plotinian idea of "the flowing" is the concept of upward ascension (later made explicit for Emerson by the evolutionary theory of natural science). Thus Emerson's own term of "the spiral" admirably hits the combination of circular movement with upward progress which is the heart of his aesthetic. Optimism controls Emerson's idea of the circle becoming a spiral, ever rising even as it revolves upon itself. Though Emerson's concept of a benevolent necessity gives little room for consideration of evil, we shall find that element more fully treated in his aesthetic than in his general philosophy.

The term "aesthetic" rather than "literary" is used, to embrace material on the fine arts as well as on literature. Since Emerson, even in recognizing differences between literature and the fine arts, traced them back to the same creative source, a study of his theory cannot maintain true balance unless both aesthetic and literary judgments are considered. Though he is a literary man rather than a critic of fine art, Emerson has made a number of provocative observations on painting, sculpture, and architecture. If his theory of aesthetic creation is drawn for the most part from the experience of writing poetry, his concept of organic form in art appears most clearly in what he says of architecture, and his ideas of aesthetic experience proceed from some awareness of all the arts. Although he resembles Mme. de Staël and the German romantics in tracing all the arts back to the same informing spirit, he yet discovers conditions prevailing in fine arts somewhat different from those in literature. Clearly Emerson's statements about the fine arts are too important to be ignored.

The prevailing view of early-twentieth-century critics, that Emerson had little to say about art, derives from a statement made by Henry James. Visiting the galleries of the

Louvre and the Vatican with Emerson in 1872, James, shocked
to discover that Emerson got very little from the great paintings, concluded that "there were certain chords in Emerson
that did not vibrate at all." [1] Failing to contrast this Emerson
of the "twilight phase" with the keenly observant Emerson
of the mature years, James was further unaware of Emerson's
essays on art and of the lectures concerning Italian art (1834)
and Greek art.[2] Other scholars, following James' lead, concluded that Emerson derived little enjoyment or understanding from the plastic arts.[3] The publication of the *Journals*
(1909–14), with their considerable body of comment on
Italian art as well as on American exhibitions, helped to place
Emerson's art criticism in proper perspective. It was not, however, until Régis Michaud wrote *L'Esthétique d'Emerson*
(Paris, 1927), that scholars actually realized the extent of
Emerson's statements about the fine arts. Though pretending
to little interpretation, Professor Michaud's book offered a
valuable summary of Emerson's statements concerning genius,
art, and the beautiful, rightly interpreted the mystical basis of
his aesthetic, and placed the fine arts along with literature in
his synthesis.

If twentieth-century readers had looked carefully at the
periodical criticism of Emerson's immediate successors in the
latter part of the nineteenth century, they would have found
frequent mention of his name and quotation from his works
in connection with sculpture, painting, and architecture. Although Ruskin had become the "grand old man" of art criticism in late-nineteenth-century America as in England, one
critic, tired of Ruskin's careful line-by-line elaboration of
landscapes, welcomed Emerson's ability to "flash scenes upon
the mind with a mere phrase." [4] The effect of Emerson's ideas
upon public architecture and the teaching of art is attested
by President Eliot of Harvard, who saw the direct inspira-

tion of Emerson's essay on "Art" in such diverse monuments as handsome high schools, the Columbia University Library, and the Harvard Stadium. Books on landscape architecture and principles of design, Eliot says, are "penetrated with Emerson's doctrine of art as teacher of mankind." If Eliot is over-enthusiastic in his claim for Emerson as the exclusive influence upon advances in art and architecture (he makes a similar expansive assertion that the thoughtful spirit of modern research fulfills the demand of *The American Scholar* for creative action), his praise is none the less sincere.[5] In the decades immediately after Emerson's death, he was cited as authority for the need of dignity and beauty in the useful arts, and for the greater importance in the fine arts of idea over technique. Even in music, the art with which Emerson was least well acquainted, his friend John S. Dwight eloquently attests his influence, in a chronicle of Boston's musical development from 1840 to 1870.[6]

These statements do not deny that Emerson's criticism of literature is deeper and more extensive than that of the fine arts, but they definitely show that what he says of art must be included in a true presentation of his aesthetic theory. Specific judgments on art and literature, however, will not be used in this study to evaluate Emerson as a critic, but rather to illuminate general theoretical tenets.

Since there is less change in the aesthetic than in the religious or political thought of Emerson, a chronological treatment of his aesthetic is not necessary. To study Emerson's critical statements from the chronological point of view is to follow a tortuous road which seems frequently to turn back upon itself; to analyze them as elements in an aesthetic process is to obtain an aerial perspective, which causes apparent contradictions to fall into place in a clear pattern. Where there is a significant chronological development, that fact will be indicated. For the most part, however, the core of Emerson's critical theory may be presented as well unified during his most productive years (1836–1856), while statements from earlier and later periods occasionally illuminate his aesthetic position.

Emerson's critical theory is firmly based upon his general philosophical ideas. Underlying his theory of art is his concept of nature, complex but admitting of analysis. His most inclusive term, employed in the essay *Nature*, is "the universe," which embraces natural objects, men's bodies, and men's souls. On occasion he speaks of nature as the world of phenomena — as leaves, flowers, and acorns — together with all other animals except man. It is this aspect of phenomenal nature, with emphasis on such small objects as snails and shells, to which he gives special value in his analysis of the poetic symbol. In an extended sense, he speaks of the "composition" of nature, to denote the unity of effect aroused in the observer by the horizon, the vault of night, or the rise of a mountain. When man gives unity to the varied objects caught up by his poetic imagination, he performs an act similar to the "composition" which he has observed in nature's landscapes. Emerson's special interest in the dynamic powers of the universe leads him to denote behind the flowing river, the surging tide, the floating cloud, a creative force which he terms Nature (upper case) as process and result, a mover similar to the Plastic Nature first defined by Aristotle and further explained by Plotinus as that deputy of the Divine which animates both the phenomenal and the human world (nature in lower case). If artistic creation gives the effect of flowing rather than freezing, of moving rather than standing still, it is proof that the artist has caught, not so much by imitation as by identity of inspiration, this energetic power which represents Nature's creative activity. In Emerson's view of the universe, furthermore, each individual man is subtly linked to the rest of human nature by the all-embracing spirit which is described in "The Over-soul" as "that unity within which every man's particular being is contained and made one with all other."

Through the concept of correspondence, which affirms that the phenomenal world and man's spirit are meant to be united, Emerson establishes the rationale of his aesthetic. Man reacts to the spirit which exists in phenomena, but he also infuses such objects as stars and stones with the subtle fluid of his own spiritual insight. Just as in the natural world Emerson takes the dualistic rather than the monistic position, recognizing the actuality of tree, flower, and bird, so in art does he admit the reality of the artifact.[7] But his fascination with the idealism expressed by Berkeley and the Hindu philosophers confirms his native disposition to place greater value upon spirit than upon matter. Stimulated by such thinkers as Oegger and Swedenborg, Emerson asserts the mutual dependence of matter and spirit: "I believe in the material world as the expression of the spiritual or the real." The importance of art in the universal scheme lies in its representation of the spirit perceived by man in the natural world. Aesthetic creation becomes man's means of showing his likeness to God. The interpenetration of the aesthetic and natural worlds appears in Emerson's dream of a future genius who would "carry art up into the kingdom of nature." If that is a dream, the fact still remains that man in his creation and enjoyment of art is making the nearest possible approximation to an ideal union of spirit with matter.

The "applied psychology" which shows Emerson's interest in the working of the human mind, published under the title "Natural History of Intellect," [8] has importance in relation to the creative and the receptive experience of art. Emerson's starting point was his reaction from the association theory of

Locke, which Coleridge criticized for giving only the *how* of mental operations, not the *what*. Despite his hostility to Locke, Emerson could not of course abandon altogether the important discoveries which Locke had made about psychology. As late as 1866, Emerson is grading men's memories by their "quality of association," placing a higher value on memory through cause and effect than on memory through accidental resemblances. The theory of association also formed the basis for Alison's critical theory and Blair's rhetoric, both of which remained as a background for Emerson's critical thinking even while he sought elsewhere for a more central explanation of art's meaning.

In Coleridge's analysis of mental processes, Emerson discovered the key to understanding the mind's action. "Coleridge alone," he said on one occasion, "has treated the mind well." Coleridge's analysis of creative power especially satisfied Emerson, because Coleridge considered the mind as a unit, not as an assortment of such faculties as sensation, judgment, memory, and will; and because he viewed the mind from within, analyzing its autonomous power, rather than considering it an instrument acted upon from without, as in the theory of association.

The Kantian distinction between Reason and Understanding, as Emerson found it in Coleridge [9] and Carlyle,[10] offered an explanation of that general division of powers corresponding to the philosophical distinction between spirit and matter: Reason, which deals with intelligibles, and Understanding, which controls the phenomena of sense perception. Though Emerson shows some grasp of the true Kantian distinction between the two faculties,[11] for the most part his use of the terms is to extol Reason as the immediate intuition of truth by a genius, above the journeyman Understanding which the genius shares with other men. On occasion Emerson speaks of

reason as sentiment, a vision which "simply perceives." [12]
Carlyle's definition of reason as direct intuition of truth, controlling both poetry and religion, Emerson found particularly
applicable to the world of aesthetic creation. On the assumption that the same mental power governs both aesthetic creation and religious experience, one can easily transfer intuitions
from one field to another. Thus Emerson asserts that the artist,
through Reason, attains direct contact with the Divine mind,
deriving his intuition for creation from a single illuminated
moment.

Both the concept of correspondence, which links the artist
with the natural world, and that of Reason, which justifies
the artist's creative power, are strongly rooted in mysticism.
It is, in fact, only by taking account of the strong mystical
cast of Emerson's thought that we can really understand
Emerson's aesthetic theory. Actually Emerson himself never
made sharp separation between his religious and his aesthetic
ideas. Stating his qualifications for the ministry at the age of
twenty-one, for example, he says nothing of saving others'
souls, but speaks of his strong imagination and his love for
poetry and eloquence. Later, as he moves away from religious
ritual, he applies the terms of the liturgy to poetry. Although
he objects to the "miracle" in religion, as implying a special
intervention of God whose every evidence is good, he "requires" the miracle of poetry. Nor does reluctance to ad-
minister the Lord's Supper prevent him from terming poetry's
deep insight "transubstantiation, the conversion of daily bread
into holiest symbols." In *The American Scholar* he describes
the creative process in terms redolent of the New Testament:
"It came into him life; it went out from him truth. It came
to him short-lived actions; it went out from him immortal
thoughts. . . . It was dead fact; now, it is quick thought.
It can stand, and it can go." [13]

Emerson's interchange of religious and aesthetic terms does not indicate that his aesthetic theory is to be interpreted through any single religious tradition. When he did long for a religion "of the people" which might nourish the cultural life of his time as Puritanism had sustained the thought of seventeenth-century England, he turned with nostalgia not to "the icehouse" of Unitarianism, but to the Calvinism of his own family background. Comparing Calvinism to a "Sabbath peace" in the New England countryside, he commends its stern virtues, its emphasis upon suffering and upon "the Spirit's holy errand" through the souls of men. Although he recognizes that the Copernican system has destroyed the Calvinistic assumption that "our little speck of an earth was the central point of nature," Emerson still wishes on occasion for the return to New England of that "dear ghost," with its "pervasive and controlling sentiment." Even after he has lost faith in the "legend" of Calvinism, he retains a respect for its moral sentiment and its metaphysics. When Emerson accepts the Plotinian theory of the immanence of Divine spirit in natural forms, his grasp of the Calvinistic concept of an omnipotent God saves him from an irresponsible pantheism. However vividly he perceives the Divine Spirit flowing through natural forms, he still maintains a firm notion of the *difference* between that spirit and the forms it penetrates. One might say that the system of Calvinism considered as a whole embodies the "instant dependence of form upon soul" which Emerson demands of poetry. In the religion of his aunt, Mary Moody Emerson, he finds the essence of Calvinism, with emphasis upon the same qualities of "the good, the beautiful, and the true" which make up the essential elements in his definition of poetry.

Had Emerson drawn only from the Calvinistic tradition, however, he would have found difficulty in justifying the importance which he assigned in the creative process to phenomena in nature. Assurance that the creative artist may discern spirit directly in the forms of nature he discovered in the thought of Plotinus. By stating that objects in nature do actually receive the impress of inflowing spirit, Plotinus indicates that the contemplative soul may discern spirit by means of natural objects, as well as through direct union with the Divine. In the importance given by Plotinus to the human soul, also, Emerson finds a different concept from the Calvinistic position, and one which is very important for his theory of creation. Instead of a poor worm before the footstool of the Maker, the intuitive spirit becomes an indispensable conveyor of spiritual energy. In Plotinus' theory, the human soul does not, as with Calvin, find itself fulfilled merely by "searching out the ways of God," but by sharing in the process of informing matter with spirit, through its own energetic activity. In "Poetry and Imagination" Emerson terms this creative dynamism "the habit of saliency," "a sort of importation or domestication of the *Divine* effort in a man." Without destroying his belief in the moral sentiment which he derived from Calvinism, then, the Plotinian system gave Emerson assurance that an immanent world spirit flows through nature's forms, and that the creative artist, by his interaction with that spirit, also contributes to spiritual energy in the world.

The mystical quality of Emerson's world view appears in his disposition to look at time and space *sub specie aeternitatis;* to consider earlier historical periods important only in their reinterpretation by the current age; to value the method of intuitive discovery of truth in a single moment by the power of Reason, above the slow methodical investigation of phenomena by the understanding; to consider the artifact as most significant not because of its material form, but through its revelation of spirit.

That the quality of Emerson's mysticism is intellectual rather than emotional scarcely needs assertion.[14] Unlike the visions of Plotinus, Emerson's intuitions of truth come by flashes rather than by extended trance. Nor does he, like Swedenborg, recount conversations with spirits of the departed dead. Emerson differs from Jacob Boehme, a mystic whose depth of faith he appreciated, in translating his perceptions of the other world into broadly human rather than theological terms. But these qualifications of Emerson's mysticism should not obscure the fact that for him the truths proclaimed to society must first be deduced from a perceptive solitude; that the valid illuminations are those received from a power outside himself, not those produced by the mind's conscious labor; and that, whatever the starting point of the soul's journey — be it a sight of Walden Pond, a statue of Michelangelo, or a verse of Homer — a conviction of truth, not to be shaken by any reasoning, characterizes the ultimate perception of the rapt intellect.

True appreciation of the mystical basis for Emerson's aesthetic will correct the overemphasis which has been placed upon his moralism, in which his Moral Law is read as the inflexible, uncompromising commandments of the Medes and Persians. Granting the importance of the moral element as the bedrock for his developing conceptions, reaching back to the Calvinism of his inheritance for a basis, one may perhaps readjust the emphasis by recalling that Emerson speaks more often of the "moral sentiment" than he does of the "moral Law." Clearly religion rather than moralism dominates Emerson's aesthetic. If the profession of faith with which he finally emerged was of a sort never before seen on sea or land, it represents always a deep religious consciousness, believing even in its moments of skepticism.

Santayana, the first systematic philosopher to take cognizance of Emerson's aesthetic, hits the right note when he terms Emerson "the Psyche of Puritanism," and his thought "a religion expressing itself as a philosophy," "veiled in various tints of poetry and science." [15] He thus recognizes the religious cast of Emerson's theory. Santayana has, however, oversimplified Emerson's view of nature, assuming that he passed at one leap from the gloom of Calvinism to the joyful atmosphere of Earth, the fruitful mother. By ignoring the Unitarianism which forms a bridge between Calvinism and Transcendentalism, and the doctrines of German idealism which gave intellectual substance to Emerson's aesthetic thought, Santayana denotes the subtly reflective Emerson as a happy, spontaneous child of Nature, thus giving encouragement to Irving Babbitt's emphasis upon the "Rousseauism" in Emerson.

In Irving Babbitt's "Conclusion" to *Modern French Criticism* occurs the first instance of the neohumanist attempt to grasp the Protean body of Emersonian thought, to hold fast that which fits the creed of absolute critical standards, morality in art and literature, and the norm of the "human" as opposed to the animal and the supernatural elements in man. In justice to Babbitt, one must recognize that he saw, as his followers have not always seen, the empirical element in Emerson's thought, even though he distrusted and sometimes misinterpreted that empiricism. Curiously, Babbitt finds in the last paragraph of the essay on "Illusions," one of Emerson's most mystical passages, some indication that the doctrine of relativity can be retained along with the search for absolute values. In so far as Emerson indicates this possibility, Babbitt finds that he can assist in establishing critical values that combine "masculine judgment" with feminine sympathy.[16] Certain elements close to the heart of Emerson's aesthetic have, however, either been ignored or twisted in Babbitt's interpretation. In the whole idea of "becoming," integral to Emerson's concept of spiral form, Babbitt could see nothing but disaster for critical insight. Babbitt's preoccupation with the "human" level of aesthetic production rendered him incapable of appreciating a critical theory like Emerson's, which places chief value upon transcendent qualities, but also takes account of hidden psychological depths in man's being. In discrediting, furthermore, the democratic emphasis of Emerson's critical thought, Babbitt was alienating himself from a tenet which lies at the heart of Emerson's confidence in art's value.

From H. L. Mencken's attack on Emerson as an arch-conservative and the epitome of that Puritanism which in Mencken's limited definition meant simply restriction of man's creative impulses,[17] it was the business of another great humanist of our time, Professor Norman Foerster, to rescue Emerson. Through his chapter on Emerson in *American Criticism* (Boston, 1928), Professor Foerster restored to better balance the critical scales which Mencken had tipped, and caused thoughtful Americans to appreciate Emerson's importance as a theorizer about art and literature. If Professor Foerster's study of Emerson, which touches his critical theory at all points except the aesthetic experience, seems less successful than that of some other figures treated in the book, the weakness lies in his ignoring certain important ideas in Emerson's theory in order to claim him for the neohumanist tradition.

A significant recent contribution to the study of Emerson's aesthetic thought is the section devoted to Emerson in the late Professor F. O. Matthiessen's *American Renaissance* (New York, 1941), a stimulating interpretation in which Emerson's affinity to Coleridge, his retention of some Calvinistic conceptions, and his deep interest in the art and literature of his time are sympathetically shown. Besides numerous scholarly studies which assist the understanding of Emerson's aesthetic by indicating the relation of his thought to other traditions,[18] the definitive biography of Emerson by Professor Ralph L. Rusk (New York, 1949) throws new light on Emerson's experience in art and literature, his personal friendship with other writers, and the general cast of his thought.

With due respect to previous scholarship, it is the purpose of this study to include a broader scope of Emerson's critical comment than has yet been presented, by drawing on the unpublished as well as the printed material, to organize Emerson's aesthetic ideas in a cycle of three phases which embodies his concept of "the spiral form," and to show the mystical element of his thought as the subtle link which binds all three phases into a harmonious whole.

Before considering the creative process, the first term in the creative cycle, we need to know something of the artistic genius. Some aspects of Emerson's concept of genius closely resemble the romantic idea as expressed by Coleridge and Wordsworth. Emerson thinks of the genius as a man of keener than ordinary vision, both physically and spiritually. He is a link between God and man; although a "geographer of the supersensible regions," he is yet no "air-fed, unimpassioned, impossible ghost." One might consider him a conductor between infinite Reason and the crowd of lesser men. His work is characterized by spontaneity, simplicity, and originality. Like Wordsworth, Emerson finds certain qualities of character necessary for the highest genius: love and courage. Although Emerson's idea of genius closely parallels that of romantic tradition, it is free from certain current views: he is impatient of such concepts as that of "the lonely genius," unhappily separated from his time by great gifts; or the ravening sensualist, who must run the whole gamut of experience before he can create; or the hypersensitive artist, who shrinks from the touch of ordinary persons. If on occasion Emerson shares Carlyle's admiration for pure daemonic power, as for example in Byron, he corrects this by his main emphasis on the high aspiration needed for the best creation. Furthermore, while Carlyle's concept of hero worship demands excessive humility in the common man, Emerson's attitude is democratic. Since even the greatest artist must dwindle by comparison with the world soul, the common man must retain a sense of proportion even in admiration. He must heed the advice of *The Divinity School Address*: "Thank God for these good men, but say, 'I also am a man.'"

With this brief introduction into the background of Emerson's aesthetic, we may proceed to the first phase of the aesthetic cycle, the process by which the artist "ultimates his thought in a thing."

CHAPTER I

The Creative Process

Theurgists . . . say, that there is a God, and deliver to us the discipline of it, by which we are enabled to excite it to become visible; and . . . also, they celebrate it as older and younger, and as a circularly revolving and eternal God, not only as the image of eternity, but as eternally receiving it . . . And besides this they assert, that it is infinite in power. For its circulation again and again is the province of infinite power. Together with these things likewise, they say that it is of spiral form.

Proclus.

INSPIRATION

Creative effort, Emerson affirms, begins with the inflow into the artist's mind of ideas from a source beyond himself. Creative inspiration is based on the fusion of the human soul with the Divine. In this assertion Emerson is at one with English romantics like Wordsworth, Coleridge, and Shelley, whose confidence in the divine afflatus as a source of poetry distinguishes them from such neoclassic theorists as Pope and Johnson. Emerson does not, however, look to his English contemporaries to confirm his view of inspiration, so much as to the Neo-Platonic writers, Plotinus, Proclus, and Iamblichus. The

divine visions of Socrates, Plotinus, and Porphyry are cited in
"The Over-soul" as genuine experiences. Like Coleridge,
Emerson finds in these writers corroboration of his own experience: that the soul's intuitions in an inspired state are inexplicable, but valid.[1] Thus in "The Over-soul" he borrows
Proclus' symbol of a man looking at his image in a river to
epitomize the soul watching the body, borne along the stream
of generation.[2] Emerson says:

> When I watch that flowing river, which, out of regions
> I see not, pours for a season its streams into me, I see that I
> am a pensioner; not a cause but a surprised spectator of this
> ethereal water; that I desire and look up and put myself in
> the attitude of reception, but from some alien energy the
> visions come.

Not only in valuing the ideas of an inspired soul, but in
trusting the validity of the poetic (or creative) mania, Neo-
Platonic thought provides a basis for Emerson's theory of inspiration. Citing the four manias of the *Timaeus*: the musical,
telestic, prophetic, and amatory, Proclus places the musical
(or poetic) mania below the telestic and prophetic, but finds
it effective in human discipline.[3] Emerson goes a step further
than Proclus, in ranking poetic enthusiasm equally with the
philosophic. *The Divinity School Address* and the essays on
"History" and "Inspiration" bear witness that the creative
artist as well as the philosopher derives his motive power from
mystical experience, from the "leaping-lightning" which the
"horse-power" of the understanding cannot measure.

Once the artist enters the "Holy ground" of oneness with
Spirit, Emerson asserts that he attains it without effort, much
as light enters the eye. In this uplifting experience, variously
termed trance, inspiration, enthusiasm, time and space fade
before the immediate awareness of soul, and the seer has a

sense of unlimited power. That this is only a foreshadowing of a future complete freedom of the body appears in Emerson's statement: "When we read true metaphysics, we shall jump out of our skin." [4] Of course the experience may occur in stronger or weaker solution; from a complete possession of soul by spirit, it may dwindle to a mere suggestion of emotion. In contrast to the long intervening stretches of dullness, even the bright illuminations occur for a brief time only. So intense an experience could not in fact continue long, lest the mind be blinded by excess of light. But while it lasts, Emerson says, "there is no miracle so stupendous as this moment's health, thought, apprehension." [5]

The precondition of entering this state is submission of the individual will. One who would tame the Holy Ghost must first put aside his individuality. To show how spirit overwhelms man's will, Emerson uses metaphors of elements possessing irresistible force: rivers, currents, and winds. Whether he is termed a "vascular organ," a channel, or a boat carried along by the stream, the artist must maintain passivity: watching, beholding, quietly waiting for Divine inflowing.

The need for individual submission, as Emerson interprets it, carries a religious emphasis that implies obedient trust in Divine power. Emerson's conviction of the necessity for the soul's submission springs from his own experience and is reinforced by his awareness, not only of Plotinian thought, but also of Calvinistic theory and Quaker discipline. Calvinistic speculation on the will, like other matters of religious doctrine, formed a haunting shadow in Emerson's youth behind the daylight Unitarianism of such enlightened ministers as his father, William Emerson. An early journal passage (1823) indicates that Emerson is investigating the problem of freedom of the will, and he mentions Jonathan Edwards' treatise, *Freedom of the Will*, as an authority for the conditioned will.[6] Edwards' speculation may well have assisted Emerson in shaping his theory of the submissive creative will. Considering the will not as an agent, but merely as an instrument, Edwards traces the human chain of action back to its first act, locating the original determining act of the will in God, who thus conditions — at least indirectly — every following act of human will.[7] Edwards also emphasizes the delightful sense of union with God which man experiences when his "supernatural sense" is opened so that he becomes possessed of grace, and enjoys "the gracious affections" — harmonious sensations of unity with God.[8] In this state his soul is so closely united with the Divine that he understands spiritual truths not merely with understanding, but with sympathy. Though Emerson makes use of the broader terms of mysticism rather than those of theology, his analysis of the will's submission, and the consequent delight of union between subject and object, bears marked similarity to that of Edwards. From the Quaker theory of mystical experience, which he liked to discuss with his Quaker friend Miss Rotch, Emerson absorbed the idea that the soul has no choice in its need to submit to Divine power. His favorite quotation from George Fox concerns submission: "Lie low in the Lord's power."

Since the mystical state of ecstasy denotes a union between the *subject* and the *object* of knowledge, as a theory of creation it emphasizes the *ease* by which the artist derives intuitions. Terming the subject "I," for example, and the object "the Abyss," he states that the number of steps may vary before the genius reaches the edge, but that the experience is always the same, once achieved. Wisdom, in this state, resembles electricity; men capable of wisdom can absorb it simply by being placed in the right conditions, as a conductor picks up an electric charge. Thus, in the essay "Inspiration," he says: "Knowledge runs to the man, and the man runs to knowledge." This emphasis upon ease of absorbing knowledge recalls Plotinus' assertion that *wisdom*, the knowledge acquired by illuminated souls through intuition, excels *reasoning*, the knowledge which ordinary men struggle to attain by ratiocination.[9]

To indicate inspiration's power, Emerson compares it to the magic which transforms a neuter of the hive into a queen bee. Thus he describes man's nearness to inspiration, his attainment of the state, and the moment's fast fading:

> We are always on the brink of an ocean into which we do not yet swim. . . But suddenly, in any place, in the street, in the chamber, will the heaven open, and the regions of wisdom be uncovered, as if to show how thin the veil, how null the circumstances. As quickly, a Lethean stream washes through us and bereaves us of ourselves. After exercising the powers of reflexion for fugitive moments, we move about without them, quite under their sphere, quite unclothed. (Ms. J. RO, 1835)[10]

The difficulty with this mystical theory of inspiration is that the artist is prevented by reverence for the Deity from complaining when intuitions fail to flow into his mind. Aware of this problem, Emerson denotes the term *instinct* as the special source of power for the arts and literature. Instinct differs from the Divine Spirit in serving the lower needs of the apparent world as well as the higher demands of the arts. In "Natural History of Intellect" he calls this power "a certain blind wisdom, a brain of the brain, a seminal brain." It bears some relationship to Proclus' notion of an essence between soul and corporeal powers, inferior to soul but superior to bodies, and containing a generating, vivifying principle.[11] The action of instinct, in Emerson's theory, is negative rather than positive; though not itself a light, it is the source of illumination for creative artists. Thus he speaks of instinct in taunting terms, as a "slumberous giant," a "drowsy genius," which man seeks to stimulate to speech by all the arts in his power.

The whole matter of instinct as a secondary source for creative power suggests that Emerson may have some more practical suggestions for stimulating thought, on a lower level than the watchful waiting which is the condition of high inspiration. And he does indeed offer hints from his own experience. Character is the first requisite, especially the traits of love and patience, which not only help the artist to wait for inspiration, but render him fit to express the intuitions when he receives them. Next comes the need for a "frolic health," whose value Emerson appreciated because he had experienced the sagging of the mind in time of illness. With character and health, the mind attains equilibrium.

Besides these basic elements, the writer may use more calculated methods of provoking inspiration. Books are exerting their proper influence when they inspire the creative mind; poets like Horace or Shakespeare, factual writers like Plutarch, imaginative writers like Proclus. Even from poor mental food the mind may be nourished, as when a man picks up a good phrase from a bad sermon, or leaves a page of inept phrases to set out on his own word hunting. Antagonism to reading, as well as sympathy, may set the mind in readiness for creative intuition.

Although his own work progressed better in solitude, Emerson does not make that an invariable rule. House guests who stayed two or three days usually drained his physical energy, leaving him unfit for work. On the other hand, an afternoon's visit with Alcott, Margaret Fuller, or George Sampson frequently jolted him out of a rut into a working mood. Although he places little importance on the passions in the creative process, he sometimes finds that anger, love, or ambition expands the mind like yeast.

Perhaps he most often sought inspiration in nature — the outer world of stream, sky, and wood — since he considered natural forms not only the substance of creative imagination, but also catalysts to stimulate the mind. The ideal was a walk through the woods with Channing or a row on the river with Thoreau. While he was formulating his ideas for *The Divinity School Address*, he walked on the cliff with Thoreau on a misty April day, listening to a crow cawing through the air and a frog piping in the lake. Going out again at night and seeing one star, he wondered if these were not enough: "Ponder it, Emerson, and not like the foolish world, hanker after thunders and multitudes and vast landscapes, the sea or Niagara." [12] Sometimes the placid surroundings of Concord were not enough, and he would set off for the White Mountains or Nantasket Beach to set the gas free in his brain. When the verses he had promised Margaret Fuller for *The Dial* would not materialize at Walden Pond, he rode into Boston to "explore the Athenaeum, nay, even the wharves and the salt water, to pluck up my drowned muse by the locks." [13] Particularly through their variety the phenomenal forms of nature have a special place in opening the mind to inspiration.

The importance which Emerson places on inspiration in the creative process appears in the fact that his simplest concept of imagination is "an arm or weapon of the higher energy." In this light, the imagination is seen as identical with the expansive power which the artist derives from Divine spirit. Thus, in "Poetry and Imagination," Emerson defines imagination as "the little chamber in the brain where is generated the explosive force which, by gentle shocks, sets in action the intellectual world." Although Emerson's central

theory of imagination includes more than this simple definition, his occasional identification of imagination with inspiration underlines the value he attaches to this inbreathing
power.

Familiar with Plato's expression of divine afflatus as the
source for poetry, Emerson could not believe, as Shelley did,
that Plato's concept of the "divinely mad" poet sufficiently
explained poetic creation. Emerson's view of inspiration may
in fact be highlighted by comparison with Plato's statement
in the *Ion*. "A poet," Socrates explains, "is a thing light, and
volatile, and sacred; nor is he able to write poetry, till the
Muse entering into him, he is transported out of himself, and
has no longer the command of his intellect." [14] Plato explains
the poetic gift as a Divine madness, during which the poet
creates without consciousness either of his matter or his form,
acting as a scribe to write down God's words. After the experience is over and the poem is written, the poet cannot say
how it has been done. Here is the same emphasis which
Emerson has placed upon the source of power beyond the
control of the creative artist.

The divergence of Emerson's theory from Plato's appears
in Emerson's fuller account of the imaginative process which
follows inspiration. What we have shown to be Emerson's
simplified form of imagination is for Plato the whole story;
that is, the beginning and end of poetic creation with Plato
consists of the influx of Divine power into the poet's mind.
Emerson himself has commented upon the inadequacy of inspiration as the complete process of imagination, in his criticism of Father Taylor's oratory. Lecturing on Father Taylor
in 1866, he praised the rich fertility of that preacher's speech,
which gave the impression that he was drawing ideas from
the "tripod of the ancients," but regretted that Father Taylor
had "sold his mind for his soul." Control of as well as sub-

mission to inspiration, Emerson concluded, was necessary for the best oratory.

A further difference appears between the Emersonian and the Platonic attitude toward poetic inspiration. However lyrical his descriptions of poetry, Plato's distrust of that kind of Divine seizure as a method of knowledge causes him to relegate the poets of the *Republic* to a low position, while he places his faith in dialectic. Emerson, on the contrary, maintains that the creative artist as well as the philosopher can attain a direct intuition of truth. When, on occasion, Emerson denies the value of the arts, he does so not because he shares Plato's distrust of their ability to reveal truth, but rather because he finds the moment of union between the individual soul and the Divine so satisfying that outward artistic expression becomes unnecessary.

When the "divinely inspired" artist of Emerson's theory comes into contact with the objective forms of nature, we have passed from the first phase of the creative process, inspiration, to the second, imagination.

IMAGINATION AS "SYMBOLIC SIGHT"

Keen sense perception is the basis of Emerson's theory of imaginative creation. His ideal poet is sensitive to sounds, touch, and taste, with "solar eyes" which pierce the dark like meteors. His poetic description of the bard indicates that he is a kind of wandering harp to catch all the tunes of nature, feeling good and bad strokes equally — "He asked, he only asked, to feel." In his friend Henry Thoreau, Emerson found the best human embodiment of that sensitivity to outward impressions which is the poet's first requirement.

Emerson's analysis of sense perception may well be compared with that of Thomas Reid, whose *Inquiry into the Human Mind* Emerson had studied as a college text. Accept-

ing Reid's idea that sensation, the raw material of consciousness, must precede memory and imagination,[15] Emerson dis-
cards Reid's distinction between sensation and perception.
Reid had denominated the feeling of a pain as sensation; the
seeing a tree, as perception; the first, having no existence but
in a sentient mind; the second, involving reference of the act
of perceiving to the object perceived.[16] As we shall see,
Emerson reserves the term "perception" for the mind's interpretation of sense impressions; for the simple act of transferring to the brain objects photographed by the retina, he uses
the term "recipiency" or "percipiency," which he denotes "a
virtue of space, not of man." [17]

In his creative writing, Emerson draws more from sight
than from any of the other senses. This emphasis is partly
explained by the greater keenness of his own sense of sight,
which led him to term his "musical eyes" compensation for
his lack of musical ear. Another influence is the Neo-Platonic
concept that the sight is of all senses the least material; as
Plotinus says of the souls on the upper regions, "There everybody is pure, and each inhabitant is as it were an *eye*." [18]

This immaterial aspect of vision leads to Emerson's special
interpretation of sense impression, as emblematic or symbolic.
Simple sense impression may be considered the introduction
to the more important adaptation by the mind of objects presented to it. Thus Emerson uses the term "perception," not in
Reid's sense, to denote reference of sensation to a specific
object, but as an act of generalization, in which the will aids
the mind, and in which creative insight "assimilates the thing
seen." Emerson indicates the high value he attaches to this
term: "The birth of perception throws him [the artist] on the
party of the Eternal. This is the ichor of the gods, pulsing
already in our veins, and converting us into powers. For this
eye, once opened, does not shut" (lecture on Instinct, Percep-

tion, and Talent, 1866). So closely is this perception allied to creative power that Emerson finds poetic images necessary to its definition. Thus he quotes Plato's description of it: "A light as if leaping from a fire will on a sudden be enkindled in the soul." [19]

A like symbolic meaning attaches to Emerson's use of the term "sensibility," which in "Poetry and Imagination" is denoted as the poet's ability to find emblems in the smell of elder blows or the sight of nesting ants. In this interpretation, the poet's "sensibility" implies a power to interpret willows, weeds, and snowflakes, rather than merely to receive them as sense impressions. The action of soul as well as mind is involved in Emerson's descriptions of Thoreau's "oracular" scent and Dante's "transcendent" eyes.

The understanding of these terms illuminates Emerson's theory of the imagination. Actually, in Emerson's reading, the "perception" or "impression" of an object on the mind indicates that it is well on its way to becoming an "image" of the imagination, since the mind's "perception" of the object implies the interpretation which will inform the work of art. Emerson's stress on the importance of images in the mind as the first stage of creative expression clearly indicates that he did not share Reid's antipathy for the Platonic notion that sensations are images of material objects.[20] Instead of Locke's *tabula rasa*, Emerson represents the mind by the figure of an iodized plate, which seizes and retains the images of sensations correspondent to the material objects which inspired them.

Memory, as well as sense perception, plays an important role in imaginative activity. It is one of the ironies of Emerson's personal history that he should have written some of his finest statements on memory for the Harvard Lectures of 1870, a time when lapses began to appear in his own powers of recollection. Conceiving of the memory as organ-ically related to man's imagination, Emerson states that the memory understands in a prophetic way the value of the materials which it accumulates, and that man gradually comes to read the meaning of those Scriptures which memory has inscribed on the walls of his mind. As the mind grows and the character deepens, lines written by the memory in invisible ink suddenly become visible to the mind. The methods by which man remembers, Emerson lists as tenacity, accessibleness or sudden rendering, pace, and logic. To the same degree that perception excels mere percipiency by interpreting images, does creative memory surpass ordinary recollection, by its deeper retention of significant ideas. For the creative mind there is the continual surprise of discovering the fruitful effect of what he remembers, upon what he sees. As the arch supporting a building never sleeps, so is the past always working, sending up rays of light into the present moment, touching long buried facts with new meaning.

Keenly aware of the advantages of memory, Emerson also warns against its misuse. A poet who so depends upon memory as to repeat his old poems will not be open to new intuitions. This overdependence on memory is mere indigestion. "Memory is not a pocket," Emerson asserts, "though in England they may think so." [21] In Alcott's lack of memory Emerson finds the chief fault of his thinking. "Though he built towns, towers, and empires in his talk of yesterday," Emerson says, "tomorrow he cannot find a vestige, but must begin again from the sandy Sahara." [22]

As Emerson's definition of perception involves a symbolic interpretation, so his analysis of memory includes the mystical sense of reminiscence, by which the philosophic mind excels other memories in its power to behold the best of its own experience. It is this sense of recollection which Emerson has in mind when he says, "Memory is essential to Reason; Reason to Memory." The Platonic interpretation of reminiscence appears in the poem "Bacchus," where remembering, compared to winds and wine, becomes a fountain of true poetic images. From Plato's analysis in the *Philebus* and the *Meno* of the soul's recollection, Emerson derives his emphasis upon the ease with which the soul remembers. The Plotinian distinction between memory and reminiscence also enters into Emerson's theory. Plotinus distinguishes memory, a power of the intellect ever conditioned by a sense of time, from reminiscence, a power of the soul, which always possesses certain innate conceptions, but energizes according to them only when it becomes elevated above body. For Plotinus, reminiscence is distinguished from sensation, by being independent of body; and from intellection, by the greater power with which it possesses ideas.[23] In the Plotinian theory of reminiscence, Emerson found an assurance not indicated by Plato's conception, that the creative artist may derive energizing power therefrom for his own creation.

Finding memory's "high antiquity" more inspiring than the pyramids in age as well as in its mysterious hieroglyphic, Emerson comments on its "myriad-fold" method:

> Its order comprehends a thousand lines, right, left, oblique, curved, and waving. Every point lives, and is centre or extreme in turn. As the lightning shineth out of one part of heaven even unto the other part, so one thought in this firmament flashes its light over all the sphere. (*J.*, 1833)

Thus by the figure of shifting lines and points, Emerson indicates the complex, often inexplicable working of memory; by the figure of lightning, he shows memory's power to set the whole mind in action. A modification of the theory of reminiscence appears in "The Poet," in the statement that a sensitive poet can hear from such natural objects as mountains, ocean,

and flowers, "overtones" from a kind of preëxistence, audible
only to a keen ear.

On occasion Emerson equates the memory to the imagination, since like imagination, memory opens the eye of reason
so that the soul's earlier experience, a fruitful source for creative expression, is revived. In Swedenborg he finds an identification of active memory with strong imaginative power.[24]
Emerson's conviction that memory greatly assists creative
thought is symbolized by his whimsical longing to get some
slips for the Botanic Garden from the famous Indian Parajati
tree, which perfumed the earth for miles around and enabled
all those within smelling distance to recall an earlier existence.

Sense impression and memory thus supply the initial stages
of Emerson's theory of imagination. In their simple function
of presenting objects to the mind, both sense impression and
memory feed the imagination; but they have an even greater
value in their higher functions of sensibility and reminiscence,
by which they show the creative mind the spiritual significance of objects in nature. In Emerson's analysis of the mind's
image-making power, therefore, we may expect a greater
emphasis upon the spirit than upon the material of the image.

The Introductory Lecture to the 1835–36 series on Literature defines imagination not as a separate power, but as "the
act of the total mind." This lecture gives special attention to
the poet's perception of analogies in nature:

> He converts the solid globe the land the sea the sun the
> animals into symbols of thought; he makes the outward
> creation subordinate and merely a convenient alphabet to
> express thoughts and emotions. This act or vision of the
> mind is called Imagination. It is that active state of the mind
> in which it forces things to obey the laws of thought; takes
> up all present objects in a despotic manner into its own
> image and likeness and makes the thought which occupies it

the centre of the world . . . Not less readily does it seize a resemblance to the small and obscure and dignify the object by uniting it to its emotion.

Here Emerson focuses on the converting power of the imagination, which molds material objects in the new form of its vision. In "Poetry and Imagination," contrasting imagination with common sense, he calls imagination "second sight," with a power to use facts as types to signify creative ideas. As authorities for this interpretation he cites Zoroaster, Bacon, and Swedenborg.

He might also have cited Carlyle, whose conception of the poet as "seer" is closely related to this idea that the poet perceives analogies in nature. Carlyle, who uses "seeing" in the Wordsworthian sense of piercing "into the heart of things," exclaims: "The seeing eye! It is this that discloses the inner harmony of things; what Nature meant, what musical idea Nature has wrapped-up in these often rough embodiments . . . To the Poet . . . we say first of all, See." [25] Emerson's theory of "second sight" closely resembles Carlyle's, especially when in "The Poet" he terms poetic insight "a very high sort of seeing, which does not come by study, but by the intellect being where and what it sees." Curiously enough, Carlyle, who was no poet, places more emphasis than Emerson does upon the music which true poetry must derive from Nature's heart.

A difference appears, however, between Carlyle's and Emerson's attitude toward phenomenal forms. Adapting Fichte's theory of the "Divine Idea," Carlyle conceives of the forms of nature as essentially a "vesture or sensuous appearance" which the poet must pierce, if he would reach the underlying reality.[26] For Emerson, the specific forms of nature do actually contain spirit; and the poet will attain his intuition not by penetrating them to reach an essence on the other side, but by actually living in these forms.

Although Emerson derived the distinction between fancy and imagination from Coleridge, this differentiation was never central in his thought, and decreased in importance for him after 1836. A more useful element absorbed from Coleridge was the concept of imagination as image-making power. Coleridge considered that the mind could not grasp pure or disembodied truth without some fleshly clothing. "An IDEA," he says, "in the *highest* sense of that word, cannot be conveyed but by a symbol." [27] In his creative work, Coleridge demonstrated the power of imagination to alter the objects presented to it by sensation, in much the same way that Emerson speaks of the poet's despotic power over nature. In his theory, however, Coleridge places greater emphasis upon the poet's reproduction of natural objects, comparing his use of them to the reflection of a green field in a calm, transparent lake. In Coleridge's analysis, then, Emerson finds a faith lacking in Carlyle's theory, that material objects do themselves contain spirit; but he finds an emphasis upon the *likeness* of an imaginative picture to the original, which diverges from his own disposition to show the poet *changing* the objects which he treats.

The core of Emerson's "symbolic sight" may best be understood by its relation to the Plotinian theory of "the flowing." Thus Emerson conceives of the movement of soul through the brute matter of the natural world: "As the river flows, and the plant flows (or emits odours), and the sun flows (or radiates), and the mind is a stream of thoughts, so is the universe the emanation of God. If anything should stand still, it would be crushed by the torrent it resisted." (Ms. J. TO, 1855) In this interpretation, "the instinct of the Universe" is shown as "becoming somewhat else," death, on the other

hand, as "the penalty of standing still." The very essence of
freedom is "the power to flow." [28] This moving soul not
only vivifies but elevates objects:

> The good soul . . . warms, suns, refines each particle,
> then drops the little channel, thro' which the life rolled
> beatific, to the ground, — touched and educated by a
> moment of sunshine, to be the fairer material for future
> channels, through which the old glory shall dart again in
> new directions, until the Universe shall have been shot
> through and through, *tilled* with light. (Ms. J. TO)

Plotinus' thinking clearly dominates this Emersonian concept. To show the energizing of matter by the intellectual
principle, Plotinus employs the image of a fountain which
sends its water out to all rivers at the same time that it remains
self-contained. Plotinus asserts that the illuminated soul assists
in driving matter toward spirit: "We follow the circulation
of the universe . . . As each part of us partakes of our soul,
so likewise we . . . participate as parts of the soul of the
universe." [29]

When Emerson defines the poetic imagination as a power
of "sharing the path or circuit of things through forms," he
uses Plotinian terms: the term "intellect" in the Plotinian
sense of a power shared by man with the gods, a power above
soul but below pure essence; the term "energy" in the sense
of infusing spirit through matter. Thus in "The Poet"
Emerson defines the heart of the creative imagination as the
ability to "name" those things which in themselves are silent:

> Beyond the energy of his possessed and conscious intel-
> lect he is capable of a new energy . . . by abandonment
> *to the nature of things* . . . beside his privacy of power
> . . . there is a great public power on which he can draw,
> by . . . suffering the ethereal tides to roll and circulate

through him; then he is caught up into the life of the Universe, *his speech is thunder, his thought is law,* and his words are universally intelligible as the plants and animals. The poet knows that he speaks adequately then only when he speaks somewhat wildly, or "with the flower of the mind" . . . If in any manner we can stimulate this instinct, *new passages are opened for us into nature*; the mind flows into and through things hardest and highest, and the metamorphosis is possible. (italics mine)

The poet is here conceived as sharing in the driving, upward motion of the World Soul, speaking and thinking in the language of natural objects through his complete sympathy, but being in a sense superior to things by his spiritual power to melt whatever adamant resists his creative impulse. Clearly the Plotinian concept of "the flowing," through its indication that the artist attains creative insight by sharing the spirit that energizes nature's forms, is central to Emerson's theory of "symbolic sight."

The connection between this concept of imagination and that of inspiration is evident. The original condition of passive reception still obtains, but instead of being directed to the Deity himself, focuses on his projection in natural forms. Emerson also shows that a direct contact with Divine spirit usually *precedes* the capacity to discover that spirit in nature. Here of course he may be making theory out of his own experience, since he had formed his idea of a powerful immanent God through study and reflection before he became keenly sensitive to that spirit's extension into phenomena. Thus in *Nature* he defines imagination as "the *use* which the Reason makes of the material world." Since Emerson thinks of Reason as "the eye of the soul," we may interpret this statement to mean that Reason first opens the inner eye, so that the imagination may see the actual world as the stuff of creation.

How is the poet to achieve this unsettling of the land and sea, so that they revolve around the new axis of his thought?

First he must live in nature, absorbing himself in her various forms. If he does this, his work will show the imprint of organic form — that is, it will give the same impression as natural objects. Thus the poet's speech becomes "thunder," the winds take flesh and the mountains talk in his verse, and the bard himself becomes "a crystal soul/Sphered and concentric with the whole." These phrases show that Emerson thinks of the poet as joining the elements, actually "going with" or "accompanying" them, while they in turn give life to his poetry. If nature in the aspect of *natura naturata* gives the artist material, Nature as *vis naturans* — shaping power — shows him method. He may even get direct hints for poetic structure from Nature's dynamism: thus birds' mating suggests an idyll; a storm, an ode; a summer, epic song. The poet who lives in outer nature will discover a plan for his work taking shape almost insensibly within his mind. If a man goes into the fields "under the influence of strong passion" (that is, with an intuition for a poem), Emerson says that he will find material expressions leaping to meet his ideas. Furthermore, if he has long studied the face of nature, his mind will be stored with natural images which will spring into the mind "in the hour of passion" — the time of actual creation. On one occasion Emerson compares the poet's living in nature to "a mesmeric state" in which he becomes oxygen, and the state of creation to the "normal state" in which he can readily express the laws of oxygen, because he has not merely observed that gas, but has actually identified himself with it. Even the words seem to flow spontaneously, as from a source richer than himself.

The simple concept of organic form, then, represents Emerson's first answer to the question of how the creative insight actually penetrates nature. From the specific objects in which the poet has been absorbed, he derives substance; from the driving spirit behind the phenomenal world, he gains hints for poetic structure. The finished poem thus gives the same impression of vitality as do plants or animals.

A deeper answer appears in Emerson's stress upon the *symbol* as the chief evidence of creative imagination, for the symbol represents the very heart of the poet's "second sight." One may merely suggest here its importance in the creative process, since the concept of the symbol as well as that of organic form will be more fully developed in the second chapter.

We recall that perception, with Emerson, denotes not merely the reception of an object on the brain, but a realization by the mind of that object's significance. Furthermore, before one can attain that perception, his inner eye must first be opened. To discover the spirit in objects — in Emersonian sense, to "perceive" it — represents a long step toward interpretation. Thus, when Emerson speaks of the poet as living *in* the forms of nature, he recognizes some value in the forms themselves, but a greater worth in "the divine aura" which breathes through them. Again, in "The Poet," when he calls art "the path of the creator to his work," he adds: "the paths or methods are *ideal* and *eternal*." The answers to all difficult questions exist in nature, and will speak to the sensitive ear. While the artist's perceiving of spirit in objects does represent an activity of his own mind, it also constitutes a *response* to the spirit that exists in natural forms. When the artist's "inner eye" really opens, the spirit in nature plainly manifests itself to his vision.

In this theory, the poet's "microscopic and telescopic"

vision exists not in his *eye*, but in his *mind*. It requires a lively comprehension to perceive the possible development of the ideas suggested by nature. Furthermore, although the senses are indispensable as "feeders" of the mind, the inner vision may sometimes be better seen when the outer eye is closed, for the immediate enjoyment of the senses may get in the way of imaginative second sight. In order to approach in his work that quality of upward ascension which characterizes the flowing of spirit in nature, the poet must advance beyond the object to the idea, and beyond the single idea to new interpretations of significance.

Like inspiration, the creative state must be preceded by a discipline, which involves a keen, active mind, well versed in nature's forms. This idea of disciplined imagination, however, does not imply a Coleridgean emphasis upon active will and understanding, so much as upon a prepared spirit. Using physiological imagery, Emerson suggests the "unwilled" way in which the creative mind works: as when he compares mental assimilation to digestive power, or the intellect's "newest" (and most useful) knowledge to the outer layer of a tree's bark. Once the creative artist has found the way, he will easily attain the intuition which informs his work.

From Emerson's talks with Charles Woodbury, one of the young Williams College students who listened to his speech before the Adelphi Union in 1854, some provocative suggestions appear.[30] Emerson advised Woodbury to seek his inspiration in nature during the early years, when the mind is plastic. Later, when there would be less danger of imitating others, he might draw from books also. "Do your own quarrying," he advised the young man. "There is a great secret in knowing what to keep out of the mind as well as what to put in."

The core of Emerson's theory of imagination, then, is the

power of the creative mind to refashion the objects of nature, with which he has long been familiar, into symbols of his own thought. Into that conception enter Carlyle's concept of the poet as "seer," Coleridge's idea of the mind's re-creation of objects "perceived," and the Plotinian view that the creative imagination not only perceives spirit flowing through forms, but also contributes to that spirit by its own energetic activity. Sensation and memory, in their primary mode, stimulate the creative mind; but they have even greater effect as perception (interpretation) and reminiscence, activities in which the intellect not only receives, but reacts upon its material.

The defect of this theory of imagination is easily noted. Emerson has little to say of the fusing power of imagination, by which disparate objects are forced into a new unity. Comparison of Emerson's "second sight" with the Coleridgean interpretation of imagination as a shaping power under the control of will and understanding, reveals a certain fragmentary quality in Emerson's idea. Although some of his own work shows a strong integral development — for example, the essays *Nature*, "The Poet," "Thoreau," and the poems, "Sphinx," "Brahma," and "The Snowstorm" — his theory gives inadequate recognition to the Aristotelian "beginning, middle, and end." Emerson's concept of the imagination as "symbolic sight" explains the overemphasis which he places in criticism upon the single line of poetry, the single sentence in prose. Seeking the heart of imaginative expression in single symbols necessarily involves emphasis upon isolated elements at the expense of the whole. Conversely, the consideration of the symbol as the container of an idea also leads to valuing a work's general expression, what one might call the "smell" or the "taste" of it, exclusive of its separate parts in relation to each other and to the whole. Emerson's praise of design in *Paradise Lost*, for example, shows awareness of the poem's devout purpose, and vivid recollection of a few lines, but no real sense of the relation borne by separate incidents to the "justification of God to man." This view of imagination as "symbolic seeing" holds up best in its application to lyric poetry, or to an art form like sculpture or painting, one observation of which gives a definite impression. It helps us least when applied to a long play, a symphony, or an epic poem.

On the positive side, Emerson's theory of imagination supplies what he was seeking in his tireless speculations about the creative mind — an imaginative theory of the imagination. Like Coleridge, Emerson was reacting from such analyses of the imagination as that of Dugald Stewart, for example, who defined that power by listing its various faculties: conception, abstraction, judgment, and fancy.[31] Such a definition seemed to Emerson logic-chopping metaphysics, failing to explain the inner working of the creative mind, as the Locke-Hartleian theory of association had failed to explain mental processes in general. Emerson's definition of "perception" avoids this facultative division by concentrating attention on one single act of the mind. By adding to the vivid reception of images by the mind, a sense of their aesthetic significance, Emerson's "perception" is actually Coleridge's primary imagination, raised to a higher power. Ignoring the fusing and shaping quality which Coleridge emphasizes in the secondary imagination, Emerson's theory represents a simpler interpretation than that of Coleridge, with a mystical rather than a psychological emphasis.

Besides the advantage of its "imaginative" quality, Emerson's theory of "symbolic sight" harmonizes closely with his theory of inspiration. The "inspired" artist is ready for contact with the natural forms which will supply the body of his art. As Nature is the source of material as well as structure, the artist will respond to that spirit and increase the supply when he objectifies his own thought in new things. If this view lacks completeness as a theory of imagination, by over-emphasizing ease and swiftness of creation, it has the advantage of keeping faith with Emerson's central philosophical conviction that Nature is the source of "the good, the beautiful, and the true," and that the creative artist attains fulfillment when he becomes in tune with her.

To complete Emerson's analysis of the creative process, we must see what he says of the expression which follows imaginative "second sight."

EXPRESSION

The emphasis which Emerson places upon influx of spirit into the artist's mind carries over from the first two phases (inspiration and imagination) to the third phase of the creative process, external expression. Works of imagination, for example, are considered valid because of a quality of free expansion which may be considered the direct result of the spiritual "flowing" discovered by imagination in nature. Placing a certain value upon *quantity* of insight, Emerson writes in his journal that "imagination is not good for anything unless there be *enough*." In "Poetry and Imagination," he says: "The sole question is how many strokes vibrate on this mystic string, — how many diameters are quite drawn through from matter to spirit." Thus he praises Proclus' "vigor and breadth," Aeschylus' "grand effort" in *Prometheus Unchained*, and George Herbert's "liquid genius." This emphasis upon sweep, spread, and expansion does not of course imply a recognition of the architectonic sense in art which was lacking in Emerson's theory of imagination, but simply a demand that the finished work of art show the same freely extended spirit which the artist's imaginative "eye" perceived in nature. The importance of the spiritual element in expression appears also in Emerson's use of the term "the newness," to denote not a neoclassic sense of novelty, but an indication in the finished work that the artist has received a fresh intuition of the Divine. Thus Miss Woodbridge's poems are rejected by *The Dial* because they lack "the newness," which appears so clearly in the authentic inspiration of Ellery Channing.

Expression is further connected with inspiration by the need for a submissive will. Emerson censures both Alcott and Goethe for letting will, in the aspect of caprice, interfere with valid expression. Once the perception has been formed in the mind, Emerson insists that the artist must not try to interpose his conscious will between the perception and its expression; the perception must be allowed to have its way. Both egotism, "the lust of imparting as from *us*," and overconcern with artificial arrangement of parts in a work, will close "the sovereign eye of Proportion." Just as in receiving the first intuition, the artist was obliged to subordinate his will, so now in imparting the vision, he must not let the will come between idea and expression. If the "meddling intellect" distorts the expression, the artist must suppress the intellect, letting the idea develop in its own fashion.

In analyzing creative expression, Emerson speaks chiefly of the *ease* with which it may come about. In "The Poet," for example, he says, "When the soul of the poet has come to ripeness of thought, she detaches and sends away from it its poems or songs," clad with wings by which they "ascend and leap and pierce into the deeps of infinite time." This beautiful view of poetic expression of course ignores the mental agony which most poets experience in the process of "detaching" their melodies. Emerson even asserts that Nature, wishing to preserve the spirit living in these poems, will protect them from critical or "unwinged" censure just as she scatters many spores over the world to ensure the propagation of trees. Emerson speaks with like optimism of the "perceptions" which animate all the arts, born by the "marriage of souls," detached, then proceeding to animate the materials of wood, stone, and iron into which they pass. Here he borrows an astronomical image to illustrate the conversion of "perceptions" into objective expressions:

> It is a steep stair down from the essence of Intellect pure to thoughts and intellections. As the sun is conceived to have made our system by hurling out from itself the outer rings of diffuse ether which slowly condensed into earths and moons, by a higher force of the same law the mind detaches minds, and a mind detaches thoughts and intellections. These again all mimic in their sphericity the first mind, and share its power. ("Natural History of Intellect")

The sense of inevitability which characterizes the creation of the planetary system gives color here to the "fated" growth of the mind's intuitions.

Comparing human creation to God's creation of the world, Emerson notes three steps:

> 1. Intellect pure is the thought; stands with us for Being; 2. Intellect passing into act is the Creator; 3. And the realization of Intellect is Nature . . . Now who does not see that this was nothing else than a copy in colossal of the process familiar in every human mind? (Lecture on Genius, Imagination, and Taste, 1866)

Although Emerson shares this conception of the poet as "like unto God" with such romantic writers as Wordsworth, Coleridge, and Blake, he has expressed the idea here with a sharp, individual clarity which makes it memorable.

Like most critics who emphasize ease of expression,

Emerson gives a definite place to the subconscious mind in creative activity. The mere passage of time, Emerson indicates, will reveal affinities and sequences of thoughts within the mind. He compares the effect of time on mental development to the process of vegetation, in which the mind does not gain thoughts from without so much as it "inveterates itself in its own quality." Even when our minds seem inactive, thought actually proceeds beneath the surface; as a traveler home from Spain finds that gradually, without his intervention, the things he has seen begin to fall into a pattern. Emerson liked his aunt Mary Moody Emerson's phrasing of this idea: "Bitter as inactivity of all kinds is, it is a kind of sleep and may be better for minds which occasionally awake, than that endless round of employment which leaves the soul untouched." [32] While Emerson's statement of the effect of the subconscious on creative activity seems limited in comparison to the quantity of such discussions since Freud, he does give it some recognition.

What is the relation of technique to this "effortless" embodiment of thought in a thing? Although we have discovered little emphasis upon technique in Emerson's theory of imagination, we shall find some consideration of the problem in his discussion of expression.

Emerson's simplest statement about the relation of technique to "easy" expression appears in his affirmation that the artist possesses an essential affinity for his material. The same "natural" relationship which he finds between the poet and the outer world obtains also between the artist and his material, so that the stone is soft in a sculptor's hands; pencils and chromes, plastic in a painter's fingers. Thus Phidias and Michelangelo cut marble as easily as if it were snow. The very force of genius, Emerson asserts, implies the power of transferring ideas into oils, colors, or poetic sounds. In his talk with young Woodbury, Emerson indicated that intuitions may more readily be transferred into painting, statuary, and music, than into literary composition. Although he attributes the reason for this difference to the fact that the symbols of writing are arbitrary and artificial by comparison to those of the plastic arts and music, one suspects that the real reason for his finding writing harder was that he had written, whereas he had never attempted painting or sculpture.

In Swedenborg Emerson sees the signal exception to his belief that true perception means good expression. Keenly aware of the correspondence between mind and matter, Swedenborg somehow lacked "the apparatus of poetic expression" which a keen intuition should carry with it. Why, Emerson asks, did Swedenborg fail? Was he so involved in his material that he could not find adequate words, did his "reporting angels" hinder him, or did he see the vision with his intellect rather than with his whole soul? Convinced that Swedenborg had right intuitions, Emerson cannot explain why he failed to make poetry of them. Comparing "the entire want of poetry in so transcendent a mind" to a hoarse voice in a beautiful person, Emerson places Swedenborg as the exception that proves the rule, that the creative artist with a strong intuition will find his materials flexible to his touch.

Emerson also shows marked preference for a genuine intuition, though roughly executed, to a skillful expression of a second-rate or derivative idea. In the early poetry of Tennyson, for example, Emerson finds excellent command of technique, but mediocre ideas. This paying greater attention to the finish rather than the argument of verses results in "music-box" poetry.[33] The same fault appears in some modern painters. In contrast with earlier artists who were not afraid to pour their vision on canvas, despite their incomplete mastery of form, these moderns produce work that is finished, but lacking in fire.

Far superior to these artists who have been trapped by technique are the creators whose rough work still reveals a vigor of ideas. Some poetry of Wordsworth exemplifies this quality of unfinished but vital thought. Chiefly in the poetry of his friend Ellery Channing Emerson detects this "poetic soul" beneath carelessness of execution. So highly does he prize the sense of being present "at the secret of creation" that he is often willing to overlook Channing's neglect of revision, which he compares to "brushes of noblemen's clothes."

Of course Emerson places the highest value on poetry and art that shows perfect fusion of spirit with form. Annoyed with Samuel Ward and Margaret Fuller for upholding Channing in his refusal to alter his verses for *The Dial*, Emerson asks, "Is the poetic inspiration amber to embalm and enhance flies and spiders?" To Channing himself he writes, frankly: "Certainly I prize finished verses, which yours are not, and like best poetry which satisfies eye, ear, heart and mind." Furthermore, it is Emerson's usual assumption that a true perception will find its way into the form that belongs to it. Lecturing on The Seven Metres of Intellect (1866), Emerson says: "The secret of human power is, that whatever is intellectually seen is by that sight already mentally accomplished; and 'tis easy to embody it in words." The conclusion is that genuine ideas inadequately expressed are better than technically perfect embodiments of derivative thoughts; but the ideal (and in fact, the usual) result of the true intuition is an equal expression. A statement from the essay on "History" is a good summary of Emerson's attitude toward the problem of expression vs. technique: "By a deeper apprehension, and not primarily by a painful acquisition of any manual skills, the artist attains the power of awakening other souls to a given activity."

How far does Emerson's own creative experience bear out this conception of *ease* of expression? Though we ought not to demand that a theorist's individual experience should correspond exactly to his generalization, we may expect some relationship between the two.

As early as 1823 we find Emerson complaining in his journal of the ebb and flow of his thought: "The worst is, that the ebb is certain, long and frequent, while the flow comes transiently and seldom." By 1848 he has arrived at one explanation of this phenomenon, that it resembles extremes of weather, impossible to change: "There is a sort of climate in every man's speech running from hot noon, when words flow like steam and perfume, — to cold night, when they are frozen." Commenting on his delivery of lectures, Emerson frequently suggests that his expression does not keep pace with his ideas. This sense of inadequacy arises not from intellectual difficulty, nor from defect in character, but rather from a temperamental coldness, which sometimes froze his personality so that he could not establish direct contact with other people. His success as a lecturer, on the other hand, indicates that his flow must surely have been more frequent than his ebb.

In writing, Emerson also takes note of some difficulty. When preparing *Nature* for the press (1836), he writes to Hedge about the length of time required to achieve even a few lines:

> There are not many greater misfortunes to peace of mind than to have keen susceptibility to the beautiful in composition, and just to lack that additional wit which suffices to create it. So shall a man weary himself and spend good oil in

vain attempts to carve Apollos which all turn out scare-crows. My versification of this ancient lament is

> Happy Bard or Dunce! but hard
> Is it to be half a bard.

This statement ill accords with Emerson's general empha-sis upon the ease of expression, the genius that "makes fingers." Does his sense of failure mean that he feels himself not really a creator, but one of the "secondary men"? To some extent this is the case, for he asserts that in an age richer in genius he would not have been a writer. Thus he calls himself a poet "of a low class," a "husky" singer. Writing to Margaret Fuller in 1839, he says: "I pine to write verses, and cannot. The wind, the water, the ferns do all but coin them-selves into rhymes before me, yet the last step of the alchemy fails." On the other hand, in the letter to Hedge, he is speak-ing of the poetic prose of *Nature*, certainly his most original contribution to American thought.

In "The Poet" he examines further the feeling of discrep-ancy between intuition and expression, where the poet feels the contrast between the steadfast and abundant natural ele-ments, and his own scattered power. He exclaims:

> Merge me in the brute universe,
> Or lift to a diviner dream!

In a bitter sense of his own inadequacy to carry out his vision, he asks the stars for compassion:

> Clothe these hands with power
> In just proportion,
> Nor plant immense designs
> Where equal means are none.

The stars reply in a curious fashion:

> Means, dear brother, ask them not;
> Soul's desire is means enow,
> Pure content is angel's lot
> Thine own theatre art thou.

The stars' answer, "Soul's desire is means enow," contains the same element already emphasized in Emerson's theory of ease of expression, that a true intuition will find its material embodiment. The stars also introduce another idea: that some sense of discrepancy between intuition and expression is the inevitable accompaniment of the human state. Such divine discontent as Michelangelo felt in his productions, for example, is part of being a man and an artist. If a poet resembles the spirits in having a divine aim, he shares with the rest of mankind the limitations of matter which obstruct the adequate expression of the spirit which he has seen. As the stars phrase it, "pure content is angel's lot" — not yours; and you must work in your own theater of human action. The stars do offer the further reassurance that a vital connection exists among themselves, man's spirit, and all of nature:

> See, all we are rooted here
> By one thought to one same sphere;
> From thyself thou canst not flee, —
> From thyself no more can we.

To the poet's eager request whether he may have access to the full tide of inspiration, the stars answer in true Emersonian language, without a "yes" or "no":

> Brother, sweeter is the Law
> Than all the grace Love ever saw;
> We are its suppliants. By it, we
> Draw the breath of eternity;
> Serve thou it for daily bread, —
> Serve it for pain and fear and need.

According to this answer, the feeling of inadequacy to express an intuition is finally compensated for by character. Just as love and patience assist the creative mind in attaining the original intuition, so do they offer consolation in the state where means to express the artist's conception do not readily appear. In this poetic statement, as well as in the letter to Hedge, Emerson indicates that these difficulties will finally be resolved by one who watches and waits.

Sometimes Emerson speaks of a difficulty with the structure of his compositions. The famous "crack" which he hoped to mend in *Nature* resulted from his original conception of the work as two essays, the first, "Nature"; the second, "Spirit"; nor was he ever completely satisfied with his joining of the two parts. A similar problem occurred with "The Sphinx," for which Margaret Fuller was holding up the proof of *The Dial*. In 1840, Emerson wrote to her: " 'The Sphinx' has fourteen verses and only wants one to complete it, but that is unluckily in the middle and like Aladdin's window." Since the finished version contains not fifteen, but seventeen verses, Emerson must have underestimated the amount of mortar needed to fill in the gap.

Some letters concerning Emerson's "Boston Hymn" present an amusing instance of an occasion when Emerson's divinely guided spirit struggled to meet a deadline.[34] With less than a month to prepare the poem, Emerson composed four separate drafts. Despite the contradiction which the experience gives to the theory of *easy* expression, it corroborates the idea that Divine inspiration may not be hastened. The attitude of "waiting" appears in Emerson's note to Dwight on December 30, 1862, advising him to print the program without Emerson's name, though he may still "at the eleventh hour, pray to be admitted." Since the "Hymn" was actually read in Music Hall on New Year's Day, 1863, one can only conclude that God on that occasion must have smiled upon Emerson and Boston as well.

Emerson's personal experience thus reveals some discrepancy from his theoretical statement concerning the ease of expression. The story of his own creative struggles recognizes that the fact does not always give the form, that words and images do not invariably come readily to hand, and that the divine vision may sometimes loiter unexpressed in the creative mind. In this sense, he by no means makes thoroughgoing application of his theory to his own work. But the drift of his experience does bear witness to his faith that without a strong informing intuition the work of art is useless. And the person who seeks in vain to put his intuition into external form has always the refuge of character.

The mystical emphasis in Emerson's theory of expression leads to the question: If spirit is the important element, why place *any* value upon external expression? Absorbed in the "perceptions" drawn from the soul of the "All," is not the creative artist likely to ignore the objectifying of these perceptions in some form? Does not the mystical theory, if pushed to the ultimate point, destroy the value of art?

On occasion Emerson takes exactly this position, that the arts may well commit suicide. By no means his considered view of expression, this self-destructive conception does have a place in his theory. The soul, for example, discouraged with inability to express, may find a cure for all its literary ills by "the mere apprehension of the Absolute." In this interpretation, mystical experience alleviates the artist's sense of inadequacy in creative expression.

On the other hand, the soul in a state of ecstatic communion may be disturbed by an effort to come out of it and make an expression. Direct contact with the source of spirit is so rich that the creative imagination is reluctant to leave it for the task of realizing its intuitions. The desire to objectify a thought becomes unimportant if the artist, by renouncing expression, may become a vessel "filled with the divine over-flowings, enriched by the circulations of ominiscience and omnipresence." In this connection, Emerson mentions the romantic conception of an earlier age in which all men were so imbued with spirit that they felt no need to impose on it the "bolts and bars" of stone, music, or canvas.

It is through comparison of his expression with the spirit that inspired it that the creator feels the same sense of disappointment that characterized the collector of shells in "Each and All," who found that these "sea-born" treasures had left their beauty behind them on the shore.

> What we record as a key-thot [*sic*] of the Universe [Emerson says] turns out in our record glistening tin, and no world wisdom. The universe had glowed with its eternal blaze, and I chipped off this scale thro' which the light shone, thinking this the diamond, and put it in my jewel box, and now tis a dead scale. (Ms. J. TO, 1855)

Emerson once discussed this matter of destruction of the arts with Henry Thoreau on an autumn walk to Walden Pond. Beginning with Thoreau's dislike of farmers' fences, the talk progressed to the statement that all the arts represented similar obstructions to man's spirit. Agreeing with Thoreau that poetry, sculpture, and architecture were mere "sparks and cinders" to the soul dwelling in the universe, Emerson asked:

> Why should we covetously build a Saint Peter's, if we had the seeing Eye which beheld all the radiance of beauty and majesty in the matted grass and the overarching boughs? Why should a man spend years upon the carving an Apollo, who looked Apollos into the landscape with every glance he threw? (*J.*, 1838)

The ridiculous phrase, "looking Apollos into the landscape," merely represents the extension to an extreme point, of Emerson's theory of imagination: that the artist forms intuitions by "perceiving" the spirit in nature's forms, and interfusing his own spirit with that discovered in nature. The fact that this is an extreme rather than a central conception of Emerson's theory may be observed by comparing this negative attitude toward Apollo and St. Peter's with the number of appreciative statements he has made about these same works.

Expression may also seem superfluous to the creative artist, not so much from an unwillingness to desert the mystical state, as from a sense of abundance of power to express. In "Modern Literature," for example, Emerson speaks of the poet's "boundless power and freedom to say a million things." Here there is a tendency to emphasize the power rather than the objective expression. Of Stewart Newton's sketches (drawn, one must remark, while Newton was insane), Emerson notes their "rich invention," asking, "Why draw any line, since you can draw all? Genius has given you the freedom of the universe, why then come within any walls?" In his own writing Emerson sometimes had this experience of coming out "into the free air of thought," sensing a freedom in the city of the Muses, and ability to continue expression indefinitely. Perhaps it is not strange that this sense of power should include an indifference toward the putting of ideas into plastic molds. "The state given," Emerson says, "a little more or a good deal more or less performance seems indifference."

Shakespeare represents the chief example of this power which exceeds any need to express. For Emerson, Shakespeare's skill in turning deep perceptions into verse so excels the work of earlier poets that he has added a new problem to metaphysics, a fresh fact to natural history. A symbol of creative expression, Shakespeare also teaches how to dispense with what he has done. "He is the chief example," Emerson writes in *Representative Men*, "to prove that more or less of production, more or fewer pictures, is a thing indifferent." Shakespeare's attainment of complete power, like a scientific discovery, can be understood without further expression. Thus, by comparison with the creative imagination itself, the arts become "poor toys," "vaunted evidences" of higher things.

By a religious analogy we may demonstrate the place of this extreme view in Emerson's general theory of expression. Although the central position of the church is that faith should be embodied in good works, the mystic may assert that his experience of communion with the Divine possesses such complete validity that he need not give it objective realization. Emerson's central conception of the value inherent in external forms resembles the normal position of religious experience; that "literary faith" should, and does, become embodied in the "good works" of art. On occasion, however, Emerson's idea of the creative experience resembles the mystic's attitude: that this state of mind is in itself so satisfying that it needs no external expression to render it complete.

As we approach Emerson's central theory of expression, we may ask what place in that theory is occupied by *communication*. Does Emerson find that the creative artist feels the need of communicating his perception to others? The existence of communication in artistic expression Emerson grants when he says that every mind is "an *impartable* essence," "communicable in the same proportion with its amount or depth." In his theory of eloquence he makes his most marked recognition of the need for communication, valuing "a certain creative heat" which can inflame the hearers' minds, and the powerful voice which can command their ears. Well aware of his own skill in communicating truth by speaking, Emerson prizes "phlegm" in a companion "that it is a triumph to disturb."

In his general theory of art and literature, however, Emerson places little value on communication. Significantly, in the *Dial* essay on "Art," Emerson speaks of communication, not in the sense of the artist speaking to an audience, but rather as "primary communication with absolute truth," that is, receiving its strength from Divine power. The poet will in fact defy his readers in exact proportion to the strength by which he grasps his thought. Perhaps Emerson values Channing's verses most of all for their neglect of an audience. Emerson's advice to Woodbury also underlines the *saying* rather than the *communicating* of ideas. "Expression," he tells Woodbury, "is the main fight. Then what is it? Say it! Out with it! Don't lead up to it. Don't try to let your hearer down from it . . . *Say* it with all the grace and force you can, and stop."

The unimportant place given to communication in Emerson's theory of expression may be demonstrated by comparing Emerson's emphasis with that of Carlyle. Both writers think of the poet or artist as representative of the people, as "seeing" the spirit in the world to which most people are blind; but Carlyle keeps always in mind the "hungry mouths of the people waiting to be filled," while Emerson thinks of the poet as *saying* rather than *communicating* his message.

Expression has its chief value in Emerson's theory of the creative process by providing a necessary complement to the taking in of inspiration. Thus the creative life parallels the alternation of powers in the physical life. Just as the lungs breathe in and exhale air, just as the body takes in food and gives out energetic action — so, Emerson says, does the creative mind, after receiving the influx of spirit, feel the need of expelling that spirit in some objective form. In "Natural History of Intellect," Emerson speaks of expression as a tightening power contrasting with the freedom of inspiration:

> The daily history of the Intellect is this alternating of expansions and concentrations. The expansions are the invitations from heaven to try a larger sweep, a higher pitch than we have yet climbed, and to leave all our past for this enlarged scope. Present power, on the other hand, requires concentration on the moment and the thing to be done.

To put the idea in a favorite metaphor of Emerson: "We like the girding belt; we like to be dissolved in liberty." Applying this metaphor to the creative process, "liberty" represents the intake of Divine inspiration; the "girding belt" signifies the need which the creative artist is under, to concentrate his inspiration at some point of expression. Expression thus involves a narrowness, a need to neglect "the All" in order to concentrate on one object; for this, the artist who has delighted in the sweep of inspiration must feel some regret. On the other hand, the ability to express involves a certain control. "Our thoughts," Emerson says, "at first possess us. Later, if we have good heads, we come to possess them." He places the essence of success in "the balance of retention and expression." Pleasure attends this materializing of ideas, for the progress of a mind from passivity to activity denotes an extra charge of electric thoughts within the mind.

Using physiological imagery, Emerson brings home the point that the creative mind has a need to make expression of what it has received. "The health of man," Emerson says in "Perpetual Forces," "is an equality of inlet and outlet, gathering and giving. Any hoarding is tumor and disease." On a day when Emerson's creative thought was particularly active (he had just written out the sentence that was the germ of the poem "Days") he quoted Hafiz in his journal, praising the "vent" of his knowledge. Deliberately lowering the conception of the work of art, in order to emphasize this "outgo" as a result of "intake," he compares the expansive writing of Hafiz and Shakespeare to perspiration. He does not go so far as to equate art with bodily excrement, though he approaches it when he approves the precept of health, "Keep the body open." The comparison of the creative mind to the physical body emphasizes the *necessity* of creation; just as the body's assimilation of food results in acts of bodily energy, so does the creative mind proceed from the first stage of inspiration to the second, the energetic act of forming a work of art.

The need for "outgo" as a result of "intake" becomes more evident when we observe that in creation, as in receiving inspiration, the artist is doing what he was meant to do. "Creation," Emerson says, "is always the style and act of these minds." Emerson scouts the idea that the "passivity" which is the heart of the creative imagination denotes laziness, by insisting that genius is always "insatiable for expression," eager to take that "stupendous step" of realizing its thought. He suggests that a kind of compulsion is even imparted to the spiritual *perception* itself, in the mind of the artist, so that it seeks to embody itself in some thing.

When a creative mind fails to realize his ideas, he misses his calling. In his friend Charles Newcomb, for example, he sees a waste of potential spiritual power: "an arrested mind, a bud that is principled against flowering, a resistance of the eternal flowing and transition of nature." *The Divinity School Address* contains Emerson's most succinct expression of this idea of "intake vs. outgo": "It is the effect of conversation with the beauty of the soul to beget a desire and need to impart to others the same knowledge and love. If utterance is denied, the thought lies like a burden on the man."

In this conception, then, that expression represents a necessary "outgo" as a result of the "intake" that was spiritual inspiration, we find Emerson's justification for the whole creative process. If by a special favor of "grace" the creative artist has been enabled to "see" into the heart of things, to form inner "perceptions" that pierced to the white of truth, now, by recognizing the need he is under to express that "perception," he justifies his place in the scheme of things by performing good "works." Through the freely expanding quality of his expression, the creative artist contributes his share to the energetic spirit that informs the world. To express the need for outgo as a result of intake, as Emerson does, in physiological terms, is merely to make more vivid the connection between this spiritual expression and man's entire human nature. Furthermore, the use of physiological imagery enables him to maintain here the same value which prevails throughout his theory of the creative process: the worth of the submissive will. By drawing an analogy between the act of aesthetic expression and man's physical life, Emerson shows the need for "activity" as a complement to "passivity," without placing undue emphasis upon the work of the conscious will in expression. For Emerson, creative expression represents an objective realization by the artist of an intuition originally derived from the spirit dwelling at the heart of nature. While the artist shows energetic activity in that realization, it is not an effort that involves wide combination of varying materials into a separate whole, demanding the ratiocinative power of the understanding. As in his original "perception," so in his expression, he is guided by the "high seeing" of the mind when its "inner eye" has been opened by the soul, rather than by the understanding or the will.

At first sight it may seem that Emerson's theory of expression is anticipating the philosophic aesthetic of Benedetto

Croce in our own day. To examine that relationship, one needs first to understand Croce's view of expression. Contrasting intuitive knowledge, or imagination, which controls art, with conceptual knowledge, which controls the sciences, Croce distinguishes "intuition" (the Idea in the artist's mind) from sense perception, from association, and from representation, identifying intuition very closely with expression. The original intuition, he says, grows in the mind in the line, color, or words whch will be the elements of its external form. Denying that one can have an idea which he is unable to express, Croce insists that clear *possession* of the idea within the mind implies the ability to express. Nor do ordinary men possess the same kind of idea as artists, to which artists merely *add* technical elements. Raphael's ability to paint did not come from the skill of his fingers, but from the depth and strength of the original intuition. Admitting that all men possess a little of the artist, Croce exclaims: "How little!" For Croce the intuitive knowledge of the artist is "expressive knowledge": "To intuit is to express; and nothing else . . . than to express." Although he attacks the romantic confusion of the arts, Croce asserts that all arts derive from spirit, and that the science of art can progress only by connection with the general spiritual life of the day.[35]

Emerson's theory clearly resembles Croce's in distinguishing the artist's intuitive power from that of other men, in finding the source of creative activity in spirit rather than matter, and in maintaining the relative indifference of the external, completed form. On the other hand, Croce's conception of spirit implies artistic reorganization within the imagination of material derived from sense perception and passions, while Emerson's spirit is that of the Divine, or of its extension in natural forms. The two theories also present different points of view on the formation of the intuition

within the mind. Although Croce seems to imply what
Emerson has stated — that once the intuition has been derived, expression is easy — Croce has thought of the intuition
as developing within the creative mind *in terms of* the form
which it will later take. While Emerson is on the whole indifferent to technique, indicating that it is unimportant if the
artist can only manage to reproduce his original intuition in
its "essence," Croce says exactly the opposite. For Croce, the
elements of technique can never be separated from the intuition, since they have existed with the intuition as it has grown.
Furthermore, the casual attitude which both show toward the
completed work of art proceeds from contrasting reasons.
Emerson considers the external expression disadvantageous,
if it destroys a state of ecstasy in the creative mind; or unnecessary, once the artist has demonstrated his power of attaining right intuitions. Croce, on the other hand, looks upon
the objective work as relatively unimportant, because he believes that the intuition, when in its complete form in the
mind, already exists in terms of its expression, and the actual
transference may be made at any time.

Despite the resemblance which Emerson's theory bears to
Croce's, then, the comparison shows that in no real sense did
Emerson foreshadow Croce's theory of expression. Placing
Emerson's theory beside that of Croce's reveals certain weak-
nesses in Emerson's conception: his neglect of the element of
technique, his occasional confusion of the arts, his disregard
of the element of human passion in aesthetic creation.

But we do injustice to Emerson's original and stimulating
theory of expression by comparing it too closely with the
systematic thinking of a twentieth-century philosopher.
Through his experience as well as his reading, he attained a
fresh view of the creative act. His concept of expression as
the necessary complement of intake went beyond the ideas

of the romantics as well as those of the eighteenth-century rhetoricians, anticipating some of the psychological interpretations of our own time. One must also indicate that Emerson's neglect of the element of technique was based not merely upon lack of interest, but upon his conviction that the theorists of his day exaggerated the importance of external form. In "The Poet" he strikes out at the critics of poetry and fine arts who know only rules for color and form, following a shallow doctrine of beauty which has "lost the perception of the instant dependence of form upon soul." Seeing in the American journals a complete disregard of what he considered the heart of aesthetic expression, Emerson tended even more than he might otherwise have done, to emphasize almost *ad nauseam* the importance of spirit, as the word which creative artists most needed to hear. Emerson's concept of expression has value also in insisting upon genuine rather than secondhand intuitions. By realizing the spiritual intuitions which the artist attains through inspiration and imagination, expression completes Emerson's theory of the creative process.

CONCLUSION

Throughout Emerson's discussion of the creative process, we have found an emphasis upon the enrichment which the creative mind receives from a source outside itself, rather than its action under the domination of its own conscious will. Just as, in receiving inspiration, the creative artist becomes one of the "elect" by accepting the "grace" of Divine power, so in his final expression of that power, he justifies that favor by his good works.

The weak points in this theory are easily discovered. It is a simple matter to push the doctrine to its logical extreme — as Emerson himself did, upon occasion — and show the receptive artist, in waiting for inspiration, as a mere feather tossed about by Divine winds; to show the poet, in the act of imagination, as an empty vessel who allows the forms of nature to "pour" its songs into him; and of expression to say — with some sanction from Emerson — that no need exists for putting that experience of Divine ecstasy into objective form. To emphasize these points on the periphery of Emerson's theory is more quickly done than to discover the essential value at the heart of his theory.

Emerson's insistence upon inspiration as the first condition of the creative process represents merely a heightening of the experience which most writers and artists find true in their own lives: that waiting is often the first condition of artistic work, and that an element always exists in the finished job which seems not to be their own. Despite the mystical emphasis which may embarrass the twentieth-century thinker, one must note a healthy soundness in Emerson's concept of inspiration: it avoids the opium fumes of De Quincey, the egotism of Byron, the sensualism of the young Goethe. The contrast with Plato's theory of the "divinely mad" artist shows that Emerson's creed of inspiration represented no abandoning of responsibility by the artist, but rather a forsaking of lesser concerns to fulfill the higher responsibility which is his rightful function.

If, in Emerson's concept of the imagination as "symbolic sight," we miss certain elements such as the emphasis upon larger unity, the control of the will, and the understanding, we must still allow the essential rightness of Emerson's statement that the creative artist forms his "inner perception" by a mental and spiritual response to the spirit dwelling in natural forms. Whether or not the critic shares Emerson's view of the "inflowing" spirit throughout the phenomenal world, he must agree that every creative artist will find Nature the source of creative power.

The Emersonian insistence upon spirit rather than mere technique in the arts has never been more needed than today. Critics of such widely differing disciplines as J. Donald Adams, Irwin Edman, and Allen Tate, have recently cited Emerson as authority in affirming that expression has little value unless it is suffused by the light of a strong idea. That individualism, furthermore, which accompanies the idea of "saying" rather than "communicating" a message, if rightly applied, can help to correct the present overemphasis upon the social value of the arts. Audience reaction to an idea expressed in words or stone is of course one measure of its value; but surely the social criterion of art achieves undue importance if it excludes attention to the clear formulation of the aesthetic idea.

As the first arc in an upward-ascending spiral, the creative process gives the dynamic impulse to the aesthetic cycle. If Emerson's theory of creation must await the analysis of the next two terms of the cycle, the completed work of art and the receptive experience, before it can be fully understood, considered in itself it offers a conception rich and fertile in its implications, whose three terms: inspiration, imagination, and expression, all bear an integral relation to the "spirit" which is their source.

CHAPTER II

The
Work of Art

She spired into a yellow flame;
    She flowered in blossoms red;
She flowed into a foaming wave:
    She stood Monadnoc's head.

Through a thousand voices
    Spoke the universal dame;
"Who telleth one of my meanings,
    Is master of all I am."

                                     "The Sphinx"

The "ultimation of thought into things" carries us to the second phase of the aesthetic cycle, that objective work of art which results from the creative process. Since Emerson thought of the fine arts and literature as issuing from the same shaping spirit, analysis of the work of art must be based on both aesthetic and literary production, if one would see Emerson's theory in balance. In the history of American criticism, Emerson's statements about the fine arts represent a new departure; his range of experience and search for underlying principles in this area are unequaled by any other contemporary American critic. Placing full historical value on these statements about the fine arts, one recognizes that Emerson

speaks with more authority of poetry, in which creative experience gives the ring of conviction to his theory.

We need first to understand Emerson's general concept of
form, in relation to the fine arts and literature; second, to see
the application of that concept to architecture, sculpture, and
literature, with special emphasis upon poetry.

AESTHETIC FORM

Art is defined in the *Dial* essay as "the spirit creative,"
"the conscious utterance of thought, by speech or action, to
any end." [1] Emerson finds philosophical sanction for art's
value in the analysis presented by Ralph Cudworth, in his
True Intellectual System of the Universe (1678) of "plastic
nature," which acts as deputy of Divine wisdom in shaping
the material world. Emerson assigns to human art a similar
energizing and fashioning power, placing art on a level with
Cudworth's "plastic nature" as an executor of Divine com-
mands. Thus art and nature have different functions within
an integral relationship, and art no less than nature bears a
responsibility to Divine power. [2]

We have observed the correspondence which exists in the
Emersonian system between the artist and material nature. As
a result of that correspondence, a finished work (if well done)
will bear the stamp of the phenomenal world. The likeness between a work of art and a natural object (or force) may be
termed its organic form. Thus masterpieces of art and literature have as normal a place in creation as plants, crystals, or
rivers. Art's power of "spiritual" reproduction compensates
for its lack of the physical reproductive capacity possessed by
plants and animals.

Though man's creation is sometimes directed toward more
trivial objects than God's, he rises to great height in building
Egyptian pyramids and Gothic cathedrals, where he makes

available for man's uses the grandeur of Nature's caverns or forests. Emerson looks hopefully to a future in which art and nature may achieve an even closer relation, when the vision of some great man will "carry art up into the kingdom of nature, and destroy its separate and contrasted existence." But for the present he must be content with establishing a blood relationship between art and nature.

Besides the organic form which art derives from nature, there exists the spiritual aspect of form, which the artist derives direct from the Divine. The consanguinity of Art, Nature, and Divine Spirit in the Emersonian aesthetic trinity leads us to expect a harmony in the finished work of art between organic and spiritual form. Before seeking that relation, let us first consider the aspect of spiritual form.

"The art," Emerson writes in *The Dial*, "resides in the model, in the plan, for it is on that the genius of art is expended, not on the statue, or the temple." The spiritual concept of form is described in Neo-Platonic terms as "one of the possible forms in the Divine mind," "discovered and executed by the artist, not arbitrarily composed by him." Some slight development of the form within the artist's mind, at the time of intuition, appears in Emerson's statement: "In the moment, or in the successive moments when that form was seen, the iron lids of reason were unclosed."

Like Plotinus, Emerson recognizes that extension of the "plan" of art into matter weakens its spiritual strength: "The aim of art is always at somewhat better than nature, but the work of art is always inferior to nature." [3] Emerson's skepticism about the possibility of complete transference of the spiritual concept into the completed form appears in his assertion that the *life* of creative moods is "untranslateable by words." On a lower level Emerson records the comment of the Attleboro jewelers concerning the stubbornness of material to accept the domination of form, that "the devil is in the gold and it will not be malleable." [4] Man's discontent in this respect resembles God's (again he uses a Plotinian conception), since the artist's intuition surpasses his completed work in the same way that God's purpose in the Creation excelled his realization. Recognizing the difficulty which the artist experiences in making his work a "print" of the mind's "seal," Emerson judges a work excellent in the degree to which it does express the ideal intuition. Such a realization he finds in Michelangelo's Justice, whose beauty convinces him of a heavenly archetype; and in Raphael's painting of the angel driving out Heliodorus, which he terms "a dazzling creation of the moment, a divine wrath, as the resisted wave bursts into dazzling foam."

In his ability to "discover" an art form in the Divine mind lies the artist's chief superiority to Nature, and the power through which he is able to create works equally vital with natural objects.

Spiritual and organic form are connected through the capacity of the material to realize ideal form. In this sense, matter becomes not a crippler, but an objectifier. Thus Emerson translates Michelangelo's poetic expression of this idea:

> Never did sculptor's dream unfold
> A form which marble doth not hold
> In its white block . . .

In this interpretation, the uniting of spiritual form with matter ceases to be an *imposing* of form from without, and becomes a *freeing* of the possible plan contained in matter itself.

With the help which Nature may give the artist in objectifying his divinely inspired plan, we have reached the principle of organic form.

In its simplest sense, organic form states that a work of art derives excellence from its resemblance to natural objects. First, it may look or sound like a natural phenomenon: a painting looks like an apple, a statue recalls the human body, a symphony sounds like a river. The principle of imitation enters into this conception, though Emerson and Coleridge are reluctant to admit it — partly because they had developed "organic form" to supplant "imitation," a term which neoclassic usage had crusted with artificiality.

The second and more subtle definition of organic form is the development of details in a work according to one controlling purpose, so that the whole presents a union of integrated parts, as a mountain or a rye field. This is the Coleridgean sense of "organic" as distinguished from "mechanic" form.[5] In this signification of a strong design shaping details, Emerson recognizes the principle of selection. In the essay on "Beauty," he writes:

> Our art saves material by more skillful arrangement, and reaches beauty by taking every superfluous ounce that can be spared from a wall, and keeping all its strength in the poetry of its columns. In rhetoric, this art of omission is a chief secret of power, and . . . proof of high culture to say the greatest matters in the simplest way.

Underlying this theory of selection is a confidence in the *simplest* method in architecture or writing. Lecturing on The Naturalist, in 1834, Emerson calls the attention of his audience to Nature's wonderful "Composition," in which a strong contrast appears between "the simplicity of the means and the gorgeousness of the result." From Nature's "cheap architecture" the artist can learn how to use straight lines and short distances. Impressed by recent physical discoveries in the conservation of energy, Emerson, lecturing on Economy in 1851, indicates Nature as a laboratory for the artist in search of form: "She watches for the crumbling atoms, seizes them as they fall, redistributes them instantly into new bodies." In the skull's arch, the eagle's quill, the fish's bones, the artist may find the secret of "the best and cheapest form." Thus Emerson speaks in the essay on "History" of observing natural forms which undoubtedly suggested their artistic counterparts: a cloud resembling an architectural cherub, with wings outspread, a thunderbolt in the sky from which the Greeks undoubtedly drew Jove's symbol, a snowdrift that may have suggested the architectural scroll. The artist who thus follows Nature's economy will avoid ornament for its own sake. "Vicious ornament," Emerson says, "is like those excrescences on plants which the ignorant may mistake for a flower, but which the botanist knows to be a diseased growth around the eggs of a worm." [6] Since Emerson thinks of Nature as working "after the same method as the human Imagination," he concludes that artists can learn much about form from watching nature in action.

Conversely, the artist may sometimes learn (though he will find this more difficult to follow) something of the extravagance of art, from watching nature. Thus Emerson records Ellery Channing's whimsical annoyance with Nature's prodigality: "Nature puts us out. Nature too green; badly disposed as to light. The horses are leggy, and the birds feathery. Nature then is not only green, but too windy. Too many leaves." [7] When Emerson showed Channing a beautiful sunset, with a telegraph pole standing in the midst of the color, "like the spear of Uriel," Channing said, "Why yes, Nature lies like the Irish." [8] In this instance Channing was the means of rescuing the concept of organic form from too strict an interpretation, by indicating that the artist may occasionally tell an extravagant untruth without going beyond the lines indicated by Nature.

For the most part Emerson's discussion of form shows little

recognition of architectonic sense, as "one design controlling manifold details." Occasionally he admits the principle, as in the essay "Art and Criticism," where criticism is judged an art in so far as it passes beyond a poet's words, and looks "at the order of his thoughts and the essential quality of his mind." In the second essay on "Eloquence" (1870) Emerson mentions method, or the power to arrange facts, as one of the orator's requirements. The need for form in a speech is more fully expressed in the 1867 lecture on Eloquence, in which he says:

> The form is much, for geometry, masonry, level and square, firm cornerstone and foundation, and symmetrical rising through the useful parts to the tower and the pinnacle are as necessary in a speech, a sermon, or even a poem, as in a house, or a mathematical demonstration.

Advising young Charles Woodbury on how to achieve the "marble" or "crystallized" state which goes a step beyond the "limestone" condition characteristic of most writers, Emerson speaks of the importance of design. Here he recognizes that the achievement of design is usually made psychologically rather than logically; that is, by a gradual assortment of the scattered ideas which come into the writer's mind.

More often Emerson's analysis of design emphasizes purpose, or end result. In the first essay on "Art," he speaks of art as *contraction*: "What is his [man's] speech, his love of painting, love of nature, but a still finer success — all the weary miles and tons of space and bulk left out, and the spirit or moral of it contracted into a musical word, or the most cunning stroke of the pencil?" The principle of selection is usually considered simply as omission, by which the artist leaves out dull details and retains only "the spirit and splendor" of nature.

Organic form, then, in its first meaning, concerns art's resemblance to natural objects; in its second, the control of one design throughout the details of a work. A third sense of the term appears in a work's being judged organic if it produces upon the observer an impression similar to that caused by nature's works. Though subjective, this third criterion may not be dismissed as invalid. Thus a work is deemed *healthy* or *sound* if it reminds one of similar well-built objects in nature. In the essay on "Beauty," for example, Emerson praises a fine statue for the healthy grace that has resulted from the sculptor's careful adjustment of bones in their sockets. And Phidias' designs are strong as trees or stones. He urges scholars to give up their "sickly" indoor thoughts and write the "fresh, blooming, out-of-door thoughts of sound men." Apples and apple trees seem to occur naturally to Emerson's mind as standards of comparison for the "healthy" in art and human nature. Thus an apple tree which bears fruit only once a year is still acceptable to his mind when covered with ice in the January wind — not so some "past and future birds" who never produce any fruit, but merely attitudinize in his parlor.[9] "Windfalls" is his term for other "inwardly sick" people, "patched up for a day or two, but unsound to the core": "I see young people, men and women, who resemble with fair outside and ready wit without faith or hope the wind-fallen apples under a tree with bright red cheek and yellow side but diminutive in size, and rottenness and wormy within" (Ms. J. D., Pt. II, 1839). The demand for health is paralleled by a standard of *wholeness*; as the works of nature give an impression of completeness, so should the work of art produce "a new and fairer whole." Difficult as this subjective measure is to evaluate, it supplies the critic with a whole field of "natural" metaphor by which to express his observation of art.

The development of Emerson's conception of organic form is complex. He may well have met the idea first in Francis Bacon's criticism of the Platonic forms. Agreeing with Plato that forms are "the true object of knowledge," Bacon attacked Plato's consideration of "forms" apart from matter. Instead, he proposed to study motion, heat, coldness as forces integrally connected with matter and more capable of being known than abstract forms.[10] The fact that Emerson's interest in Bacon's discussion did not involve complete understanding is shown by his query: "What were Bacon's forms?" Through his contrast between two types of virtue, however, Bacon presents a very clear picture of what the romantics called "organic form":

> This [organic virtue] is indeed like the work of nature, whereas the other course [superficial] is like the work of the hand; for . . . when a carver makes an image, he shapes only that part whereupon he worketh, as if he be upon the face, that part which shall be the body is but a rude stone still . . . but, contrariwise, when nature makes a flower or living creature, she formeth rudiments of all the parts at one time.[11]

Bacon here states an idea that enters into Emerson's "organic" theory: the notion that the artist can never make his work grow all at once, in the living way of a flower, a leaf, or a tree. Emerson's one answer to this unanswerable objection is to say that works of art are "spiritually reproductive," in contrast to nature's "organic reproduction."

Ironically enough, Bacon, who presented Emerson with an early expression of organic form, became the target of Emerson's censure for failing to embody strong structure in his writing. Lecturing on Bacon in 1835, Emerson finds his work lacking in the "intrinsic unity" which characterizes *Hamlet*:

> Bacon's method is not within the work itself, but without. This might be expected in his *Natural History*, but . . . in his *Essays* it is the same. All his work lies along the ground a

vast unfinished city. He did not arrange but unceasingly collect [*sic*] facts. His own Intellect often acts little on what he collects. Very much stands as he found it — mere lists of facts . . . The fire has hardly passed over it and given it fusion and a new order from his own mind. It is sand without lime . . . The order is much of it quite mechanical things on one subject being thrown together; the order of a shop and not that of a tree or an animal where perfect assimilation has taken place and all the parts have a perfect unity.

This criticism not only represents a fair judgment of much of Bacon's writing, but is the most consistent evaluation which Emerson has made of an author, in the light of organic form. Perhaps Bacon had taught him better than he knew.

Bacon's desire to turn from the consideration of final causes to more measurable elements was well known also to Goethe, who in turn supplied a thread for Emerson's "organic" texture.[12] Of the many aesthetic suggestions which Emerson derived from Goethe, the element which he borrowed here was Goethe's idea of a beneficent necessity as opposed to fate (which may include an element of evil). Thus Emerson's definition of the beautiful echoes Goethe: "Arising out of eternal Reason, one and perfect, whatever is beautiful rests on the foundation of the necessary. Nothing is arbitrary, nothing is insulated in beauty. It depends forever on the necessary and the useful." [13]

Coleridge, whom Emerson began to read in 1830, and whose influence continued during his productive years, supplied Emerson with the application of organic form to literature. Though Coleridge more often uses the principle in its architectonic sense, that is, the development of a work according to one design, and Emerson more often in comparing works of art to natural objects, the principle is the same.

From certain mystical writers Emerson received confirmation of his belief in correspondence between man and external nature, the basis for organic form. He is attracted by Sampson Reed's analysis of the mind through chemical metaphors, terming it an "active solvent" of the subjects presented to it, and comparing the mind's arrangement of ideas to the process of crystallization. "The most perfect understanding of a subject," Reed says, "is simply a perception of harmony existing between the subject and the mind itself." [14] In Swedenborg, with whose thought Emerson first became acquainted through Swedenborg's disciple Reed, the whole concept of correspondence was extended and particularized. Study of a stone's magnetic powers, for example, Swedenborg terms an excellent approach to "the nature and laws of the material heavens both visible and invisible." [15]

Emerson's concept is also fertilized by the explanation of man's relation to nature which he finds in *The True Messiah* of the French mystic, Oegger. Praising Oegger's attempt to "put his hands like Atlas under nature and heave her from her rest," Emerson adopts in *Nature* Oegger's description of material objects as "scoriae of the substantial thoughts of the Creator." The idea of a necessity controlling works of art as well as of nature, frequently stated by Emerson, is strongly affirmed by Oegger, who insists that the forms and colors of man's creation are as definitely determined as the objects of the material world. Oegger throws some light on the relation between aesthetic form and that of God's creation when he says: "The Universe in its minutest details existed for God as really before the creation, as after it; because it existed in him substantially as the statue exists in the block of marble from which the sculptor extracts it." [16]

From these mystical concepts of Reed and Oegger Emerson derived a fresh statement of the "God-like" nature of organic form, and also a confirmation of his native disposition to conceive a form growing in an artist's mind with the same mixture of mystery and calculation which prevails in the combination of chemical atoms. From the experimental attitude of Bacon he was encouraged to take a more tentative position on the development of aesthetic form than if he had derived his "organic" concept from Plato's "ideal" forms. Goethe helped him to see the whole world of art as a universe of equal importance with the natural, though always dependent upon it, and Coleridge assisted him to apply the idea to literature. From these varied strands taken from other writers, Emerson wove his own "organic" web.

One might expect that an organic theory of art would give some attention to the relation of ugliness to aesthetic form. Since Emerson regards evil philosophically as "privative" rather than absolute, one is surprised to discover that he does consider the problem of ugliness in art. Lecturing on Beauty in 1858, he remarks on the discrepancy between man's love of beauty and his moral feeling, which appears in his amusement at the useful though homely donkey, and his making emblems of those "handsome cats," the lion, leopard, and tiger. Emerson is disturbed by the victory of beauty over morality shown by this favoring of fiercely beautiful animals over the good but ugly donkey. His instinctive feeling is that inner beauty of character should also make the outer person attractive. When character fails to have that effect — as with Turner, whose face remains ugly despite his creation of beautiful paintings — he asserts that character makes up for the lack of outer grace. Conversely, a handsome person who expresses ignoble sentiments becomes suddenly ugly in Emerson's eyes. These compensations, however, never quite make up for his disappointment when "inner" qualities of character fail to match outer manifestations of grace, or vice versa. The reason is that in the perfect working of organic form, the two should be consonant. Emerson's position is humorously illustrated by his comment on the squinting servant in his house, who was dishonest as well as ugly. When she returned the money she had stolen, it seemed to him that her strabismus should have been healed at the same time as her moral character.

Though Emerson treats the relation between beauty and moral character chiefly as an individual matter, his lecture on England (1849) recognizes the effect of social conditions on personal beauty:

> These fair ruddy muscular well-educated bodies go attended by poor dwarfed starved short-lived skeletons. There are two Englands: — rich Norman Saxon learned social England, — seated in castles, halls . . . and poor, celtic, peasant drudging chartist England, in hovels and workhouses, cowed and hopeless.

Here Emerson implies (at least by indirection) how this bodily ugliness may be turned in the direction of beauty. For the most part, however, such consideration of man-made conditions is only incidental to his study of the more important fashioners of organic form: the phenomena of nature, and the driving natural Spirit which forces matter into beautiful patterns.

Certainly Emerson's concept of organic form does not demand that art adopt a nature "red in tooth and claw." But he does indicate that artistic expression would profit by the removal of artificial barriers. He regrets that the nose cannot be mentioned in poetry, he speaks of the limitation which the teeth impose on the human frame — even children, he says, are considered prettier with their mouths closed — and he finds that painters will not show men eating, though they paint birds pecking at fruit and oxen browsing in the field. This last restraint he lays at the door of civilization, not of the painters, since the custom of eating "sodden" bread indoors has taken away the poetic association which once accompanied primitive outdoor eating.

Perhaps Emerson has given more place to evil in his aesthetic than in his general philosophy because he is able there to show its place in a definite scheme, as no one can do so adequately in life. He recalls Swedenborg's statement that "the hells were not without their extreme satisfaction." "What would painter do," he asks, in "Considerations by the Way," "but for crucifixions and hells?" Here he has in mind, however, not concentration upon the torment in itself, but upon the "marvellous balance" of beauty and disgust. Thus in "Circles" he suggests that "our crimes may be lively stones out of which we shall construct the temple of the true god." On reading a terrifying story of murder, Emerson's sense of gloom cleared up when he discovered the story's purpose: "a systematic long-sought accurately-measured revenge." Once the horror was shown to have meaning, it became bearable.[17] In his lecture on Byron (1836) Emerson censures that poet for cursing at too great length in the fifth canto of *Childe Harold*, reminding him that the place of malevolent feelings in poetry is "only for a short time or in company with and under the counter-action of others." His general view is that evil may appear in art, if subordinated to the plan of the whole. That "melancholy show of bones, of distortions and diseases" which Emerson witnessed at the Medical Rooms he denoted as a limitation "which the man must recognize to draw his plan true." A good epitome of the place of evil in Emerson's aesthetic is the tortoise which Plotinus describes as obstructing the movements of the dance: "If the tortoise had arranged itself with the dance, it would not have suffered from those that composed it." [18] The artist who keeps this symbol in mind will not allow the elements of evil to conceal the ruling purpose of his work.

As the artist gets from nature the secret of form, so may he learn from her how to "absorb" the evil aspects — he will find, for example, that greener grass grows on patches where cattle have dropped dung. Nature's absorption of the ugly is well epitomized by Emerson's description of a hawk, "wheeling up to heaven in spiral flight":

> What [he asks] could be more in unison with all pure and brilliant images. Yet is the creature an unclean greedy eater, and all his geography from that grand observatory was a watching of barn-yards, or an inspection of field-mice . . . Yet observe how finely in nature all these disagreeable individuals integrate themselves into a cleanly and pleasing whole. (*J.*, 1834)

Thus nature demonstrates to the artist that the unpleasant is the potentially beautiful, which has not yet been absorbed into design. The success of seventeenth-century poets in using ugly material Emerson compares, in the essay on "Literature," to a similar adaptation in nature and art:

> As nature, to pique the more, sometimes works up deformities into beauty in some rare Aspasia or Cleopatra; and as the Greek art wrought many a vase or column, in which too long, or too lithe, or nodes, or pits and flaws are made a beauty of; — so these poets were so quick and vital that they could charm and enrich by mean and vulgar objects.

If Emerson's consideration of ugliness in organic form is not extensive, it is nevertheless fuller than his usually sanguine view of life might lead us to expect. He takes account of the exceptions to the dominant idea that outer grace should accompany inner beauty; he indicates that the apparently ugly

may acquire charm when placed in a general design; and he
points to nature as a guide to achieving that assimilation.

ORGANIC FORM IN THE FINE ARTS

Greek art. Emerson shares with English and German romantics, as with the men of the Greek Revival in America, the
enthusiasm for Greek art as an early embodiment of organic
form. In his lecture on Beauty (1859) Emerson underscores
his appreciation of Greek art by saying: "It is impossible to
speak of art without rushing to the Greeks." Probably his first
acquaintance with criticism of Greek art came from Alison,
whose *Essays on Taste* he read in 1830; he extended his reading to Flaxman in 1832; to Christopher Wren in 1836; [19] to
Winckelmann and Lessing in 1838. A number of statements
from Goethe about the Greek temperament, manly beauty in
sculpture, strength in architecture, are translated in his journal
of 1836 and in the Goethe Transcript. The liking for Greek
art, especially for sculpture, once established, continued
throughout his life.

In commenting on Greek art, Emerson praises the objective
qualities of proportion, fitness to an end, economy of means;
and the subjective traits of health and temperance which underlie this external beauty. The general tenor of this appreciation
follows the drift of romantic criticism.[20] The lecture on Beauty
praises the strict form implicit in Greek art:

> Greek architecture is geometry, — as peaceful and sure as
> mathematics. Its temples are diagrams in marble, — a sort of
> flowering of geometry in the sense that a globe is the power
> of the circle, — a cube is the power of the square, — and a
> cone is the power of the right-angled triangle.

Speaking to an audience in Manchester, England, in 1847,
Emerson denotes temperance as the keynote to all the Greek

arts: rhetoric, painting, sculpture, architecture, adding that the quality also implied restraint in character, as in mixing water with wine.

Although Emerson's comments on Greek art hew closely to the line of romantic criticism, they are not literary only, but based on personal observation as well. In a lecture on Art and Criticism (1859) Emerson looks back to the year 1823, when Augustus Thorndike, on Canova's advice, presented the first casts of Greek statues to the Boston Athenaeum. He lists the Belvedere Apollo; the Laocoön; the Venus de' Medici; the Gladiator Borghese; the Discobulus; the Torso (of Hercules); the Antinous. These, he says, at a time when few people traveled to Italy, "fed the eyes of young men like nectar." When Emerson sees the originals of the Apollo and Laocoön in Rome, and the Venus in Florence, he finds that earlier acquaintance with the plaster casts has better prepared him for appreciation of their marble archetypes.[21]

On his second voyage to England (1847–48) Emerson discovered the Elgin Marbles with a delight only slightly less intense than that of Keats. His lecture on Beauty in Art (1859) praises Lord Elgin for acquiring the Parthenon Marbles for England, and Haydon the painter for attesting to their genuineness. He deems the imaginative feat of reconstructing the temple comparable to Owen's rebuilding of the antediluvian Dinornis skeleton from a single bone. Finding as much cause for every rosette as for the foundation or the roof, he admires the fitness of the temple's ornament, in which ten statues, for example, represent ten cities, and dove, snake, and crab stand for the various city emblems. Making little distinction between the Greek Marbles and the Xanthian (Lycian) Marbles brought from Asia Minor by Sir Charles Fellows, Emerson recounted to his audience in his lecture on London (1849) his pleasure in seeing the Xanthian collection under the immediate guidance of Sir Charles Fellows himself. Emerson's criticism of both collections takes a practical turn when he condemns the arrangement of the marbles, without names, numbers, or skillful order. A young scholar, he suggests, might well prepare himself to guide visitors through the display by reading Winckelmann and Visconti.

Perhaps the most important way in which Greek art fulfilled Emerson's concept of form was its demonstration of functionalism, particularly in architecture. The "functional" critic judges a building beautiful in the degree to which it fits means to ends. Doubtless Alison first suggested this idea to Emerson, when he proposed, in place of the earlier conception that Greek beauty is "intrinsic," the idea of fitness of means to ends, as the reason for that beauty.[22] In this interpretation, the building is beautiful if the walls seem adequate to support the weight of the ceiling, the temple large enough for worshippers, the ornaments related to religious or political ideas. Emerson himself employs the principle chiefly in statements about the useful arts.

With Greek art before us as an embodiment of organic form, let us see how Emerson applies the principle to architecture and sculpture.

Architecture. Architecture presents the clearest demonstration of Emerson's theory of organic form. Emerson terms it a "mixed" art, combining the useful with the beautiful; serving man's needs, but drawing its inspiration from Divine power. The architect's dependence on nature appears in his deriving plans for buildings direct from her phenomenal forms: sea shells, birds' nests, spider webs. In an eloquent passage in the essay on "History," reminiscent of Bryant's description of the groves as "God's first temples," Emerson finds the origin of the Gothic church in an adaptation of arched trees in the forest.

A road through pine woods in winter recalls to his mind "the low arch of the Saxons," and the sunset seen through bare branches, the stained-glass windows of Gothic cathedrals. One who looks at the old Oxford buildings, he says, must feel "that the forest overpowered the mind of the builder," so that his implements reproduced not only the larger pattern of arches, but smaller ones of ferns, flowers, and pine cones. Thus, Emerson concludes: "The Gothic cathedral is a blossoming in stone subdued by the insatiable demand for harmony in man. The mountain of granite blooms into an eternal flower, with the lightness and delicate finish as well as the aerial proportions of vegetable beauty." [23] His intense appreciation of the cathedral as an embodiment of natural beauty appears in the phrases which show it taken up into the universal "chain of being" — the "mountain of granite" "blossoming in stone," "blooming into an eternal flower."

In Italy in 1833 Emerson experienced a splendor of church architecture for which the bare simplicity of Boston's Unitarian churches had ill prepared him. In Naples he found nothing remarkable in the exterior of the six or seven churches he visited, though he delighted in their inner spaciousness and lofty decoration. In Rome at the festive season of Easter, Emerson gives highest praise to St. Peter's, which he describes in his journal as "the sublime of the beautiful." In that gem of Italian churches, Santa Croce in Florence, he takes keen delight, finding the stained-glass windows most beautiful after sunset, at the hour of candlelight. Although he employs the catch phrase of "frosted cake" to describe Milan Cathedral from a distance, he admires its "profusion of slender pinnacles shooting up their ornamented forms into the sky, and every one surmounted by a saint," and on more careful inspection finds the cathedral "impressive and glorious without and within," admiring "the grand perspective of its ribbed Gothic aisles seen by light which is all coloured by the stained windows but mostly yellow."

The journal comments on Italian architecture show Emerson's fondness for surveying a city from a high prospect, which reveals the buildings "taken up into nature," becoming a part of clouds, sky, and landscape. Here his own experience furnishes a basis for the principle later to be expressed in the second essay on "Art," as "adventitious beauty." [24] Looking down upon Pompeii from the temple of Venus, he admires the unique view of half a mile of roofless houses. In his first lecture on Italy (1834), Emerson tries to recapture for his audience the charm of the spectacle seen from the theater at Pompeii:

> Wide around lies the green and fertile land sprinkled plentifully with white villages and palaces and monasteries, washed by the sea adorned with islands and close at hand on the other side the solemn mountain, author of all the ruin and now black recent streams of lava, without a green shrub or so much as a blade of grass upon its side and a little smoke stealing out of its summit as if to say — the fire that once and again has ravaged this garden is not quenched.

Here the vista's charm is enhanced by the contrast between the impression of outer peace and the potentially destructive power of the quiescent volcano. In Rome Emerson enjoys a similar perspective on the ruins of aqueducts, their successive arches running for miles. From St. Peter's cupola there is the view of the Campagna, with the Appennines on one side, the sea on the other, many-peopled Rome, and "Tiber flowing through this marble wilderness." In Florence his eye is charmed by the "curve" of Ponte de Trinità, and "the fine old towers of the city, the rich purple lines of the Appennines broken by the bolder summits of the marble mountains of Carrara."

Through the "distant" view, Emerson was able to see the

place of single buildings in the larger scheme of Nature. Not only in the "adventitious" beauty contributed by natural surroundings, but in the size and mass of great cathedrals, he discovers organic form. Of the Cathedral Church of St. Agatha at Catania, he exclaims: "What exhilaration does the mere height of these prodigious churches produce! We feel so little and so exalted upon the floor that we are reminded of the sensations that arise from an extended mountain prospect."

Here structure does not consist in resemblance to natural objects, but in the artist's use of such natural laws as the principle of gravity. In his journal of 1840 Emerson explains his feeling of elevation in the presence of great buildings:

> In architecture, height and mass have a wonderful effect because they suggest immediately a relation to the sphere on which the structure stands, and so to the gravitating system. The tower which with such painful solidity soars like an arrow to heaven apprizes us in an unusual manner of that law of gravitation, by its truth to which it can rear aloft into the atmosphere those dangerous masses of granite, and keep them there for ages as if it were a feather or a scrap of down. Then, great mass, especially in height, has some appreciable proportion to the size of the globe and so appears to us as a splinter of the orb itself.

Thus, by his use of the principle of gravity, which is in a sense his enemy, the architect gives the impression of having created a "splinter" of the great orb, the world. This organic structure is developed, not as a bird builds its nest, but as the earth holds its place in the solar system. More than any of the other arts, Emerson explains, architecture must make friends with the elements of sun, wind, and rain, as well as the physical laws of gravity, lest it be in turn destroyed by the very force of nature.

In Egyptian temples even more than in European, Emerson

discovers a relation between the architect's plan and the universe. In a lecture on Memory (1871) he remarks the discovery of carving on the under side of old Egyptian structures, indicating the ruins of a still older civilization. The quality which he chiefly notes in Egyptian architecture is the tremendous size of the temples, built in proportion to the globe. Emerson's interest in Egyptian architecture dates from 1838, when he copied in his journal several quotations from Heeren's *Historical Researches*, concerning the frightening effect upon observers of the vast conceptions which produced the great Egyptian temples. Heeren points out the relation between the huge masses and shapes built by Egyptian architects, and the natural caverns from which their designs were drawn.[25] To Elizabeth Peabody in September of 1838, Emerson writes his enthusiasm for Heeren's researches, saying that he has read the Persian and Egyptian history, and is now alternating between the Phoenician and the Indian. "If I were not bound so fast to my two acres," he says, "I should have looked in the newspapers last week for passage to Alexandria, and have studied the ways and means of seeing for myself the vast saloon of Karnac and the temples of Luxor." In 1840 he is studying the plates in Baron Denon's *Travels in Upper and Lower Egypt*, at the Athenaeum, finding the illustrated plates "a rich spectacle" after his reading in Heeren. Lecturing on Art and Nature in 1868, he speaks of the simple, "natural" form of the pyramid:

> The Egyptian pyramid is in the first place a cairn or pile of stones, as our Indians had the custom of never passing certain historic spots without throwing a stone. 'Tis the simplest form that gravel dumped down from a cart will take. The Egyptians gave this pile a square foundation, and hence the pyramid. Of course, it cannot fall. That is the

type of Egyptian architecture, superfluity of base, made stronger still by truncating the pyramid at the top.

As in Greek art Emerson detects the moral quality of temperance, so in Egyptian sphinxes he finds health and an expression of "complacency and tranquillity" — qualities which he puts to poetic use in his composition "The Sphinx."

Not until 1872 did Emerson at last visit Egypt. From Alexandria he writes to William Forbes that he can still "wake to the wonders of this strange old land," seeing in the colossal Egyptian temples an achievement which men of the nineteenth century can no longer attain. The size and profusion of sphinxes and statues is more forcibly borne in upon him by the "small and limitary" look of the country: "no breadth — nothing but the two banks of the long Nile."

Emerson's appreciation of grandeur in Egyptian architecture shows a flexibility of taste unusual in a period when the Greek was the measuring stick. Though other critics and connoisseurs at this time showed an awakening interest in Egyptian art, few were willing, as was Emerson, to consider Egyptian art not merely as the bizarre, but as a production indigenous to its people and in its way as important as the Greek. Recognizing that the Greeks made technical advances over Egyptian art, Emerson still finds the pyramids an excellent reflection of Nature's colossal design. In a sense, Emerson's reference to Egyptian as well as to Greek art for architectural standards is but a symptom of his catholic taste, as in his lecture on Art and Nature (1879), where he lists the five orders of architecture recognized by the textbooks: Egyptian, Doric, Ionic, Corinthian, and Gothic, but asks: "Where was the Chinese, and the Hindoo, and the Persian, and the Saracenic? Five is a very narrow counting for the styles of men."

The English counterpart of the pyramid is Stonehenge,

which Emerson visited with Carlyle in 1847. The two clambered about the rocks for a day, comparing notes on the structure. "Only mastodons," Emerson reflected, "could have piled these huge stones on each other." Carlyle compared the rude formation to "the flight of ages and the succession of religions." The grandeur of the rockpile led Emerson to conclude the early architect God-like, and to agree with Stukeley's comment (1740) on "the Deity who made the world by the scheme of Stonehenge."

When Emerson applies the organic principle to American architecture of the nineteenth century, he indicates that changes in building should be adopted to supply man's altered needs:

> The wise man [Emerson says] will prize and obtain the luxuries of baths, of ventilated houses, of gardens . . . Is not thought freer and fairer in a house with apartments that admit of easy solitude than in a foul room?
>
> Justice can be administered on a heath, and God can be worshipped in a barn. It is, nevertheless, fit that Justice should be administered in a stately hall open to the sun and air . . . and that God should be honored in temples whose proportion and decoration harmonize with the works of nature . . . (*J.*, 1838)

Emerson wishes to see these so-called luxuries adopted by American houses, courts, and churches, if they fulfill genuine necessities. In his search for a typically American architectural form, he is not willing to accept Margaret Fuller's ideal of the Western log cabin, gradually expanded to accommodate the settler's growing family — perhaps because his western tours had shown him too many "temporary" log cabins put up overnight and abandoned after six months, ruins of sagging boards and leaking roofs. Nor, as a family man, could he accept Thoreau's one-room hut as the ideal. The house which

Thoreau compared to a burden carried on a man's back for fifty years meant to Emerson a satisfaction of various human requirements. Although his own home in Concord could hardly have been run without servants, it provided him a comfortable dwelling for some forty years, with adequate space for his own study, his children's play, and guests' entertainment. The house lacked the elevation which he would have liked, but it offered a wide view of surrounding fields. In one early-morning look from his own doors he sees "an astonishing magnificence": "When I see this spectacle so near, and so surprising, I think no house should be built quite low, or should obstruct the prospect by trees." Little changed today from its state in Emerson's time, the Emerson house still embodies the combination of austerity with comfort which typifies the best New England home building.

"A country person's" ideal for a home is cited with approval in Emerson's lecture on Hospitality and Homes (1868). The house is to be built low, so that one need not climb stairs all day, wood rather than stone to be used in construction, since the house need not last forever, and special attention to be paid to the orientation — that is, openness to the sun on all sides. Emerson's practical sense of building appears in his criticism of flats he visited in Philadelphia and New York, where light entered only from front or rear, leaving the inner chambers dark. He takes note also of the sacrifice of convenience in some houses to a piazza, or an overgrand staircase; even of such mundane matters as ill-built chimneys and leaking cellars.

To show man's dwelling as an epitome of his human needs, Emerson employs an anatomical figure:

> Every work repeats in small the nature of the workman, a house is a sort of statue or mask of the builder, the underpinning being the feet; the cellar, the abdomen; the kitchen,

the stomach; the windows, the eyes; the chimney, the nose;
the sitting room, the heart; the library, the brain; and the
lower members with their uses are not wanting in the vents
and vaults of the house. (Ms. J. W., 1845)

Emerson's conception of organic form in American domestic architecture admits of more grandeur than is allowed
in the strict functionalism of some modern designers.[26] Making
allowance for amplitude of design to fit changing needs, Emerson also seeks a spaciousness which will satisfy the "aesthetic
eye" rather than mere bodily demands. In his memory lingers
the recollection of Stafford House, that "best house of the
English kingdom," [27] and he seeks to acquire for the American
scene a touch of Europe's "monumental solidity."

Though Emerson has offered less criticism of public buildings than one might wish, a few perceptive comments appear
in the journals, letters, and lectures, concerning government
buildings and churches. Speaking at the centennial celebration
of the Boston Latin School in 1876, he mentions Bulfinch as
the architect of the State House and of the Capitol in Washington. His comment on the Capitol, written to Margaret
Fuller in 1843, includes praise for its mass, its commanding
position, and its imposing entrances, again with a practical
criticism of the "inconveniently small" interior passage. From
London in 1847, Emerson describes to his wife the "dusky
magnificence" of the West End buildings, which makes his
walking "dreamlike," and which he compares to John Martin's
pictures of Babylon — "light, darkness, architecture and all."

It is not surprising that Emerson should have been most
sensitive to church architecture. As early as 1829 he writes
from Hartford to Abel Adams to praise the Gothic structure
of the unfinished Episcopal church there, finding it superior
to the new Trinity Church about to be dedicated on Summer

Street in Boston. From Naples in 1833, he expresses to his brother William his desire for one temple built in America after the magnificent Italian manner:

> Every people is just as much padlocked to its own customs whether of eating or architecture or worship or what not, and we, no doubt, shall continue, in America, fancy free though we be, to build mean churches with pews for a thousand years to come, instead of those sublime old temples so lofty and many-chapeled, covered with the marble and gold of ages . . .

Yet he could revert to an admiration of simplicity in church building, as in his fine observation of the church clock in Concord, heard ticking at night "like the step of time": "You catch the sound first by looking up at the clock's face. And then you see this wooden tower rising thus alone and stable and aged, toward the midnight stars. It has affiance and privilege with them."

The keen perception which these comments reveal makes one wish that Emerson had spoken more fully about specific monuments of American architecture. One must admire his application of the general principle of organic form to the buildings he observes, his desire to see American builders absorb the best of European styles while maintaining their own integrity, and his appreciation for the grand in architecture, combined with a practical sense that leans toward functionalism.

The similarity of Emerson's theory of architecture to that of Horatio Greenough is to be explained as interrelation rather than influence. When Emerson met Greenough in Florence in 1833, the chief theoretical point which Greenough discussed was his admiration for the Greeks. Though Greenough's first article, "Remarks on American Art," was printed in 1843 in

The United States Magazine and Democratic Review, Emerson seems not to have read it until 1852. The summary of
Greenough's theory, presented by Emerson in *English Traits*,
closely parallels his own concept of organic form:

> A scientific arrangement of spaces and forms to functions
> and to site; an emphasis of features proportioned to their
> *graduated* importance in function; color and ornament to be
> decided and arranged and varied by strictly organic laws,
> having a distinct reason for each decision; the entire and
> immediate banishment of all make-shift and make-believe.

Greenough's statement presents a well-organized formulation of an idea which Emerson had held for some time.
Emerson's theory clearly corresponds with Greenough's
definition of functionalism as "the external expression of the
inward function of the building — adaptation of its features
and their gradation to its dignity and importance." [28]

A friendly interchange of ideas was carried on between
the two men. Emerson read the manuscript of Greenough's
articles, which were not published in book form until
Greenough received Emerson's approval. In both theories the
concept of functionalism is applied particularly to the useful
arts; Greenough's discovery of functional beauty in yachts
and steam engines might be termed a confirmation of the
value placed by Emerson on "the familiar, the low."

Beneath the similarity, some difference exists between the
two theories. Greenough, as a practical artist, places more
emphasis upon the technique by which functional principles
are executed; and he finds functional beauty only in Greek
principles (even though his own practice diverged from the
strictly Greek ideal). Emerson is less concerned than
Greenough about the danger of adapting European styles to
American architecture; quite naturally, each writer is wor-

ried about the evil of imitation in the art he knows best —
Emerson in poetry, Greenough in architecture.[29]

Both writers, by their admission of the moral element,
must be disqualified as strict "functionalists." The moral element appears, for example, in Edward Garbett's treatise on
architecture,[30] called to Emerson's attention by Greenough
as an expression of the functional theory. Writing to
Greenough in 1852 about the work, Emerson remarks that
Garbett is Ruskin's scholar, but "a better teacher than the
master." Nor does Emerson see any difference between
Greenough's theory of functionalism and that expressed by
Garbett. At the very beginning of his treatise, however,
Garbett seeks another principle than that of *use*. For "architecture proper" he proposes the objects: politeness, beauty,
expression, poetry, which show a departure from the idea
that a building's beauty lies in fulfillment of function.
Garbett, stating that a building may fulfill its aim and still
look ugly, finds the answer to that ugliness in a curious place
— Emerson's essay on "Art." Supported by Emerson's reference to the "selfish and even cruel aspect" of modern
machinery,[31] Garbett concludes: "Is not an unarchitectural
building ugly simply because it looks selfish?" While the
main emphasis of Emerson's essay is functional rather than
moral, it is significant that Garbett fastens upon Emerson's
moral statement, and that neither Greenough nor Emerson
sees any inconsistency in the fact. Perhaps it is well to have
before us this "moral" impression made by Emerson upon his
contemporary, lest we go too far in equating his theory of
organic form in architecture to that of modern thinkers.[32]

First awakened to a perception of form in architecture by
his view of Italian churches, Emerson was encouraged by
Goethe to see natural patterns in architectural design. Always
hospitable to other thinkers' speculation, he strengthened his

own concept of organic form in building by interchange of ideas with Greenough.[33] Emerson has best applied his concept of architectural form to domestic building, in which the theoretical starting point, a concern for human needs, is reinforced by observation of homes in America and abroad, and admits of some grandeur and beauty beyond the strict satisfaction of necessity.

Between the functional theory that a building's beauty depends on its fulfillment of purpose, and the "decorative" conception that some beauty lies in ornament, Emerson offers a compromise: "Architecture, the skeleton, the resistance to gravity, and the elements make one extreme; florid, petulant anthropomorphism, which carves every pump-handle and door-knob into a human face, is the other; midway between these is the sobriety and grace of art" (*J.*, 1850).

While this idea is actually less characteristic of Emerson's theory of architecture than the functional concept, it exemplifies the middle position which holds true for many of Emerson's general statements about literature and art.

Sculpture. Sculpture presents a simpler aspect of organic form than does architecture, since its chief basis is the human body. Temperamentally more sensitive to sculpture than to painting, Emerson notes the "organic" advantage of sculpture over painting, in educing the life out of the marble block, instead of putting on paint and gold. Reluctant though Emerson is to limit criticism by the method of comparison, he states in the *Dial* notes on "Painting and Sculpture" (1841) that sculpture, especially that of the Greeks, is "the result of all the other arts, the lofty interpreter of them all; not in the order of time, but in the truer one of affinities." Considered historically, "sculpture is the pause of art in the swift current of the life of nations."

Emerson's observation of real sculpture dates from his visit to the Academy of Sciences at Naples in 1833. His first impression of the Academy is that of an embarrassment of riches — "many noble statues Cicero Aristides Seneca the Farnese Hercules Floras Dianas and Apollos without end." Against the greedy cicerones and frivolous sightseers, the severe purity of "the fine old heads" speaks to Emerson as a "moral admonition." The quarter mile of statues in the Vatican gallery increases his sense of being loosed in a wilderness of beauty, though here he gravitates to the Belvedere Apollo, which becomes a standard for all other sculpture, and to the Laocoön, of which he recalls the description "tragedy in stone." The Torso Hercules seems "as familiar to the eye as some old revolutionary cripple." In the Vatican he also sees three statues of Canova, the Perseus, and two fighting gladiators, on which he does not comment.

In Rome he visited the studios of Thorwaldsen, and of the English sculptors Gibson and Wyatt. He saw Thorwaldsen's statue of Byron (later placed in Trinity College, Cambridge), and his Christ, with which Emerson was not impressed. Apparently he discussed art with Thorwaldsen, since he records in his journal (April 1833) the difference between Thorwaldsen's view and his own, concerning art's purpose. Later he recalls with approval Thorwaldsen's description of sculpture: "The clay was the life, plaster the death, and marble the resurrection of sculpture." At Gibson's studio he saw a clay model of the statue of Huskisson and at Wyatt's, the marble of Girl at the Bath. Before going to Florence, he had heard much of Greenough, whom the American artists considered the most talented of the young expatriate sculptors, and superior to the Italian, whom they considered tame. At this time Emerson was disappointed in Greenough's achievement, for the Achilles, which he saw in clay at Florence, despite its "colossal" qualities, seemed to him a poor subject. The statue of Washington, which he saw later at the Capitol, he admired wholeheartedly, merely agreeing with Greenough that it was badly lighted.

The opening of the Athenaeum gallery of sculpture in July 1840 was a landmark in the aesthetic culture of Boston, since it brought into one gallery the statues which had been scattered throughout the building, and added some new pieces. The most famous of the new acquisitions were the casts of Michelangelo's Night and Day, which Greenough had presented to Colonel Perkins for deposit at the Athenaeum. The Athenaeum catalogue of the first exhibition carried Greenough's explanation of their value, since they were "proof casts, made to try the moulds ordered here by the king of the French," "for all purposes of study and criticism identical with the originals," "in the best state and quite new." The fact that Boston was not quite ready for this exhibition is indicated by the catalogue's cautious note on the Laocoön: "These figures, as well as most of the casts in the Athenaeum, are nearly naked, but the conventional costumes of the heroic and mythological times allowed little dress."

Emerson attended the exhibition with great interest. Coming home from the gallery on July 27, he wrote to Margaret Fuller that he wished he had had her notes on the sculpture (published in *The Dial*, October 1840) before going. He admires the Night and Day very much, reproves his friend for not mentioning the two antique Floras, and says that he has admired sculpture on this occasion more than he has for a long time. It is interesting to note that he finds something attractive in every piece except the modern busts. Of eighty items in the exhibit, thirty-seven were modern busts. One might expect that Emerson's great interest in representative men would have aroused his admiration for some of these marble heads. (Margaret Fuller, for example, makes extensive comparisons between the busts of Napoleon and Byron; those of Everett and Allston; and the two heads of Webster, one by Clevenger and one by Powers.)

Although Emerson's comments on the Athenaeum sculpture are not extensive, one cannot question that his frequent views of the statues on visits to the library made a strong impression on his mind. On one occasion, seeking to demonstrate the difference between the philosophy of the Scotch metaphysicians and German idealism, he states that as wide a gulf separates these two as divides the statue of Uncle Toby (one of a sentimental group by Ball Hughes, in which Uncle Toby is shown extracting a cinder from the Widow Wadman's eye) and the figures of Phidias.

The epitome of organic form in sculpture Emerson discovers in the work of Michelangelo. First led by Goethe to admire this sculptor, Emerson proceeded to study him independently. The essay on "Michael Angelo" approves his definition of beauty as "the purgation of superfluities," which of course underlines Emerson's own demand for selection, in artistic form. In his sculpture, Emerson sees that demand for design fulfilled, in "every figure, every hand and foot and finger." [34] Emerson also admires in Michelangelo's sonnets his expression of Platonic idealism, where material beauty is considered the revealer of a higher idea, and external grace termed "the frail and weary weed, in which God dresses the soul which he has called into Time." Thus the exemplar of organic form in practice also shows a clear verbal expression of spiritual form. Emerson's increased enjoyment of Michelangelo's art through reading of his sonnets differs sharply from the attitude of a modern critic, Bernard Berenson, who says that his understanding of Michelangelo as a man, through his letters and poems, has not assisted his appreciation of the artist's statues or paintings.[35] Emerson, on the other hand, even when he read adverse criticism of Michelangelo's extravagant "romanticism," did not renounce his god of sculpture. So long had he enjoyed the artist's work that he was willing "to regard the grandiose as grand."

The choice of Michelangelo for his ideal in sculpture indicates that Emerson's concept of organic form in that art differs sharply from the "classic" ideal. The turbulence as well as the design, the "far-off glimmering" of a distant ideal as well as the integration of idea with form, are the keys to Michelangelo's appeal for Emerson throughout the years.

Despite his admiration for sculpture, Emerson has moments of boredom with it. In the first essay on "Art" he terms sculpture "a merely initial art serving to teach the poet how deep is the secret of form," sympathizes with Newton's scorn for the Earl of Pembroke's collection, as mere "stone dolls," [36] tires of the Greek portrayal of manly beauty, and exalts in its place the "living" beauty of woman, "moving in waves before the eye." In such sculpture as the gargoyles on medieval cathedrals he sees vice, tyranny, and ignorance reflected: a cruel Fate instead of a beneficent Providence. In his journal he goes further, seeing in sculpture and painting "the dislocation of man's mind," "the dances of the savage," classing them below the arts of architecture, poetry, and eloquence. "It cannot be," he says, "that anything so stark dead as Sculpture should be found in a highly improved society." [37]

But this censure reflects the periphery rather than the center of Emerson's aesthetic position, and merely indicates that sculpture was not the first in Emerson's hierarchy of the arts. His more central view is that sculpture's portrayal of the human body gives it a universal appeal to all men. His lecture on Art (1836) sounds as though he were correcting that extreme statement of denying life to sculpture, when he reminds his audience that even antiquated, grotesque pieces reveal the people and time which wrought them:

> Why say sculpture is dead. Every thing has a dozen successive meanings and in the light of a new thought we shall come back and see that the most stiff and misshapen Chinese/Indian idol is a thoroughfare for some human thought and has its beauty considered as a piece of inevitable history.

As for American sculpture, Emerson praises the Mills-Greenough plan of an obelisk instead of a column for Bunker Hill Monument. Aware of the expense of such projects, he censures the extravagance of the Bunker Hill Society, which ended by mortgaging the monument, contrasting it with the good management of the Washington Statue Society, which had enough money left over from paying Horatio Greenough to buy from the Stuart family the unfinished heads of Washington and his wife.[38] Emerson remarks on the situation that it is easier to find architects to build a hall than sculptors to erect monuments.

Although one might expect fuller comment from Emerson on the work of such modern sculptors as Clevenger, Powers, and Frazee, one recognizes that American sculpture had not progressed very far in the years of Emerson's maturity. In a statue called the Shell Girl, by the German sculptor Steinhäuser, he found great beauty, saying that the girl seems "all ear, or, if you look at the shells, you say, 'herself a shell.' "[39]

Emerson's concept of organic form in sculpture shows an appreciation for the well-formed skeleton, as in Michelangelo's work, though his is by no means a Winckelmann's strict worship of the Greek ideal; it is Renaissance rather than Greek, and the color of Platonic idealism suffuses it. Yet in his study of real sculpture abroad and plaster casts at home, Emerson shows an alert eye for form, and a desire, as always, to express what he has seen in terms that will be clear to others. The *Dial* "Notes" (1841) recognize that the circle of Greek sculpture is complete, but with true Emersonian optimism look for an ascension of the "spiral form" in modern sculpture, which, by a freer expression than the Greeks, will capture and interpret the complications of contemporary life. Emerson seeks a sculptor who will define Christianity through art, as Plato defined Greek culture through the *Dialogues*. "Will the gazing world wait in vain for the Christian Phidias," he asks, "who shall lift this history out of the dim twilight of experience, and plant it in marble for eternity?" His suggestion for an American figure that might combine native growth with distant dream is a strong "Yankee wood-god," whose new and vigorous expression might far excel the Greeks. For such a form we have still to wait.

Painting. Before his trip to Italy in 1833, Emerson had seen even less of painting than of sculpture. It was therefore natural that his first comments on the richness of color in Neapolitan and Roman galleries should be a kind of dazzling of the eye. Of the paintings in the Pitti Palace at Florence, he remarks to his lecture audience in Boston (1834) that no one who has not seen this embarrassment of riches could have an idea of the powers of painting.[40] Once his eyes are restored to clear sight, he finds himself not in the presence of "great strangers" in the picture galleries, but comfortable and at home.[41]

Among the works of lesser painters he took particular pleasure in Andrea Sacchi's Vision of S. Romaldo at the Vatican. "One is greater," he says, "for knowing that such forms can be." The American painters Cranch, Wall, and Alexander accompanied Emerson to the Roman galleries, no doubt giving him the benefit of their superior training in art. Although Emerson noted Cranch's keen eye for the work of Titian, whom he praised as "an original painter," Emerson apparently did not share Cranch's admiration. The next year he is comparing Titian with Michelangelo to Titian's disadvantage; Michelangelo is the Homer, Titian the Moore or Spenser of painting.[42]

Emerson's enthusiasm for Michelangelo's sculpture carries over to some extent to his painting; not deeply impressed by the Last Judgment, he is completely captivated by Michelangelo's self-portrait in the Capitoline gallery. In Florence he mentions Carlo Dolcis and Salvator Rosas "in plenty," as well as a self-portrait by Rembrandt. Although he praises a "beautiful Madonna" of Leonardo da Vinci at the Convent of St. Onofrio in Rome, he makes no comment on the Last Supper, which he saw at Milan. Later in reading Vasari he takes note of Leonardo's varied skills in engineering, painting, and statuary,[43] but he seems never to have given Leonardo's genius any recognition comparable to his enthusiasm for Michelangelo.

The height of excellence in Italian painting Emerson finds in Raphael's Transfiguration, which becomes for him the "ideal" in painting comparable to Michelangelo in sculpture. Touched by the picture's "calm, benignant beauty," the "sweet and sublime face" of Jesus, he denotes the whole "familiar, simple, home-speaking." No doubt influenced by the high critical value placed upon this painting, Emerson seems to have studied it with some care and to have been genuinely moved by it.

Although Emerson told his lecture audience in 1834 that he did not go to Italy to collect cameos, medallions, or paintings, but merely to observe what man had achieved in art, twelve years later (1846) his journal records the purchase of ten drawings, including reproductions of the Sibilla Cumaea, the Erithraea, the Persica, and the "Danie" of Michelangelo, and Raphael's Four Sibyls, The School of Athens, Poesis, and Justitia.[44] That this was an unusual departure appears in the note of individual prices, and the total, $29.75. Guido's Rospigliosi Aurora, sent him by Carlyle, still hangs in the Emerson house; though its black-and-white reproduction does scant justice to the original, it was much prized by Emerson.[45]

At home the chief painter who claimed Emerson's attention was Washington Allston, whose work Emerson observed at Allston's gallery and at the Athenaeum. His dominant impression of Allston's work is expressed by the unfavorable comment "feminine or receptive" rather than "masculine" (as on the Lorenzo and Jessica, which he says has moonlight, but no moon), but he praises Allston's landscapes as the work of a "fine pastoral poet," and accepts the current critical dictum that Allston is the only American painter who can draw hands. Allston, furthermore, fulfills the idea of organic form in teaching, when he tells Sarah Clarke to paint her trees so that a bird could fly through them, and in artistic method, when he begins a landscape "as nature does" by creating his blue sky against a first coat of deep black.[46] The painter Hicks thought that Allston worked in the right direction when he tried to get natural colors in the mixing, though he did not, like Michelangelo, dig the clay out of the garden and stir it up with glue and water.[47]

To the popular substitute for miniature portraits, the daguerreotype, Emerson gave due praise, especially to the skill of its inventor, Daguerre. From the experience of sitting for his daguerreotype, he concluded that the process encouraged in the sitter an expression of asininity, but he found the daguerreotype more "organic" than the miniature in the fact that the miniature lost its illusion when held too near the eye, while the daguerreotype was, like nature's works, "incapable of being seen too near." [48]

It would be untrue to say that experience in observing the color of painting led Emerson to look at nature with a more keenly perceptive eye, since his descriptions of natural scenes are much more vivid than his analyses of painting. He has made an occasional observation to show that he compares the outer world with that of painting — as one June afternoon, looking into the river, when the idea occurs to him that the dark shades in paintings by Rembrandt and Salvator probably came from painting the reflection of landscape in water; [49] or when he observes that sunshine is more pleasing than deep shadow in the actual world, but that in a landscape shades are needed to set off the light. [50]

Since Emerson's eye was more sensitive to line than to color, he tended to think of line as the form of painting, and color, however pleasing, as something added. Lecturing on the Eye and Ear (1837), he states the importance in art education of teaching children the variety of expression which can be given by line. The implication of the first essay on "Art" is that painting is less revealing of structure than is sculpture; for he speaks here of painting as showing the "coloring," while sculpture reveals the "anatomy of form." On the other hand, he betrays a feeling for the greater vitality of painting when he says, of his "hierarchy of the arts," "Sculpture is past, picture passing." [51]

The omissions from Emerson's catalogue of painting are as interesting as the inclusions. One who has written perceptively of the soft and delicate tones in Concord surroundings might be expected to say something of landscapes by such painters as Claude and Poussin; from this acute observer of great men in history one might look for an analysis of historical portraits. The fact that Emerson has said little about landscape or portraits, giving his admiration to such allegorical treatments as Guido's Aurora, or to such religious subjects as Raphael's Transfiguration, doubtless indicates that he thought of painting as a more ideal art than sculpture, though less ideal than poetry — in a realm midway between the actual and the transcendental. While he has made some application of the organic principle to painting, his use of that criterion in this realm is less thorough than in sculpture or achitecture. One may conclude that Emerson thought of painting as a realm of beauty supplementary to nature, less necessary to man than fitting architecture, less vital than poetry, but with a special appeal to man's desire for color and allegorical representation.

Summary. To sum up his view of the arts, we may say that he applies the organic principle in its "root" sense most closely to architecture, idealizing organic form by successive degrees in sculpture and painting. We have seen that he adopted ideas from such critics as Bacon, Goethe, and Coleridge for his concept of organic form, but shaped these varied suggestions into a new whole. Emerson gives recognition to the importance of facts disclosed by the critics Winckelmann, Goethe, Charles Bell (Bridgewater Treatise on *The Hand*), Greenough, Ruskin, Garbett, Penrose, Viollet-Le-Duc, as "joyful possessions" to be ranked close beside the discoveries of natural history; [52] of these critics, however, only Winckelmann and Goethe can be said to have made any substantial contribution to Emerson's speculation. Although he recognizes the destructive effect which machine-made tools can have on handmade art, when he mentions the Indian's hatred for the "dapper imitations" of the mills which will replace his carefully fashioned canoe,[53] for the most part Emerson differs from Ruskin in taking a hopeful view of the possibility of refining the machine-made arts. He even condones advertising as a "manly" expression of confidence in excellence which it is then the advertiser's duty to make good (perhaps we should have less blatant advertising today if we had more Emersons to remind advertisers of their "duty").

Emerson's general attitude toward professional art criticism is well expressed in his statements on the critic Gustav Waagen, whose admiration for the Elgin Marbles Emerson shares, and whose definition of art Emerson approves, as "an expression of the mind whose peculiar character cannot be supplied by anything else." But with Waagen's sorrow over the ruin of certain masterpieces of Raphael and Titian through unskillful cleaning, Emerson cannot sympathize. He grants that the obliteration of strokes of genius is sad, but disputes Waagen's inference that no such inspiration can ever reappear. "We have heard this elegy often," Emerson says, "yet to us the loss of the pictures seems not so sad as the loss of faith which this elegy implies." Granting, he says, that some art is past, it may still take on new forms, "may run railways from Arctic circle to equator and tunnel the Andes and cut canal betwixt the two Americas . . . Before Agamemnon there were heroes and volcanoes before Aetna and Vesuvius and painters before Apelles and shall be after." [54]

Here, in his difference from Waagen, Emerson clearly expresses the divergence between his concept of art and that of the historian or connoisseur. However definite the value which Emerson places on specific works of art, his regard for the spirit that creates all artifacts keeps him from sorrow at the

loss of the greatest masterpiece. A foreshadowing of this attitude appears in Emerson's journal at Naples (1833), where
his first reaction to the riches of classical and Renaissance
art is that there are no "living artists." [55] The Emersonian
concern with spirit does have the past "at its back," but its
ultimate point of rest is the future rather than the past; its
temper is that of hope rather than despair. From this optimistic point of view Emerson derives the answer to his own in-
sistent question about imitation in art. In the perspective of
spirit, he sees the "centuries and nations of imitators" as "only
the fringes and shadows and minor consequence." The important effect of art, which he sees operating in the same way on
all productive souls, is "the impulse to creation." This is the
new-springing power which can be traced down through
the ages; the imitations, which give so much concern in their
own period to thoughtful critics, will be carried off in the
current of the stream of time.

Besides its final emphasis upon the creating spirit rather
than the specific artifacts, Emerson's view of art keeps always
in mind the human needs which all art must serve. He asserts
that not body garments alone, but picture galleries, sculpture,
architecture are the "dress" of man.[56] Clearly Emerson is convinced that art is made for man, not man for art, and in his
desire to obtain the best art for his own country, from fine
paintings to exquisite gardens, he is not seeking these objects
as collectors' items, but for the nourishment which they can
give to all men's spirits. Doubtless because of his democratic
and human purpose, this "ideal" critic has placed more emphasis than any other contemporary American on the importance of filling the useful arts (which are most available to all
men) with the spirit of beauty.

In his lecture series on The Philosophy of History (1836–37), Emerson proceeds from the third lecture, on Art, to the fourth, on Literature, and defines the special place of literature in the creative world: "Whilst Art delights in carrying a thought into action, Literature is the conversion of action into thought. The architect executes his dream in stone. The poet enchants you by thinking out your action. Art actualises an idea. Literature idealises action" (lecture on Literature, 1836). For Emerson, the difference between literature and art thus appears in their expression of the ideal; literature is closer to the intellectual, the transcendental, art closer to the actual.

Deeming literature the most universal of the arts, Emerson defines it in this same lecture as "the record of human thought in written language." One can hardly name a thought or feeling which some writing has not expressed:

> Literature is the record of all; the sum and measure of humanity. Every part of man has its department in literature; his observation, in history; his love, in lyrics and novels; his wrath in satire and controversies; his mirth in comedy; his piety in psalms and sermons; his contemplation in philosophy. Even crime and folly have their books. Thus it represents all human thought showing after the passage of centuries and millenniums of years not only its average ability and aim, but also the wild follies and defeats of the mind, and thus discloses the tendencies, and fixes the divine boundaries of the human spirit.

Here in his definition of literature Emerson has indicated a breadth which covers the whole range of human life. If in his critical illustrations and his own practice he drew more often from the observation of history, the love of poetry, or the contemplation of philosophy, than from the wrath of satire, the mirth of comedy, or the crime of fiction, he corrected that lack by including these passionate and frivolous elements in his definition.

In literature even more than in art, Emerson places importance upon the quality of the age. Applying to literary criticism his concept of Necessity, a Fate made beneficent by confidence in God's power, Emerson states that a foreordained place exists for each work of literature. Necessity operates through the age as well as through the individual, so that each finished poem, play, or essay attains power partly through the general temper of the time, partly through the writer himself. Even the form in which the genius writes is beyond his choice, determined by the demands of the time and his own ability. Original expression, paradoxically enough, can be achieved only by a man "charged in his single head with a nation's force." Accepting a "wave" theory of human progress similar to Taine's, Emerson states that the activity of nations goes by great surges; the tide, full for a short time, ebbs, and the creative "water power" appears again in another place. He uses the chemical term "zymosis" to indicate that fermenting power within an age which induces literary creation. In the essay on "Eloquence" he compares the power emerging in oratory to the geologic force which causes mountains: "As the Andes and Alleghenies indicate the line of the fissure in the crust of the earth, along which they were lifted, so the great ideas that suddenly expand at some moment the mind of mankind, indicate themselves by orators." Thus the age of Cicero in Rome and that of Lord North in England exemplify periods when the earth's geologic steam was let loose from the mouths of orators.

Although Emerson's reading ranged through German, French, Italian, Persian, and Hindu literature, his theory of the integral relation between the individual writer and the age may best be illustrated through English literature, which he knew deeply as well as widely. His Lectures on English Literature (1835–36), supplemented by his Readings in English Literature (1869), present a good focus for this study.

Covering the span of English literature from the Anglo-Saxon period through the eighteenth century, these lectures analyze the interaction of literary genius with the quality of the age. Thus in the Anglo-Saxon and pre-Chaucerian period, Emerson finds individual writers of little importance; here the qualities of the age may be said to exist in the air, and Anglo-Saxon gloom or chivalric fancy to fill whatever vessels come to hand.[57] In Chaucer Emerson recognizes the first individual genius of English literature, praising his balance, his human kindness, his "hilarity of good sense," his treatment of common things, and a quality of homeliness whose later decline Emerson deplores. In the period of Elizabeth and James, which he considers in one lecture, he finds not only "matchless individuals" but also "multitudes and masses."

Although Emerson gives some attention to Ben Jonson and Francis Bacon, he reserves two full lectures for Shakespeare, recognizing that even in a great age he towers above his fellows.[58] Beginning his reading in the sonnets, whose "over-mastering imagination" Emerson praises, he later denotes the sonnets a throwback to "the old Aristotelian culture," and places them on a level below the plays, which more truly reflect their own time. His analysis of tragedy is best exemplified by his statement of *Macbeth* as a tragedy of fear, with all its parts subtly united to produce one dominating impression of horror; his criticism of comedy appears in an encomium of Falstaff. Though he ranked the heroic plays below the tragedies, he commented on them at some length, perceiving in them Shakespeare's remarkable distillation of the drama implicit in English history. In considering that Shakespeare was at his best in closet reading rather than in dramatic performance, Emerson shared the romantic view of Shakespeare held by Coleridge and Lamb rather than the prevailing modern opinion that Shakespeare was a dramatist first and a poet second. Deeply though Emerson admired Shakespeare's characters as the fusion of ideal with real — he gives special meed to Henry V, Brutus, and Antony, and like many another idealist, falls prey to the charms of Cleopatra — he presents no analysis of character comparable to Coleridge's or Hazlitt's study of Hamlet, and he neglects the element of passion.[59] Emerson cannot resist making sport of the Shakespeare Society for their interest in such items as the second-best bed. On the other hand, he makes his own critical contribution when he applies the test of verse to the moot play *Henry VIII*. Though acquainted with Shakespearean criticism, he carried that learning lightly, and gave the warning still salutary for scholars, that not critics, but Shakespeare himself, is the ultimate court of appeal.

The significant element in Emerson's criticism of Shakespeare appears not only in the elevated place assigned to the Bard, but in the amount of comment in relation to other figures which is devoted to Shakespeare in this literary survey. Despite the temperamental affinity which critics since Alcott have noted between Emerson and such seventeenth-century figures as Herbert and Thomas Browne, Shakespeare alone has received more attention from Emerson than the whole group of religious writers in the period of the Stuarts. Since much of Emerson's critical statement about Shakespeare has not been published, scholars have not so far appreciated the extent of Emerson's reading or the volume of his notes on Shakespeare. Yet the interpretation which appears in the lectures and readings shows a lively appreciation of varied aspects of

Shakespeare, and attests the fact that the transcendental theory of art, exercised by a sensitive critical temper, finds its way to masterpieces which the world calls great.

From the point of view of religious belief, Emerson finds the seventeenth century most satisfying, detecting in George Herbert, Robert Herrick, and the great "solar" poet John Milton the "pure flame" of belief reflected from the spirit of their age.

The eighteenth century Emerson denotes an arid desert, perhaps because his own search for literary values was in large part an attempt to define his difference from neoclassic thinkers. In Johnson and Burke, however, he discovers some perception of "the Necessary the Plain the True the Human," and he finds in this generally fruitless age another good quality — the increasing democratic spirit, passing from Rousseau and Voltaire to Bentham, the Mills, and Tom Paine, most clearly seen in Franklin, but soon degenerating into utilitarianism. Goethe and Coleridge, Emerson says, had to "reinstate men in the Real," by interpreting literature in the light of the Kantian distinction between Reason and Understanding.

From his survey of English literature, Emerson concludes that we have come a long way from the medieval love of fable, which resembles decorative ornament in architecture; and from the servile admiration for a king, which causes a serious flaw in so great a writer as Francis Bacon. Summing up England's achievement for the St. George's Society Dinner in Montreal, 1852, Emerson denotes Shakespeare as the "first name" in intellect; Newton, in exact science; Milton, in epic and lyric song; Bacon, in learning and reason. Though he mentions several others as lesser great, these four seem to him (at the moment) to make up the first rank.

Turning to his own age, Emerson sees it inheriting all the

advantages of political freedom, since writers speak now to a
whole people instead of to a privileged class; and in the insight of philosophical idealism he observes an inner inspiration
of even greater value than the political. With all this superiority, Emerson looks at the contemporary scene with a jaun-
diced eye, failing to see in it the "enthusiasm" of love, patriot-
ism, or religion which lifts literary production off its feet. To
a certain extent this denunciation of literature as faithless was
a critical concept first expressed by Herder in *The Spirit of
Hebrew Poetry* (1782–83). The excessive subjectivity whose
suicidal tendency Emerson notes when he says, "Our young
men all had knives in their brains," is one reason for this skepticism; Emerson finds Goethe citing it also as a destructive
quality in the German *fin de siècle*.[60] Though literary in
origin, the concept was no mere attitude with Emerson, because it expressed a lack which he, as well as Thoreau and
Alcott, sensed in contemporary writing. After a meeting with
the Transcendental Club, for example, Emerson writes in his
journal (1836) that art and literature must die because true
worship has been lost. Emerson was obliged to admit that his
own extreme liberalism had contributed to that skepticism;
nor could he seek revival of a faith, merely for the sake of art,
in which credence no longer existed. He reproves Jones Very
for making just such a false effort, when he tries to match his
"new" intuitions with worn-out religious language that has
grown "secondary and morbid." Using an organic image to
show the lack of new-springing faith, Emerson says that
modern society seems "composed of the débris of the fore-
gone structures of religion and politics, unmixed composite
bronze just as the soil we till is made up of the degraded
mountains of the elder world." [61]

For the most part this censure of his age as unbelieving,
with its related fruitless search for a "national" religion to

which he could only partially subscribe, was expressed during Emerson's early years of production (1836–41). He is still analyzing the quality of his age (though with a less negative outlook) in 1849, when he remarks that Putnam, Whipple, Dewey, and W. H. Channing, as well as Emerson, are concurrently lecturing on the Spirit of the Times,[62] and Carlyle is conducting a similar examination of England in *The Present Age*. Thus many thinkers at the same time seek to solve the problem of "the age," which Heine called "a sphinx which throws itself from the rock as soon as its riddle has been guessed." At the opening of the Civil War, Emerson's outlook is again clouded by the acute realization that the greedy monster of war is eating up man's aesthetic production:

> All [man's] arts [Emerson says] disappear in the one art of war. All which makes the social tone of Europe milder and sweeter than the miner's hut, and the lumberer's camp in America; the ages of culture behind; traditional skills; the slow secular adjustment of talent and position; the cumulative onward movement; the potency of experience, is destroyed; and the uncouth forked nasty savage stands on the charred desert to begin his first fight with wolf and snake, and build his dismal shanty on the sand. (Lecture on Art, 1861)

In 1877 Emerson again assails the lack of religious belief, comparing it to Egyptian mummies: "So dead is this faith, so dealeth it with death. Every day the people the heart and life of the youth is falling from this unsubstantial pageant."[63]

But this negative view does not represent Emerson's complete perspective on the finished or the potential production of his own time. Three months after he has denounced theological aridity in *The Divinity School Address*, he records the hope that even "the dead pond" of the Church might again become "a treasury of all fine and all sublime faculties if their objects appeared or if an electric atmosphere of thought and heroism enveloped them." [64] If an age understands its evils well enough, Emerson believes that it may be on the way to overcoming them. "I like very well," he says, "that the trials of this age should be new, — early old age, pyrrhonism and apathy; that we should find some topic that is neither classic nor romantic, some spot of virgin soil. Let us wait, and at least do that greatly" (Ms. J. H, 1841). Emerson's belief that his epoch, whatever its faults, has made some progress beyond the first twenty years of the nineteenth century, in which his father was a Unitarian leader, is shown by his terming those years "that early ignorant and transitional Month-of-March in our New England culture." [65] To that period he has no wish to return.

Beneath Emerson's whole discussion of "the age" lies a kind of deterministic conviction that certain qualities exist in the atmosphere, apart from the contribution of individuals, just as matter is made up of certain chemical combinations. Thus he traces the poverty of earlier unproductive periods to no individual fault, but to an "endemic disease" in the air, poisoning those who breathe it.[66] Although the burden of *The Divinity School Address* and of "Self-reliance" is a cry for individual effort, Emerson explains in his journals that the best art cannot proceed from one who separates himself from the tendencies of his time. Thus he values the "composite force indicating the exact amount of conviction of the necessity of self control existing in the total mind of the community," and asserts: "For every individual who scorns it, it descends; for every individual who passionately attaches himself to it, it ascends" (Ms. J. C, Pt. II, 1837).

That the art of an age must have an "unwilled" relation to the existing time spirit may be considered a corollary of the individual passivity which we have observed in Emerson's creative artist who "receives" inspiration. Thus Emerson asserts: "I cast myself upon the Age and will not resist it. Passive I will think what it thinketh and say what it saith." [67] Overstatement, this, in a typically Emersonian way; yet it serves to correct the evil of a personal pride which tries to convert the "vast Ocean" of the time into a mill wheel for the service of private and selfish interests. One must also realize that Emerson here advocates passivity to the spirit of the age rather than to its material manifestations in laws, institutions, or books, whose importance he minimizes. One might define this concept of "the spirit of the age" as the social counterpart of that more intangible Over-soul, whose mystical importance we have seen in the creative process.

The circular quality of this argument is obvious: individual artists must lead the age, but they must also depend upon the age's spiritual quality. The contradiction is not resolved, but it is given some direction by Emerson's idea of history. Retrospect over the great centuries can give inspiration to our own.

> I think not of mean ages, [Emerson says] but of Chaldean, Egyptian, or Teutonic ages, when man was not feather-brained, or French, or servile, but, if he stooped, he stooped under ideas; times when the earth spoke and the heavens glowed, when the actions of men indicated vast conceptions, and men wrote histories of the world in prison, and builded like Himmaleh, and the Allegany [*sic*] chains. (Ms. J. ZO, 1856)

Since Emerson conceives, furthermore, that each period must interpret earlier times in the light of its own convictions, he asserts that the advance made by the nineteenth century may come to light when later writers, with fresh perspective, assess its leaders in relation to its general spirit. Emerson himself is able to present a more hopeful view of the Civil War several years after its close, than he could obtain at its beginning. "In America," he says, "the grandeur was shown by our youth in the war, whilst their fathers were looking for it in the thinkers and statesmen." In 1878 he states one great advantage resulting from the recent war: "Our eyes are withdrawn from England, withdrawn from France, and look homeward." [68] Thus some dross has been melted in the crucible of conflict. If religious faith has not revived, at least a stronger, more independent national spirit emerges from the wreckage of war.

Language. Nowhere in Emerson's literary theory is the organic principle more clearly expressed than in his conception of language, the stuff and substance of literature. For Emerson language has the vitality of plants, animals, and men, and is conceived in all its complexity as a gradual growth. Thus he writes: "Language is a city to the building of which every human being brought a stone; yet he is no more to be credited with the grand result than the acaleph which adds a cell to the coral reef which is the basis of the continent" ("Quotation and Originality").

Emerson's historical conception of language is the romantic view that the savage naturally expressed his ideas in metaphors, which civilization has crusted over until they have lost their touch with life. Although this idea appeared in that neoclassic guide to composition and Emerson's college text, Hugh Blair's *Lectures on Rhetoric,* [69] it did not become an operating principle in his thought until he found it more vividly expressed in the mystic writers Sampson Reed and Oegger. [70] Comparing the original emblematic, vital quality of language with its "civilized" disintegration into "fossil poetry,"

Emerson indicates in *Nature* the way to recover its life: "Wise men pierce this rotten diction and fasten words again to visible things."

This concept of language bears out the correspondence which Emerson affirms philosophically between man's spirit and material nature; as soon as man recovers that lost harmony with natural things, he will easily attain vivid expression. He does not believe that there was any "original" relation between the word and the thing. His early experiment in repeating the words "black" and "white" until all fixed meaning vanished taught him his first lesson in idealism. Once the connection has been established, however, the word comes to fit the thing, so that students actually can, by effort, discover the "wisdom of words," and find with surprise that the common words which have lived for centuries still fit their expanding thought.

This close connection between words and vegetable nature appears in Emerson's description of the positive degree (under-statement) in writing as "the sinew of speech," in contrast to the superlative as "the fat." Thus Montaigne's language, an example of "low" or barroom style, issues from the heart of nature: "Cut these words, and they would bleed; they are vascular and alive." Modern civilization, Emerson suggests, can correct its false delicacy by recalling the plain speaking of such ancient writers as Plutarch, who could speak freely because he wrote only for one sex. "Guts," Emerson says, anticipating the "tough" school of modern fiction, "is a stronger word than intestines." It is important to recall that Emerson's own use of language, which today seems vital but certainly not racy, shocked Alcott when he first heard Emerson lecture. (Alcott was later to try to modify his own neoclassic diction by a touch of Emerson's saltiness.) The principle of restraint of course always operated in Emerson's published work. Praising Rabelais and Whitman as like masters of this "Rommany," Emerson maintains some caution in his admiration of Whitman, when he says that Whitman "has not got out of the Fire-club and gained the entrée of the sitting-rooms." Even climate may have an effect on the kind of language used, as the long frosty nights of England and New England hold those people "pretty fast to realities." Organic metaphor is used to show lack of clarity in Carlyle's style: "O Carlyle, the merit of glass is not to be seen, but to be seen through; but every crystal and lamina of the Carlyle glass is visible."

The critic, in turn, may judge by a writer's language how closely his spirit has been in tune with nature — if the language seems vital and earthborn, the work must have value.

Not only in the light of organic form, but from the point of view of a practicing critic does Emerson consider language, with a keen ear for the telling phrase. Western nicknames are cited: "Michigan wolverines," "Wisconsin badgers," "Illinois suckers," "Indiana hoosiers," "Missouri pikes," "Iowa hawkeyes," "Ohio buckeyes," to illustrate the people, "rough grisly Esaus, full of dirty strength." Emerson collects country statements that illustrate restraint: "a gun is unhealthy to Britishers"; "rain won't do hay any good"; "Preston never swum as far as he could." He delights in the colloquial terms that describe a parvenu: "upstart," "squirt," "scalawag." He comments on the triumph of philosophical over popular conception in the use of the word "devil." While in the popular mind the devil is a malignant power, in philosophy he is negation, falsehood, or nothing. Yet the people's phrases express the philosophical rather than the popular sense of Satan: for example, "the devil a monk was he" means "he was no monk." The practical writer speaks in this advice: "Blot out the superlatives, the negatives, the dismals, and the adjectives (and *very*) and finally, see that you have not omitted the thought or fact which the piece was written to state."

The modern critic would go along with Emerson's suggestion that writers use short words of Anglo-Saxon origin when possible, avoiding long Latin terms, especially "the whole family of Fero." An amusing illustration of preference for Saxon over Latin words appears in Emerson's attempt to arbitrate a dispute between Margaret Fuller and Henry Thoreau over the phrasing of his line "Nature doth have her dawn each day" (published in *The Dial*, January 1841). Concerning her proposal to change "doth have" to "relumes" Emerson writes to Margaret that Thoreau has "boggled" at "relumes" and he has agreed to restore "doth have." "Othello's melodious verses, 'that can thy light relume,'" Emerson says, "make that word sacred always in my ear. But our tough Yankee must have his tough verse, so I beg you will replace it."

Young writers may still gain by studying Emerson's list of dangerously showy words: "asphodel," "harbinger," "chalice." In his catalogue of "vulgarisms to be gazetted" there is an echo of neoclassic strictness not characteristic of his general theory: some of these "banished" terms are "moiety" for "a small part," "nothing would answer but," "in our midst," "might have to go."

On the whole, however, Emerson's view of language not only harmonizes with organic form, but also shows a practical sense of the vivid in contemporary discourse as well as in writing. H. L. Mencken must applaud his record of such terms as "dab," "cockney," "granny," "peacock," and "a cocktail House of Commons." He even shows sufficient objectivity to record Dr. Osgood's contemptuous criticism of his own sermon as "patty-cake."

Poetic form: the organic principle in meter. Poetry, Emerson's favorite literary form, clearly embodies the organic principle, since its special techniques, rhythm and rhyme, issue directly from human nature. In "Poetry and Imagination" Emerson relates rhythm not to natural objects, but to the human pulse:

> Metre begins with pulse-beat, and the length of lines in songs and poems is determined by the inhalation and exhalation of the lungs. If you hum or whistle the rhythm of the common English metres, — of the decasyllabic quatrain, or the octosyllabic with alternate sexasyllabic, — you can easily believe these metres to be organic, derived from the human pulse, and to be therefore not proper to one nation, but to mankind.

In establishing the basis of rhythm in human breathing, Emerson's theory of verse bears some similarity to such modern experiments in acoustic metrics as that of Wilbur Schramm, whose *Approaches to a Science of English Verse* (1935) analyzes by means of scientific instruments the changes of pitch and volume which occur in the reading of poetry. Emerson's theory also opposes the idea of a "national" rhythm (the consideration, for example, that blank verse is a typically English expression) by rooting meter in the ebb and flow of man's breathing.

Sometimes, Emerson says, the poet may catch from nature an auditory suggestion which controls the rhythm of his poem: "As if the sound of a bell, or a certain cadence expressed in a low whistle or booming, or humming, to which the poet first timed his step, as he looked at the sunset, or thought, was the incipient form of the piece, and was regnant through the whole." This account (doubtless of personal experience) has an interesting modern parallel in A. E.

Housman's *Name and Nature of Poetry*, where Housman speaks of a poetic idea gradually taking on rhythm and form as he walks along.

Rhyme Emerson also conceives as integral to man's nature. Fondness for rhyme, far from being an infantile pleasure, is based on the principle of repetition with difference which appears throughout nature; thus a sonnet's rhymes please by the same principle as nodes in a sea shell, shadows reflecting rocks, columns in a building. The poet's problem in rhyme is "to unite wild freedom with hard sculpture," and successful rhyme is defined in "Poetry and Imagination" as "the transparent frame that allows almost the pure architecture of thought to become visible to the mental eye." Although Emerson's poetic ear was subtly attuned to unusual rhymes, he more often conceives of rhyme as visual than as auditory. Skill in rhyme Emerson submits as a test of poetic ability; unusual and untried rhymes indicate a lively imagination. To express the combination of freedom with limitation which rhyme implies, he compares it to a bird's dartings through a wood.

Emerson discovered poetic music in a wide variety of verse — in the ballad, in Beaumont and Fletcher's "Songs," in Collins' "Ode to Evening" and Gray's "Elegy," in the Persian Hafiz, and in the work of Ellery Channing. On occasion he could read poetry for the melody, forgetting the meaning. Byron's faults could be momentarily ignored in his enjoyment of the "perfect flow" of the stanza in "Childe Harold" or "The Hebrew Melodies." Such an attainment of "sound without sense" does not, however, satisfy Emerson as it does Poe. Of the best poetry he requires a certainty of direction as strict as that of a pilot guiding a ship. He was attracted by Ellery Channing's statement of poetry's need for inner coherence: "Drive a donkey, and beat him with a pole with both hands; — that's action: but poetry is revolution on its own axis." [71]

Rhythm, Emerson finds, ascends in power according to the sense, so that the lofty thought necessarily finds rich musical expression. Dominating his whole conception of technique is the insistence that poetry's essence is not mere "metre," but "metre-making argument." His view of rhythm thus differs from theories defined in terms of music — such as Poe's comparison of poetry to musical melody in "The Rationale of Verse," or Lanier's application of musical notation to poetry in *The Science of English Verse* — and finds a twentieth-century descendant in a critic like John Crowe Ransom, who avers that meaning controls the effect of poetic sounds. Emerson's demand for ideas in poetry does not, however, imply that he lacks interest in metrical experiment. Poets, he says, must not play over the same old airs; he looks for the invention of new meters, as well as new images, "rhythms of a faery and dreamlike music" which will make the best-known English poetry sound like psalm tunes. A prophecy of this new music to come appears in some passages of prose eloquence, which he finds richer than modern verse.

In our discussion of expression in Chapter I, the young Tennyson was cited as an example of a poet whose technique excelled his ideas. Emerson's complete view of Tennyson's poetry, however, shows appreciation for his advance beyond this early stage. If Emerson found the 1833 volume of *Poems* deserving of the same admiration which might be given to a mechanical dividing machine, he saw in the 1842 *Poems* a progress beyond mere musical skill to a deeper perception: "The same fluent and apprehensive nature which threw itself with such ease into the forms of outward beauty, has now been intent rather on the secrets of the shaping spirit."

Though the clever verse and superficial thought of "In Memoriam" seemed to revoke this promise, the "Ode on the Duke of Wellington," "Ulysses," and "Tithonus" again replaced Tennyson in Emerson's rank of "thinkers" rather than mere "singers."

Form as spirit: the symbol. The ultimate test of good poetry for Emerson is its embodiment of vital metaphors. A successful symbol is the material object transformed by the creative heat of the poet's imagination. The Plotinian concept of "the flowing," whose importance we observed in the imaginative process, leaves its mark also on Emerson's conception of the symbol. We recall that Emerson describes the creative insight in "The Poet" as a perception of the flowing or metamorphosis at the heart of nature, a realization that

> Within the form of every creature is a force impelling it to ascend to a higher form; and following with his eyes the life, [he] uses the forms which express that life, and so his speech flows with the flowing of nature. . . He uses forms according to the life, and not according to the form.

The symbol is the objective realization of the poet's power to "go with" the forms of nature. Readers are electrified by a poet's glowing symbols; indeed, the imaginative effect of a symbol upon his readers becomes the test of a poet's success in perceiving nature's flowing. Since the poet finds this spirit in natural objects, his realization of it in the symbol shows the relation between symbolic and organic form; Nature, in Emersonian language, is herself a trope.

Beauty itself is conceived as evanescent, most attractive in the moment of transition. The myth of Venus born out of the sea is employed in "The Poet" to represent nature as symbol, life overflowing into body.[72] Loveliness is defined in the essay on "Beauty" as "the moment of transition, as if the form were just ready to flow into other forms." Running water, birds' flight, aesthetic dancing all show this charm of changing movement. Thus, in the poem "Beauty":

> Was never form and never face
> So sweet to Seyd as only grace
> Which did not slumber like a stone,
> But hovered gleaming and was gone.
> Beauty chased he everywhere,
> In flame, in storm, in clouds of air.[73]

In this "fluid" interpretation, the poet's symbol is most successful if it admits of more than one application; and that poet deserves most praise who finds ever new objects to contain his thoughts. Emerson's delight in reading poetry is to discover "a new glance at the fact or subject, and from the deepest centre."

Apart from the Plotinian concept of "the flowing," the strongest single influence upon Emerson's idea of the symbol is the scientific thought of the time. Without any systematic training in science, Emerson read the works of Oersted, Cuvier, Herschel, Oken and others, with growing interest. His imagination soared under the stimulus of the atomic theory, the nebular hypothesis, and the concept of progressive amelioration.

The impact of science upon Emerson's concept of the symbol differs from his general critical speculation, in revealing a definite chronological development, from an early skepticism concerning the value of science, to a confident assertion that science has the key to unlock the symbol's mysteries. At first reluctant to accept scientific advance, Emerson objects in an early journal passage (1824) to the probing analysis which destroys the flower's beauty and the rainbow's charm, terms scientific progress "the successive destruction of agreeable delusions," and desires to see Nature reclothed in the charming garments which Science has stripped from her. By 1834, however, Emerson begins to hail scientific research as a long-awaited revolution in human thought. When the scientific dawn does break upon him, it comes so gently that he perceives in its cold, clear light the garment he had sought to make Nature fairer. His wholehearted accept-ance of scientific advance, once made, shows no trace of Tennyson's tortured doubt or of Arnold's balanced pessimism.

Emerson's concept of evolution is based on the work of such writers as Laplace, Cuvier, and Herschel. Although he was reading Lyell's *Principles of Geology* as early as 1836, he found it a mere "catalogue of facts," and Darwin's *Origin of Species* (1859) came too late to have any shaping influence on his thought. Emerson's idea of evolution may better be termed "progressive development," since he fails to recognize the derivation of animate from inanimate forms.[74] This res-ervation does not proceed from any reluctance to derive man from a vegetable; the lecture on Leasts and Mosts, for ex-ample (1868), shows a fascination with Goethe's theory that the universe began "in a plant's stomach." Nor would Emerson have been unwilling to accept the ape as man's ancestor; he entertained the Pythagorean concept of metem-psychosis with something more than irony, frequently noting a wolf's fangs or a fox's teeth beneath the human countenance of certain individuals. The fact remains that his concept of evolution is simply a gradual refinement of natural forms, following a spiral upward movement. Nature is conceived as repeating the same process on different planes, from plant, to animal, to man. Optimism governs this theory, always imply-ing ascension in the successive adaptation from one plane to

another. Nor does Emerson think of man as the ultimate creation of Nature. Lecturing on American Nationality in 1861,
he says that we have indeed surpassed the saurians, whose
efforts in the aqueous ages made the earth habitable for us,
but our efforts in draining swamps and clearing forests may
be making similar preparation for a future creature superior
to ourselves.

The concept of progressive adaptation gives an upward
direction to the Plotinian idea of flux. The principle of ascension implicit in Plotinus' theory is made explicit and given
tangible proof by the scientific evidence of progressive development. The application to the poet's symbol is obvious: his
creation must show the ascension which characterizes the
method of nature: "like the metamorphosis of things into
higher organic forms is their change into melodies." Only by
perceiving the necessity which impels every form to move to
a higher form, can the poet create a symbol as vital as the
objects of nature.

From the atomic theory also Emerson's concept of the
symbol is enriched. The essay on "Swedenborg" in *Representative Men* (1850) traces the atomic theory back to
Lucretius, recognizing the contribution made to the conception by Malpighi and Swedenborg. The lecture on Leasts and
Mosts (1868) states that the same atom which makes up the
animalcule also composes man: "A man is a developed animalcule; animalcule is an arrested man." Through the atom,
man is related to vegetable as well as to animal nature;
Wordsworth's respect for "the meanest flower" appears in
Emerson's theory, with scientific rationalization, since even a
buttercup can make a finer division of matter, and "strip the
little Proteus hydrogen of his last coat." Emerson's respect for
the atom's "violence of direction" is worthy of a nuclear
physicist:

Nature is made up of atoms, but these are puissant, omnipotent, and we go in and out all our days amid the explosive atoms of nitro-glycerine, each one of which can shatter
the planet. Faraday found that a single grain of water has
electric relations equivalent to a very powerful flash of
lightning.

In Cuvier's account of the eight hundred varieties of marine
shells composing the limestone beds of Paris, Emerson finds
evidence of the small things that make up a larger whole.[75] He
observes that human art follows the same procedure of building vast structures from infinitesimal objects. As the power of
the atom in Nature, so is that of the symbol in poetry, small
but potentially world-shaking, by its relation to a larger
theater of significance.

Not only does science demonstrate the power of the small
to mirror the large, but conversely, the dwindling of large
things into small, through perspective. Emerson finds in
Herschel the demonstration that mountains and seas on the
earth's surface, when represented on a globe of sixteen-inch
diameter, appear no larger than the roughnesses of an orange
rind.[76] Likewise, in poetry, mountains and seas are tossed
about like baubles in the control of poetic imagination.

Lecturing on Poetry in 1854, Emerson uses a botanical
analogy to show "the convertibility of one thing into any
other thing." Just as the same bit of gelatin may become a fish
in water, a chamois on a mountain, a worm underground, so
the same object may be turned in poetry to varying symbolic
uses. Emerson derived this illustration from the physiologist
Camper, who converted the drawing of a man's skeleton by a
few successive strokes to a horse, a bird, a fish. The height of
this "convertibility" Emerson finds in some drawings at the
Athenaeum, which begin as a toad and end as the Belvedere
Apollo. The concept receives further illustration from the

species of infusoria called Proteus, which changes from a ball to a ribbon to a star.[77]

The Emersonian symbol is also illuminated by the contemporary idea of polarized light, which states that when polarized light is viewed through certain transparent solids, a regular succession of colors is seen. Emerson (like Thoreau and Alcott) was excited by this theorem because the production of the color band by this method involved a certain mystery, combined with regularity. In a similar fashion, Emerson finds that the raw materials of nature issue from the poet's refracting imagination, as symbols with a universal appeal for all men, but with an advantage over natural colors in the varying applications which they admit. "There is nothing," he says, "which comes out of the human heart — the deep aboriginal region — which is not mundane, thousand-faced, — so that if perchance strong light falls on it, it will admit of being . . . related to all things" (lecture on The Poet, 1841).

The capacity of the symbol to reveal universal truth is further strengthened in Emerson's mind by the relationship which he observes among the sciences, pointing to one universal law of nature. Thus he speaks — inaccurately, it is true — of chemistry's attempt to reduce the elements to two, or "one, with two poles." Oersted's discovery of the relation between electricity and magnetism leads Emerson to conclude: "Electricity, Magnetism, Light, Heat, Gravity, muscular action — varied forms of one force." Since the identity of law thus discovered has man for its typical result, Emerson concludes that "chemistry, botany, physiology cannot forget him." The poet's symbol, in fact, represents the unity at the heart of nature toward which the sciences are striving.

Perhaps Emerson shows overconfidence in the unity of the sciences, and overoptimism in his conviction of man's central importance in the universe. At any rate, his reading of scientific ideas strengthened his belief in the correspondence between man and nature, and led him to place authority on the poet's symbol, which has validity through its creator's relation to physical, chemical, and biological forces. Though Emerson himself might seek in vain to imitate in literary criticism the naturalist's patient collection of facts, according to Sainte-Beuve's ideal, he was not without scientific imagination. Of the slow development of man through time, for example, he says:

> Nature and moral laws work in cosmical and secular periods, they can well wait and work slowly. Races are insignificant, ages are a span to these long eternal powers. They can well afford to drop a race or an age out of the flowing eternity. (Lecture on Natural Religion, 1869)

The same cosmic sense characterizes his comment on space:

> Set your thought upon the space itself. Is it boundless? How can it not be? And yet again, is it? Bring home the miracle to your mind, of that space, upon whose area the works of God are a mere dot, and the far-computing thought of man can only enter on its margin. All that exists is lost in the bosom of its great night. (Lecture on the Moral Sense, 1860)

Passages like these show that science has stimulated Emerson's mind to an awareness of the immensity of space, and of the long, slow development of the universe in time.

In the writing of Swedenborg Emerson thought he had found the embodiment of the true scientific attitude. Swedenborg's appeal for Emerson is easily explained. With some pretension to original scientific research, Swedenborg was dominantly a moral and religious thinker. His conception of nature closely matches Emerson's, in his affirmation of correspondence between material nature and man's soul, his search for "the more in the less, and the great in the small," and his conviction that material things may be converted to spiritual truths by means of imagination.[78] The ascension of forms in nature is described by Swedenborg as "wreathing through an everlasting spiral"; man he terms "a very minute Heaven." His interest in the "inner Copernican system" of the mind resembles Emerson's. Impressed by Swedenborg's successful creation of symbols as well as by his view of nature, Emerson ranks him at first with such poets as Homer, Dante, and Shakespeare.

Despite Emerson's sympathy with Swedenborg's scientific grasp, he finds Swedenborg a failure at symbolic expression. As in Chapter I of this book we found Swedenborg the exception to Emerson's belief that a true intuition will find the right expression, so does he fail in creating symbols by limiting them to a strictly theological interpretation. Through a "Hebrew symbolism," Emerson says, by which a horse always signifies carnal understanding; a tree, perception; the moon, faith, he "mistakes the village church for part of the sky." Though Swedenborg's philosophical interpretation has grasped nature's subtle flowing, his own symbolic expression is so frozen that it cannot partake of the fluid interpretation which Emerson demands.[79]

But literature affords Emerson abundant examples of successful symbols. Shakespeare's "miracle of mythologizing" he compares to nature's symbolic touch, when it confers a "secondary glory" on woodpiles by means of snow or moonlight. Wordsworth, whose early poetry seemed to Emerson too pragmatic, creates symbols in *The Excursion* which arouse the same "right feeling" as that caused by stars, mountains, and winds. In the "musky verses" of Hafiz Emerson discovers a different, but equally effective type of symbol, praising this poet's skill in "naming" cedar, palm tree, and birds. Emerson's keen eye for good symbolic expressions appears in his choice of Spenser's line, "For soul is form, and does the body make," Michelangelo's, "As from fire heat cannot be divided, no more can beauty from the eternal," and Thoreau's, "Hell itself may be contained within the compass of a spark." Among Thoreau's poems, whose symbolic creation Emerson recognized as superior to his own, his favorite was "Smoke." He has offered a tentative explanation of Thoreau's famous "hound, horse, and turtle-dove." [80] Emerson's blindness to the value of Keats' and Shelley's poetry prevents him from enjoying their fiery symbols, though he commends Shelley's painting of the skylark "Like a poet hidden in the light of thought."

Of Emerson's own poems, "The Sphinx" and "Brahma" are most successful as symbols. In both these poems, idea has been so integrally fused with image that criticism cannot separate them; the "drowsy Sphinx" has become the riddle of the world, the "red slayer" of Brahma, the mystical idea of union between subject and object. Not always so lucky in finding symbolic expression for his generalizations, Emerson states in the journals (1835) that his method of thought always involves "some material symbol of my proposition figuring itself incipiently."

He then records some successful symbols: Augustine's figure of the phial of water broken in the sea, to represent the soul's absorption in God; his own image, of weeds in a stream turned in one direction, to symbolize the domination of man's several acts by his will. Seeking to express time's judgment on literary reputation, which kills some books and preserves others, he thinks of potatoes in a pail of water — some at the top, some in the middle, some at the bottom — and this image he condemns as poor. The homeliness of the picture, he says,

ill accords with the lofty idea, and the picture of "potatoes
swimming in a tub" remains in the mind after the idea of
literary reputation is forgotten.

To estimate the value of Emerson's concept of the symbol,
one asks how far the theory is structural or organic, postulating a fusion of idea with image into inseparable unity. One
notices that Emerson never looks long at the object involved,
but usually considers the symbol in terms of the writer's creative power, piercing an object's outer form to its inner spirit;
or in terms of its effect upon the observer, as exhilaration or
consolation. Spirit is emphasized at the expense of the concrete in "The Poet," where he maintains "the independence
of the thought on the symbol, the stability of the thought, the
accidency and fugacity of the symbol." "The poet," he says,
"did not stop at the color or the form, but read their meaning;
neither may he rest in this meaning, but he makes the same
objects exponents of his new thought."

Implicit in this demand for a "fluid" symbol is a value for
novelty. Thus Emerson rebukes preachers for leaning too
heavily on the evocative power of Christ's name. "You name
the good Jesus," he says, "until I hate the sound of him." [81]
As he had criticized Swedenborg for monotony of interpretation, so does he find fault with Unitarian ministers for using
"trite rhetoric" instead of a "little algebra" in their symbols.

Not merely in demanding novel images, but in its conception that not even the single idea of the symbol remains in the
observer's mind, does Emerson's theory have fluidity. Each
symbol is figured merely as a stimulus to send the reader on to
new intuitions. Emerson thinks of the symbol as having effect
not so much through perfect fusion of idea with image, as
through the expression given to the object by the idea, in the
moment of flowing through it. The idea may remain in the
reader's mind, or the object may be put to fresh uses by the

poet; but idea and image are not considered as inseparably fused in a new unity. The material object has only temporary value, in objectifying spiritual intuition. As the spirit flows on, it leaves the object behind. Emerson's search for the idea implied in the poetic symbol was amusingly rebuked by his daughter Ellen, who replied to his question whether she had learned the meaning of Dante's figures in *The Inferno*: "No, and I do not wish to: to me they mean leopard, wolf, and Lucia, and any second and interior meaning would spoil all for me." [82]

Emerson's theory of the symbol is, then, ideal rather than structural. And it is this "ideal" emphasis of the symbol which renders it an excellent epitome of his general theory of art. In "The Preacher" he shows art embodying the "vanishing Spirit" in painting, sculpture, and temples, but man failing to appreciate truly, by transferring his admiration from the spirit to the "steadfast form." Yet one need only look at Nature, Emerson says, to realize the importance of "idea": "Beautifully shines a spirit through all the toughness of matter. The Adamant streams into softest but sharpest form before it." [83] He seeks another term for "Beauty" which will express for art that "delicate future tense" which is implicit in the Latin name for nature, "Natura, *about to be born*." [84] For Emerson the core of art's interest is that "which is in ACT OR ENDEAVOR TO PROCEED, to reach somewhat beyond, and all the better, if that be somewhat vast and divine." [85] The crux of Emerson's aesthetic, as of his symbol, appears in his reverence not for the form, but for the "vanishing Spirit."

We may well recall Santayana's perceptive comment on Emerson's "fluid symbol":

> If one set of symbols is substituted for another, nothing is changed in the thing signified, in the inner life of the soul, except the vehicle of expression . . . All ideas . . . are

fluid, and . . . it matters very little what things exist or
how long they endure, since the only reality is the perpetual motion that creates, transforms, and changes them
("Emerson's Poems," *Boston Daily Advertiser* Centenary
Number, May 23, 1903).

To illuminate Emerson's theory of the symbol, one may
compare it to that of Blake, whose spiritual perception of
the meaning implicit in marble, harp, and cloud received
Emerson's praise. Blake is quoted in Emerson's "Poetry and
Imagination" on the importance of "second sight":

> He who does not imagine in stronger and better line-
> aments and in stronger and better light than his perishing
> mortal eye can see, does not imagine at all. The painter
> asserts that all his imaginations appear to him more perfect,
> and more intimately organized than anything seen by his
> mortal eye. (William Blake, "On the Bard") [86]

Using Blake's theory to illustrate his own, Emerson has
twisted the idea to his own purpose: to show the spiritual,
not the corporeal, as the abiding element in the symbol. Looking at the whole passage in Blake, one sees that his purpose
differs from Emerson's: he is defending his representation of
"spirits with real bodies." In illustrating Gray's "Bard," Blake
says, he has tried to show "a spirit"; but he cannot conceive
that spirit, even in imagination, without giving it corporeal
form. While Blake agrees with Emerson's idea that symbolic
representation excels anything seen by mortal eye, he differs
from Emerson in maintaining that inner perception cannot be
grasped without concrete form. Once the spirit has been
poured into its body, Blake believes that it cannot be separated from its objective clothing. To put the matter symbol-
ically: Emerson believes that men are spirits; Blake believes
that spirits are "organised men."

By contrast with Blake's structural theory of the symbol, Emerson's spiritual emphasis emerges. While Blake thinks of an integral fusion between matter and spirit, Emerson conceives of spirit as flowing out of the matter which it has vitalized in the moment of creation. Whereas Blake considers the form as being developed in the artist's mind in terms of the material to be used, Emerson asserts that the plan grows in the artist's mind in terms of spirit, and by lucky chance gets transferred to matter.

The famous creed of "the familiar, the low" announced in *The American Scholar*, often taken as a manifesto of realism, actually embodies Emerson's idea of the spiritual symbol. "The near, the low, the common" are not to be simply presented, but "explored and poetized"; the shop, plough, and ledger are to be related to a central cause; it is "insight" into today, not simple representation, which Emerson demands.

Evaluation of Emerson's concept of the symbol must admit its inferiority to a truly structural theory like that of Blake. If the observer is always fleeing from the material aspect of symbol to the idea represented, and from that idea to others, his aesthetic appreciation takes on a disembodied quality. Further, Emerson's theoretical confidence in the symbol's value fortifies his native disposition to read for "gleams and glimpses," embracing particulars at the expense of general design, forgiving much to a mediocre poem in which he finds "an urgent fiery line like threads of gold in a mass of ore."

But Emerson's concept has its good points. The symbol represents the result of that creative process by which the poet has participated in the flowing action of nature; if it is well wrought, it will produce the same immediate effect of spiritual elation which the objects of nature inspire. It is thus the point of contact between man and the material world.

The dominantly spiritual cast of Emerson's conception belies Professor Sutcliffe's evaluation of the symbol as the only element of Emerson's poetic which reconciles the material with the ideal.[87] Emerson's symbol represents, rather, the essence of the poet's vision, which gains rather than loses by being stripped of its material vesture. Based in Plotinian philosophy, enriched by such scientific conceptions as the theory of progressive adaptation and the atomic hypothesis, Emerson's view of the symbol is self-consistent, fruitful in its application to specific poems, and stimulating both to creator and observer.

Eager to improve American poetry, Emerson urges the writers of his time to find new symbols in the world around them. In logging, fisheries, and politics, poets should find material for original poetry. "The northern trade, the southern planting, the western clearing," he says, "are yet unsung. Yet America is a poem in our eyes; its ample geography dazzles the imagination, and it will not wait long for metres" ("The Poet"). Though his own muse favored the tamer aspects of nature: fields of cattle, birds, and calm waters, he looked for a new genius, whose "tyrannical" eye would explore America's wilderness, and interpret her barbarism and materialism as well as her grandeur. If the beginnings of satisfaction appeared in Thoreau's "microscopic" vision and Whitman's "buffalo strength," there was no one who had yet caught into symbols the excitement of American life, which, Emerson said, "storms about us daily, and is slow to find a tongue."

CONCLUSION

The extent to which Emerson's view of art represents a new departure in American thought cannot be appreciated without comparing it to the eighteenth-century ideas which were Emerson's starting point. The aesthetic perception of Alison's *Essays on Taste*, for example, though somewhat liberated from neoclassic theory, was based chiefly on the principle of association. Without denying the validity of association as a description of some mental operations, Emerson sought the secret of aesthetic creation in a much more dynamic idea: the chemical reaction between nature and the mind of man, which results in a new production — the work of art. Emerson's difference from eighteenth-century criticism appears more evident by contrast with Blair's *Lectures on Rhetoric*, which he studied in college. Consider Blair's treatment of metaphor, with an enumeration of the various figures, a reminder to writers that figures must be suited to their subject, as the "dress of the sentiments," not vulgar or dirty, but clear, and of course not mixed.[88] How different is this analysis from Emerson's concept of the symbol as the penetration by the poet of the phenomenal world, and the evocation of that spirit which lies at nature's heart.

Real comprehension of Emerson's theory of organic and spiritual form must also correct the prevailing impression that his aesthetic is rigidly moral. One has only to look at the *Dial* reviews of Menzel's *Goethe* by Margaret Fuller and Theodore Parker (January 1840) to see that Goethe is the light leading the Transcendentalists out of a consideration of the work of art an an exemplar of moral commandments, into a freer state of aesthetic appreciation. Goethe performed a similar service for Emerson, as appears when he reminds himself to look at a picture as a picture and a tune as a tune, since "Goethe laughs at those who force every work of art into the narrow circle of their own prejudices." [89] The journal of 1839, for example, finds that the complex forms of drama, epic, and novel, as well as the musical symphony, allow the writer to express his "knowledge of life by indirections as well as in the didactic way, and can therefore express the fluxional quantities and values which the thesis or dissertation could never give." Emerson's progress beyond a tendency to look at works of art as evidence of specific moral judgments has come about not by abandoning the term "moral" but by expanding "moral" to a broader signification, inclusive of all natural as well as human life.

Not only by its emancipation from earlier more restricted views, but by breadth of experience in the fine arts and literature, Emerson's conception of art has a richness not possessed by any other contemporary American writer. From the Coleridgean statement of organic form, the Goethean concept of vegetable forms in architecture, the Plotinian theory of spiritual form, Emerson freely adopted suggestions for his interpretation of organic form. Through his well-integrated concept of architectural form, Emerson illustrates his general thesis that the useful arts and the fine arts can learn from each other.

The organic principle, widely employed by modern critics, does not of course derive solely from Emerson, but goes back as far as Aristotle for its roots and includes German and English romantic thought in its growth. The idea has suffered some of the deleterious effect which Emerson observed as characteristic of all language, in becoming a kind of critical cliché whose central meaning is forgotten. Critics can, I believe, refresh their sense of the vitality of "organic form" by attention to the Emersonian interpretation of it, as the seal and sign by which the artist reveals his sympathetic understanding of the universal spirit which links his own soul to objects in nature.

The organic and spiritual qualities of form in Emerson's theory of art enjoy the same integral relation which binds together matter and spirit in his view of nature. As in nature, material objects realize spirit and are in turn vitalized by spirit, so in art the organic principle issues from a spiritual impulse. Through the concept of the symbol in poetry, his favorite art, Emerson clearly demonstrates that if one kind of form must be sacrificed to the other, it is the organic which must give way to the spiritual. Emerson's concept of the "ascension" of form in the symbol has a stimulating effect both upon creative artist and observer. The poet may not rest in satisfaction of a line well turned; the observer may not limit himself to admiring one creative artist. Each must move on to fresh discoveries, modifying former views in the light of new thought. Nor does this free creation and interpretation imply irresponsible impressionism, for the strong hand of the Divine will restrain one who seeks to follow mere caprice.

The principal lack in Emerson's concept of form is the gap which exists between the intuition in the artist's mind and its transference to objective matter. Although this lack may not be explained away, it can be better understood in the light of Emerson's distrust of the principle of imitation. As early as 1820, when he is just beginning to reflect on aesthetic matters, Emerson attributes the pleasure in observing a painting not to its resemblance to natural objects, but to the power required to produce the work.

Clearly Emerson's concept of imitation is not Aristotelian, but the neoclassic sense of the term, that of following models. A late journal passage (1862) distinguishes between photographic representation, which suggests Aristotle's "imitation of things as they are," and ideal representation, which parallels Aristotle's "imitation of things as they ought to be." Emerson's demand that a painter present "a better fairer creation than we know" comes close to Aristotelian $\mu\iota\mu\eta\sigma\iota\varsigma$. While Emerson's theory of the artist's shaping power thus bears some underlying similarity to Aristotelian imitation,

such explicit references as Emerson makes to Aristotle imply
that he thinks his criticism outmoded.[90]

Considering the term "imitation," then, as an imitation of
styles, Emerson finds it the chief error of American artists,
who exist only to ape England. "Can we never," he asks in the
Dial essay on "Art," "extract this maggot of Europe out of
the brains of our countrymen?" Especially does he regret that
we are not only taught but begotten by England, because
much of English art and literature is itself derivative. Except
for Milton, Shakespeare, and Wordsworth, he fails to find
illumination on his "idea of the poet" in Chalmers' collection
of five centuries of English bards.

His most considered view of course recognizes that Americans cannot cast off the cultural influence of Europe; he says,
in fact, that an intellectual discovery of importance for the
whole land is made by the first American scholar who reads
Homer under a farmhouse roof. Emerson grants that even
while he asserts his independence, "the artist has always the
masters in his eye." Thus Michelangelo thinks of Da Vinci;
Raphael, of Michelangelo; McKay the shipbuilder thinks of
Steers, and Steers, of Poole.[91]

But absorption of other cultures, Emerson insists, must be
carried on with creative intent. His lecture on Literature
(1836) demands that we stop printing this "vast carcass of
tradition every year with as much solemnity as a new revelation." [92] To Margaret Fuller in Italy he writes, "Ah must we
walk proudly too in Rome!" His conclusion is that after
foreign travel and reading of other literatures, each man must
find beauty in his own native spot, "in the chamber where he
sits, in the half acre where his chimney rises." The best of
alien art and literature must be cautiously adapted, lest we lose
original inspiration.

Emerson's dislike of the term "imitation," as "imitation of

models" and the typical sickness of American culture, thus kept him from using imitation, as he might have done, to explain how the artist objectifies his creative intuition in material shape.

Besides its failure to show how idea becomes realized in matter, Emerson's theory of form lacks any good criteria by which the great works of art and literature may be judged. In architecture we have the functional guide of comparing the design of a building with its purpose, thereby determining whether its beauty constitutes mere embellishment, or the stronger beauty of structural design. In the fine arts and literature, we have chiefly the subjective criterion: "Does the work give the same impression of unified wholeness that one derives from an oak tree?" Or, if it is on a grander scale, "Does it give the impression that the writer has employed universal laws with daring creative skill?"

Certainly Emerson never studied a work of art in the methodical manner indicated by a modern critic: "Under what circumstances was this work of art created? What did the artist intend to create? How successfully did he accomplish it? By what standards should it be judged? What is its value by these standards?" [93]

Of these criteria, the "intent of the artist" interests Emerson least, since he is convinced that what is divine in the work will speak directly to what is divine in him. An instance of his using this criterion appears, however, in 1838, when he writes to Alcott concerning that curious production, Psyche (still in manuscript form today), that he must decide whether he is writing a book of prophecy or a literary essay, and revise accordingly.

Emerson's study of the work of art does, however, reveal a concern with the circumstances of creation. The fact that Emerson's theory of art lays down no specific rules and that

his criticism follows no systematic procedure should not blind
us to the fact that he is aware of historical and biographical
influences in art. In his lectures on English Literature we have
observed that he relates the writers to the qualities of the age;
and that consideration of his own time shows an awareness of
the complex atmosphere of the nineteenth century, and of the
fact that individuals must reflect as well as guide their age.
English Traits reveals a lively sense of those Anglo-Saxon
ancestors who look out from the modern Englishman's eye;
Representative Men portrays rounded sketches of great individuals, placing the dynamic Napoleon against the background of French geography and history, showing in Plato a
balance of Eastern mysticism with Western common sense,
and indicating Montaigne as the embodiment of skepticism
in his time. Aware also of history's importance in the fine arts,
Emerson has wished that he might increase his understanding
of the great masterpieces by knowledge of their development
down through the centuries. The lecture on Poetry and Criticism includes an amusing comment on the changing attitudes
of historical criticism toward great men, which Emerson denotes "white and black washing." Whitewashing appears in
Froude's portraying Henry VIII as a good family man, and in
Sainte-Beuve's characterization of Richelieu as a patriot.
" 'Tis almost Caesar Borgia's turn to be a lamb and a martyr,"
Emerson wryly remarks of this "improving" tendency. On
the other hand, Forchhammer has "black-washed" Socrates;
and Macaulay, William Penn. Emerson finds these changes
representative of a healthy tendency in criticism, a passing
judgment on old forms in the light of new ideas.

Some awareness of national characteristics appears in
Emerson's comments on the English as uncreative, but possessed of a remarkable capacity for absorbing other cultures;
the French as light, clever, and humorous, though lacking in

true imagination; the Americans as "exaggerated" English-men, with quicker apprehension and keener minds. A larger division is recognized in his distinction between Eastern, or Persian, poetry, as characterized by the superlative, and West-ern, as distinguished by the positive, degree. Again, Emerson makes a racial generalization concerning creative power, stat-ing that the Semite race (Hebrew, Arab, or Syrian) has high imagination in poetry, art, and eloquence; the Indo-European races, exemplified by the Roman, adopt the Semites' beautiful creations and deduce rules from them, but lack any creative strength; and the Mongolians destroy the arts as they con-quer other nations. That this last is too broad a generaliza-tion to have value scarcely needs comment; but it serves to indicate Emerson's interested speculation about art's rela-tion to the factors of race as well as of biography and national history.

Emerson's analysis of literary history, we have observed, involves a "wave" rather than an "evolutionary" interpreta-tion, implying an ebb and flow throughout the ages, and asserting that an earlier time may have qualities superior to the present. But his very optimism about the future art and literature of his own country implies a confidence in progress. However clearly he recognizes dead spots in his own time as well as in earlier periods, he retains an underlying faith that the future will bring a cultural advance as much better than the present as the present excels the past, even though that advance may appear in unexpected places and in fashions un-noticed by the contemporary observer.

The realization that Emerson judges the highest excellence of art by a mystical standard should not be made to obscure the place which he gives, on the human plane, to historical, biographical, and national factors in the aesthetic drama. In our own day critics like C. S. Lewis and I. A. Richards, fascinated by the psychological aspects of criticism, have tended to neglect the factors of race, time, and environment. It is therefore salutary to recall that this nineteenth-century thinker, no less fertile of ideas concerning the psychology of creating and enjoying art, has by no means abandoned historical and biographical elements, but has used them wherever they could throw light on that ever fascinating enigma, the work of art.

When we turn from the human plane to that more elevated realm of spirit by which works are ultimately to be valued, we seek to define the nature of Emerson's "ideal" standard. Professor Foerster has called Emerson's high aesthetic selection the "classical conception of the ideal." [94] Emerson's criticism of sculpture, which Professor Foerster attests as one instance of his "classical" criticism, has been shown to diverge from the "Greek" ideal in postulating, not the classic Praxiteles, but the Renaissance Michelangelo as its epitome. "The unfading petals five" of Emerson's poems "The Test" and "The Solution," also cited by Professor Foerster in evidence of his "high selection," lose force in this connection when one reads Emerson's comment on them.

In "The Solution" of "The Test" Emerson lists the "five" as Homer, Dante, Shakespeare, Goethe, and Swedenborg. He writes to Lowell concerning the printing of these poems in *The Atlantic*:

> My riddle, you see, is not very deep, and admits, like other riddles, of several solutions. Mine is, five national poets, Homer, Dante, Shakespeare, Swedenborg, and Goethe. A German can, if he will, interpret it, Bach, Mozart, Handel, Haydn, and Beethoven. If you choose to print it, I can put my solution into rhyme in another number. (*L.*, V, 230, 1860) [95]

This comment and the fact that Emerson omitted these verses from his *Selected Poems* indicate that Emerson attached little importance to their "high selection."

Since Emerson does not think of a few great names in art or literature as lasting models of excellence, the strictness in his theory of form cannot be called "classic" in the usual sense of the word. Emerson indicates the direction of his "high standard" when he says:

> Works of the intellect are great only by comparison with each other; *Ivanhoe* and *Waverley* compared with Castle Radcliffe and the Porter novels; but nothing is great, — not mighty Homer and Milton, — beside the infinite Reason. It carries them away as a flood. They are as a sleep. ("Literary Ethics")

By the mystical criterion, all works of art have value in so far as they catch, for a moment, the universal spirit. The great works, which have caught a larger portion, will be longer preserved and appeal to more men than lesser creations, but no single work can absorb enough of the All-soul to keep the attention of one who can discover that Spirit itself.

To state that all aesthetic production shrinks before the Infinite Reason does not, of course, express the whole value of Emerson's theory of form. The very variety and extent of his statements about the arts, as revealed in this chapter, are evidence that before Emerson drives the arts to this ultimate suicidal point, he has much to say of their work alive.

Emerson's specific criticisms of contemporary art and literature reveal a principle of high idealism operating together with a friendly recognition of partial achievement. When he turned from contemplation of the boundless world of spirit to his own country's aesthetic production, Emerson sought to lead and drive American creative effort in the direction of the "spiral flowing." Appreciation for indigenous American growths, even though crude, appears in a lecture on Literary and Spiritual Influences (1843) where he advises American literature to turn westward, and produce more writing with the flavor of Davy Crockett's and Daniel Boone's exploits. The fact that Europeans are already avidly reading these books, in preference to more polished work imitative of England may, he thinks, indicate that the center of American literary balance is to swing from the seaboard to the middle of the continent. To get rid of Oriental culture, homage to Europe, and subservience to Cambridge, he suggests a boat trip down the Ohio and up the Mississippi.[96]

Despite the broader horizon which he visualizes for all of America, Emerson's chief literary interest still lies in New England. His lecture on Boston (1861) applies the organic principle to his home city. He asserts that a spiritual inspiration pours forth from the aerial fluid of Boston's atmosphere; the bracing quality of Charles River water makes men get up earlier; and exposure to snows, east winds, and changing skies excites them to thought. He dates the beginning of modern literature from Buckminster's Phi Beta Kappa address at Cambridge in 1820. Though Boston has made some contribution to culture through its advance in politics, science, and the learned professions, it has yet to yield a literary masterpiece. To some extent, he says, New England shares with Europe the "re-discovering" quality of the nineteenth century; of the Elgin Marbles and the city of Pompeii in art, the lost manuscripts of Cicero and Milton, the publication of the Sanskrit Vedas. With these rich cultures for a foundation, he has every hope that original and vital literary thought will proceed.

Among his own friends and acquaintances, Emerson expresses hope for the future reputation of the "wild Whitman, with real inspiration but choked by Titanic abdomen," of Delia Bacon in criticism (despite her quixotic defense of the Baconian hypothesis), of Thoreau, Alcott, and Channing.

Perhaps Emerson's own great essays come closest to the new and dynamic creation which he sought for New England's literature. Besides his own work, his contribution to *The Dial* as coeditor with Margaret Fuller is significant. Their manifesto in the first number (July 1840) shows their desire that *The Dial* bear the print of organic form: "It has the step of Fate, and goes on existing like an oak or a river, because it must." Sensing a lack of earthiness in his own writing, Emerson wanted *The Dial* to "go straight into life," covering the domestic, civil, and political topics which his essays omitted. Even when *The Dial* died, after sixteen numbers, it had done something to answer the cry which Emerson was always hearing: "My bareness! My bareness! seems America to say."

In *The Massachusetts Quarterly Review*, that "*Dial* with a beard" to which Emerson gave reluctant assistance for a year, he finds a lack of intellectual tone and literary skill, and fears that without a sudden upsurge after the January 1848 number, the periodical "will sink in a North American." Yet his editorial address in the first number represents an excellent expression of the Emersonian hope that American literature will show the ascension of "spiral form": "Bad as it is, this freedom leads onward and upward, — to a Columbia of thought and art, which is the last and endless end of Columbus's adventures." The essay, "Boston," confirms this glimpse of America's future:

> What should hinder that this America, so long kept reserved from the intellectual races, until they should grow to it, glimpses being afforded which spoke to the imagination,

yet the firm shore hid, until science of art should be ripe to propose it as a fixed aim. . . What should hinder that this New Atlantis should have its happy ports, its mountains of security, its gardens fit for human abode, where all elements were right for the health, power, and virtue of man?

CHAPTER III

The Aesthetic Experience

The word by seers or sibyls told,
In groves of oak, or fanes of gold,
Still floats upon the morning wind,
Still whispers to the willing mind.

"The Problem"

THE OBSERVER'S RELATION TO THE CREATIVE ARTIST

With its effect upon the receptive mind, the creative process, begun by the artist through influx of the Divine Spirit, and objectified in the finished work of art, now comes full circle. Emerson's theory of response to art has received less attention from his critics than have the first two terms of the aesthetic series.[1] Yet Emerson has clearly indicated the importance of the observer in *realizing* the creative idea which has only partially fulfilled its purpose through embodiment in stone, canvas, or poetic rhythm.

The body of Emerson's statements about the work of art certainly attests his belief in the objective validity of the art object. As his philosophic position is dualistic rather than monistic, so is his aesthetic grounded in a faith that the artifact does exist independent of its appreciators. The qualification of this dualism, however, in art as well as in nature, is that artistic as well as natural objects have importance not by their *existence*, but through their *realization* by a human mind. "The beauty of the object," Emerson says, "exists in the mind of the beholder." [2] Just as the creative artist, by his keen perception, touches into vital life the element of beauty latent in natural objects, so does the observer realize the potential loveliness in the work of art. No less than the pilgrim who carries with him into the woods "the beauty which he visits," painting it with his eye and singing it with his ear, does the observer of art awaken the sleeping Psyche of the poem or painting with his inbreathing spirit. Thus the reception of art in the aesthetic realm is the counterpart of correspondence in the epistemological realm.

The same concept of benevolent necessity (as opposed to malignant fate) which governs Emerson's view of the natural world obtains also in his aesthetic. A sympathetic observer will, he is convinced, appear for every great work of art: "the eye was placed where that ray should fall, to the end that it might testify of that particular ray." [3] "The poet and the lover of poetry," Emerson asserts, "are born at one instant twins." [4] The "one instant" of this passage of course denotes mystical rather than worldly time (if appreciation is delayed for a century, it is none the less real when it comes). It is Emerson's underlying trust in *Representative Men* that "nature never sends a great man into the planet without confiding the secret to another soul." "The appreciation," he insists, "never lags far after the invention. The hearing ear is close to the speaking tongue." [5]

Pondering on the miracle of his mind's quick response to the beauty of Roman art, Emerson writes to his brother in 1833 that "these things take a place that seems to have waited for them in our own minds. They are almost *recognised*, as Fontenelle said of new truth." [6] By 1837, in *The American*

Scholar, Emerson has worked out an answer to this apparent miracle; the mind's leaping to enjoy a work of art far separated from it in time does not show a special providential act by which a work exists as grub until some sympathetic observer converts it to a butterfly, but merely proves "the philosophical doctrine of the identity of all minds." The relation to a larger Divine nature, which the receptive mind shares with the creative, provides the rationale for his power to bring the creative vision into life.

Perhaps because he approached the world of literature and art with rather less reverence than the natural world, Emerson has presented a better rationalized explanation of the receptive than of the creative consciousness. What seemed pure miracle in the creative state becomes, when related to the receptive mind, more understandable in human terms. Though we shall find that Emerson places the ultimate value of the receptive, as of the creative experience, in its mystical uplift, the receptive experience is more fully explained than is the creative, on its "lower levels." Not only does this fuller psychological analysis make Emerson's theory of art more interesting to modern readers, but it presents a better balanced picture of his aesthetic than one discovers from surveying only what he says of the creative process. Emerson's recognition of the complexity involved in aesthetic enjoyment appears in the second essay on "Art," where he speaks of the "blended" rather than the simple origin of our pleasure in art.

The relation between creative artist and observer involves the whole question, much discussed by German and English romantics, of the difference between genius and the masses. Significantly, Emerson's treatment of this problem differs from that of the Germans as well as from Coleridge and Carlyle in its democratic emphasis. Confidence in the average man's capacity to appreciate art does not of course blind

Emerson to the presence, even in free-breathing America, of a group with no sensitivity at all. He is interested in Coleridge's "gradation of men" according to their power to appreciate, as in his record of Machiavelli's distinction of minds: those who invent, those who understand, those who neither invent nor understand.[7] The "blind" group are denoted in the lecture Classes of Men (1860) as "perverse" rather than deficient in sensibility, "tyrannic temperaments, stiff-necked, with the nose of a rhinoceros"; these, "the moth and rust" of quiet times, will be "whipped out of nature" at the first hint of crisis. These are the vulgar despised by Michelangelo for obscuring "every beam of beauty in the universe."

Apart from this recognition that a few men are impervious to art's shafts, Emerson has faith in the common man's ability to enjoy the beautiful in art and literature. Compensation for lack of culture in that "inarticulate behemoth," the mob, appears in its "uncorrupted instinct."[8] The precious quality of current literary criticism, Emerson suggests, might be readjusted by the clear, unsophisticated view of a committee of farmers. "All men think; but rarely," he says. "All men can." The very effort of a poet in creating implies this belief in the potential capacity of readers to enjoy his work.

Grappling with the problem of the difference which exists between creative genius and appreciative observer, Emerson sees this inequality consequent on the order of nature. Thus he compares the creator to an aqueduct whose water comes ultimately from the heavens, and seeps down by force of gravity to the receiver's level; and again, using his favorite "bi-polar" explanation of nature's dilemmas, he likens the creator to the north or positive pole, the observer to the south or negative, and asserts that each is needed to complete the other. Since in the Emersonian system the creative artist receives his intuitions from God, and passes them on to lesser men, a great man is considered as "standing on God," a small man as standing on a great man.

The sensitive observer, Emerson asserts, will always be aware of this difference between himself and the artist, even in moments when he feels most closely at one with the creative genius. Reading *Hamlet* and *Lear*, for example, Emerson wonders at "the perfect reception" accorded to "this wit and immense knowledge of life," in contrast to our inability to produce a similar work. Of the thousands whose reading of Wordsworth and Tennyson is so sympathetic that they feel they could write verse, few have that power. Emerson explains the paradox:

> So impassable is, at last, that thin, imperceptible boundary between perfect understanding of the author, perfect fellowship with him, *quasi* [*sic*] consciousness of the same gifts, — and the faculty of subordinating that rapture to the Will in such degree as to be able to conjoin and record our states of mind. (*J.*, 1838)

By the term "quasi consciousness" Emerson strikes the heart of that sense of distance which must always be a part of the observer's sense of union with the artist.

Emerson's democratic faith, not merely in the common man's power to understand great art, but in his necessity in the aesthetic system as a completer of creative intuition differs sharply from Carlyle's statement in *Heroes and Hero-Worship*, which emphasizes the great man's superiority to the average man, and the average man's need to adore (without real understanding) the flashes of genius which dazzle his sight.

The observer's kinship with the creator in Emerson's system is attested by a feeling of identity with the artist as he comes under his spell. In Montaigne's essays Emerson found so true an echo of his own thought that he felt as if he had written the book himself. Too keen a sense of oneness with the creator may abstract the attention from the work itself, as Emerson says of Carlyle's *French Revolution*: "Why should I read this book? The man himself is mine." [9] But in general the observer's feeling of identity with the artist assists aesthetic enjoyment. The cumulative effect of studying the background of Gothic architecture — the religion, the common man's contribution, the artists' coöperation — is described in personal terms in the essay on "History": "We have as it were been the man who made the minster." In the aesthetic experience the observer shares for a vital moment the creator's vision of the Over-soul; he becomes an imaginative re-creator of the artist's intuition. Emerson's flexibility in adjusting to varied types of creative art appears in his statement: "When I read a problem, I would be a geometer; poetry, a poet; history, a historian; sermons, a preacher; when I see paintings, I would paint; sculpture, carve. . . The manifold soul in me vindicates its acquaintance with all these things" (*J.*, 1835).

In Emerson's system, the ideal observer, realizing his importance as a link in the aesthetic chain, will show a self-reliance no less strong than the artist's. Each man must choose his own aesthetic fields to conquer; to defer to another's taste in reading is to "fill the stomach of a horse with the food of a fish." Man must free himself not only from present guides, but from the authoritative weight of history; the present rather than the past tense, modern reinterpretation rather than respect for tradition underlie man's independence. Of the world's churches, empires, and literature, Emerson says:

> I must and will have them subordinate and not masters. They shall accept and serve my point of view. . . Say to

such, you are greatly obliged to them as you are to all the History, to the pyramids, and the authors, but now we are here, now our day is come, we have been born out of the Eternal silence, and now will we live, live for ourselves and not as the pallbearers of a funeral but as the upholders and creators of an age and neither Greece nor Rome . . . nor the three unities of Aristotle . . . nor the *Edinburgh Review* is to command any longer. Now we are come and will put our own interpretation on things and moreover our own things for interpretation. (Ms. J. D, Pt. I, 1838)

The phrase "our own things for interpretation" demands not merely a fresh view of the classics, but independent choice of books and pictures to be enjoyed.

If Emerson sometimes exaggerates the observer's need for self-reliance, such overemphasis is natural. Always more in danger from others' influence than is the artist, the observer may degenerate from the plastic state of sensitive appreciation into mere looseness of fiber. Particularly in the realm of the fine arts, whose law Emerson feels less competent to discover than that of poetry, he insists on individual freedom, trying not to yield too completely to the painting or sculpture he surveys. Of some sketches by Guercino, Piranesi, and van Leyden, brought to him by Margaret Fuller, he says: "The difficulty consists in righting one's self before them; in arriving at a quite simple conviction that the sketch appeals to me, and coming at a state of perfect equilibrium, leaving all allowance to spontaneous criticisms" (*J.*, 1838). If this insistence on "balance" and "equilibrium" of mind before the masters seems a little self-conscious, it nevertheless shows the right tendency, toward independent judgment. Emerson's reluctance to admire "what he should admire" is amusingly illustrated by what he says of the Venus de' Medici in the Tribune at Florence. "Walking coolly around the marble lady," he grants that she deserves to be visited, and that the plaster cast in the Athenaeum has inadequately shown her beauty; yet he withholds complete admiration, making "a continual effort not to be pleased except by that which ought to please me." [10] Not until his second visit, he tells his lecture audience in 1834, is he "quite satisfied."

One recognizes a danger in this "complete self-reliance" which Emerson so vigorously states as a principle of aesthetic enjoyment. May not this "self-reliant" observer miss the beauty in great works of art by an unwillingness to make the effort necessary to enjoy them? May not his independence degenerate into idiosyncrasy?

That Emerson was aware of the problem involved in this "self-reliance" appears in some attempts he makes to qualify the term. He sees inherent in the great works of art a power which will overcome all but the most stubborn opposition. By the Divine fire which they breathe, they will kindle man's sense of beauty, whether he will or no. In Rome Emerson finds this power to subdue the visitor: "It is in vain to refuse to admire. You must in spite of yourself. It is magnificent." [11] The works of genius, Emerson asserts, exert an unquestioned influence over man. When from any part of the world a production appears "that meets all the conditions, and delights us," we all say, "*This is it!*" [12]

Recognizing that certain works will remain classics even if young men scorn them, he seeks to explain "the spirit of piety in which this old noblesse is assailed":

> It is not . . . in a bragging spirit, that philosophy now tends to disparage books, and affirm that the reader of Shakspeare is also a Shakspeare, or he could find no joy in the page. Nor does the young student persuade himself that he could bodily restore the Parthenon, whilst he affirms the ultimate identity of the artist and the spectator; but only

in the spirit of a child who says, "I am but a child, but I am the heir of all." (*J.*, 1839)

Thus the cure for extreme self-reliance in the enjoyment of art is found in a true humility of spirit. In the lecture on the Eye and Ear (1837) Emerson defines aesthetic independence as "ideal" rather than "actual":

> Whilst I persist in showing the property all men have in what is beautiful, I need not say I am very far from feeling any wish to degrade the work of art by representing every rude novice as entitled to sit in judgment on it. It is not the actual but the ideal Man that has a property and jurisdiction over the poem and the tune. In fact if we wish to know what a poem or a tune or cameo can teach us we must go to them and not bring them to us. We must passive and docile learn what the artist strove after and not too petulantly say what we like.

In the humble spirit and the ideal quality of this critical independence, then, as well as in the power possessed by great works of art in themselves, Emerson finds the safeguard to threats of brag or idiosyncrasy. In this qualification one sees the difference between Emerson's theory of criticism and the completely impressionistic view, for example, of a writer like Anatole France, who justifies the wanderings as well as the adventures of his soul among the masterpieces. With Emerson a recognition (even though implicit) always exists, of the inherent validity of great creative works. One may call this the reservation of his aesthetic idealism, the restraining judgment which keeps him from making a complete equation between Michelangelo's Last Judgment and the weather stains on the wall.

Emerson's comment on Margaret Fuller's judgment of art

illustrates what he considers extreme self-reliance in criticism. Assisted by Margaret Fuller as well as by Samuel Gray Ward in learning to appreciate the plastic arts, Emerson at first tries to see pictures through Margaret's eyes. The fact that he considers her on the whole a good critic appears in his analysis of her appreciation, as a "sympathy with the artist," a "co-perception with him of the eloquence of form." Gradually, however, as his own taste takes shape, Emerson begins to suspect his guide, particularly when she deals with technique, and he concludes that her taste, "though honest, was not on *universal* but on *idiosyncratic* grounds." In her love of nature as of art, Emerson finds a certain sentimentality, a "pleasure-able excitement rather than a deep poetic feeling," which to him seems "sickly and superficial." [13]

Emerson's detection of egotism in Margaret Fuller's aesthetic judgment does not include any rule for avoiding this fault, but his censure implies a suggestion for the right way. Just as the artist must be self-reliant in his independence of other men but submissive to the Divine Mind, so must the observer free himself from human guides — as Emerson becomes independent of Margaret — while he remains subject to the Divine Spirit as a guide to right appreciation. A hasty judgment of art, for example, is likely to show individual caprice; whereas a slower response, in which the observer waits for the spirit to speak from the work, has more chance of striking the heart of the matter.

If self-reliance can err by too quick an admiration of art, it can also stray in the opposite direction of a stiff-necked independence which refuses to submit to the aesthetic object. Possessing good potential appreciation, these stubborn men are not hopeless, like the "tyrannic" temperaments described in Classes of Men, but their eyes are clouded by egotism. Such a proud man is Alcott, who searches for his own universals in reading a book, and completely misses what the author is trying to say.[14]

To avoid these extremes of superficial admiration (as represented by Margaret Fuller) and egotistic blindness (as shown by Alcott), the observer should bring to the work of art the same passivity which the creative artist shows before the Divine Spirit. Good reading in the Emersonian sense always involves "a yielding, sometimes entire, but always some yielding to the book." This receptivity does not mean a mesmeric state in which the mind receives messages from a literary spirit; rather, the mind holds in abeyance its own method, so that it may freely follow the writer's line of development. Thus Emerson admires Belzoni's imaginative recreation of the building of the Pyramids,[15] his own fancy awake to Belzoni's lead: "My thought lives along the whole line of temples and sphinxes and catacombs, passes through them all with satisfaction, and they live again to the mind, and are now" (essay on "History").

Emerson has given us fuller suggestions about how the observer can enjoy the great masterpieces than about how a curious young man can find the classics. Despite the deficiency of his theory at this point, his own experience in literature and the fine arts included most of history's great landmarks. With a good background in the classics, including Plutarch and Horace as well as Homer and Plato, he proceeded to a wide reading in the Neo-Platonists, in English literature, in European writers like George Sand, Goethe, and Dante, Scandinavian sagas like the *Eddas* and *Ynglingasaga*, and in such currents outside the English stream as Hafiz' Persian poetry and the Hindu *Bhagavad-gita*. In the fine arts, his range extended from most of the great ancient and modern works of Italian art, the Elgin Marbles and the great English cathedrals — even the Egyptian pyramids. If he could not draw up a rule for the discovery of the classics, he could make a striking demonstration through his own experience that an inquiring mind can discover the great in literature and art.

Like the artist in his creative state, the observer can receive the impact of art best when healthy in body and free in mind. Quiet may help him to achieve surrender to a book, especially with a difficult writer like Schelling, who demands the "lamp" and the "lonely tower" and the "lustrum of silence." His own experience gives Emerson confidence in the value of the casual approach to art and literature. Young men, he insists, will gain more from reading Shakespeare as recreation than from studying him. Just as the moon is more beautiful when unexpectedly seen, so is the book more delightful when read without too much pretension for scholarship. Away from the familiar background of the library, a book may take on added zest; thus Goethe is more exciting in the woods, Agassiz in prairie taverns. In the fine arts also Emerson warns against the systematic combing of a gallery, guidebook in hand. Recalling his delight in a second visit to Santa Croce after sunset when the candles were lighted, he says: "Perhaps the most valuable impressions are those which come to each individual casually and at moments when he is not on the hunt for wonders." [16] From the "active passivity" of his mind in the presence of great writers, Emerson feels his whole being enriched, as if he had acquired "an entire new mind," and, a kind of Proteus, he "enjoys the universe through the powers and energies of a hundred different men." [17] Thus the number of artists and writers whom the observer comes to know acts as a multiplying factor to enlarge his view of life. Since the scholar has subordinated his will only to that portion of the work which shows the true Baphometic fire, and since he is active along the lines indicated by the creative artist, aesthetic experience does not humiliate him, but instead brings him to an awareness of "the absolute boundlessness" of human capacity, in which he shares.

The dynamic relation which should exist between creative artist and observer is nowhere better illustrated than in Emerson's statements concerning eloquence.[18] From a rich background in Greek and Roman oratory, a wide reading of contemporary English and French speeches, a full knowledge of the American history of public speaking from Eliot's *Address to the Indians* down to Parker's *Transient and Permanent in Christianity*, a broad experience in pulpit and lyceum addresses (he probably made and listened to more speeches than any other American of his time), Emerson was well qualified to speak of the effect of oratory upon listeners. The one art in which Emerson inherited an American tradition, eloquence is so far exalted by him as to be termed a combination of painting, sculpture, architecture, music, and poetry, "an exponent of human culture, as one of the last and finest forms of man." His consideration of it as a social art, in which the hearer, in concert with others, is raised to a higher pitch of consciousness, shows that he derived from it much the same sort of pleasure which a modern audience enjoys in drama or symphony. In the best orator, he says, the audience may see before them fused into one dominating personality, the qualities of will, memory, invention, language of nature, power of mind, which in other art and literature they view for the most part in fragments. Discarding Blair's emphasis upon organization, figures of speech, and pronunciation as the keys to successful speaking,[19] Emerson locates the orator's power over men chiefly in his depth of idea and strength of character.

As in the enjoyment of art and literature, so in eloquence, the audience must be submissive to the speaker's power. But Emerson shows a sense of difference here from the other arts, in the resisting strength of an audience which the orator must overcome. The lecture on New England Manners (1843) describes the "pinched wedged elbowed sweltering assembly" of Faneuil Hall, pushing and shouting during a poor speech, suddenly quieted as if magnetized when a commander like Webster takes the platform, "and the house hangs waiting on the lips of one man." Though Emerson prizes serenity in a speaker, "a marble texture, against which the mob of souls dashing is broken, like crockery falling on stone" (lecture on Eloquence, 1867), he finds mere serenity of no avail unless accompanied by that creative heat which is partly personal, partly intellectual, inspired by the speaker's fierce belief in the truth of what he is about to say. Emerson records Pepys' belief that Lord Clarendon's success proceeded from the confidence that his audience was below him,[20] but he prefers to explain the audience's submission to a speaker not on the basis of social inferiority, but on the higher level of interest in the message.

Nor is the audience merely hostile or merely passive; by its electric response, it inspires the speaker. Of N. P. Rogers' suggestion that he take a course of mobs to overcome his "quaintness and transcendentalism," Emerson says, "I might have found it as good for me, as the watercure for paralyzed stomachs." [21] He can think of no better sign of power than "riding this wild horse of the people." Conversely, an audience's limitation may be the cause of poor speaking. The reason for the uniform dullness of contemporary British political speeches Emerson finds in Lowell Buxton's statement that the House of Commons loves good sense and joking, but distrusts any speech that soars into ideal regions. The ideal of audience contribution to a speaker appears in a comment of Hermes Trismegistus: "O son, he that hears must co-understand and conspire in thought with him that speaks; yea, he must have his hearing swifter and sharper than the voice of the speaker." [22]

A good speaker will guide his talk not by an audience's interest in externals, but by their deeper concern with ideas. A lecturer who so defers to popular taste as to reveal "just that degree of depth which his audience can swim in, without any real originality" [23] must produce a result inferior to an orator who risks offending his audience by flouting tradition, and letting in the light of new ideas, speaking to the divine spark in his hearers' minds. Holding an audience by the ears is better than holding it by the eyes, but holding it by the mind is best of all. Thus does the speaker "excite the slumbering intellect" of his listeners.

Emerson's gratitude for those men who truly agitate, convert, and inspire him he terms "a feeling that would wash the feet of the speaker." The fact that Emerson was able to inspire as well as to be inspired is demonstrated by Father Taylor's comment on his power: "If the Devil had only his genius, the climate would alter, and the emigration would be the other way." [24]

Through eloquence Emerson has given an excellent illustration of the close relation between observer and creator which is the foundation stone of aesthetic experience. From this basis, we may go on to consider what Emerson says of the observer's psychological reaction to art.

THE PSYCHOLOGICAL MATRIX

As late as 1832 Emerson is citing, as authority for judging the work of art by psychological reaction, a philosopher of the common-sense school, Sir James Mackintosh: "Every picture, statue, poem, is an experiment on the human mind." [25] By this time, as we have seen in analyzing the creative process, Emerson was familiar with Coleridge's method of going beyond the eighteenth-century facultative psychology by considering each mental operation as "a total act of the mind," and with Sampson Reed's comparison of the mind's growth to the intercombination of chemical atoms. The reference to Mackintosh shows that in dealing with the psychological aspects of aesthetic experience Emerson seeks to readjust his background of common-sense philosophy to these newer, more dynamic concepts. Out of this effort at adjustment emerges Emerson's clear conviction that a work of art is ultimately justified not by sensuous values or architectonic power, but by its capacity to excite the observer's mind.[26] That creators of art must be aware of that "reaction" as the measure of value is brought to their attention in the essay on "Worship," where Emerson reminds them: "If you make a picture or a statue, it sets the beholder in *that state of mind* you had when you made it" (italics mine).

As in the creation of art, so in its reception, mental reaction begins with sense impression.

Sense impression. Whatever judgment man makes about aesthetic objects is, Emerson says, derived from the material furnished the mind by the senses. His first definition of aesthetic appreciation, in the journal of 1822, is "a power to decide upon the pleasures of sense." Although he later built airier towers upon this substructure, he never denied the importance of sense impression in aesthetic enjoyment. On one occasion, discussing with Thorwaldsen the aim of art, Emerson found Thorwaldsen defending the "ideal" aspect which was more properly Emerson's province in criticism. Agreeing with the artist that "the soul, not the eye," must be art's ultimate aim, Emerson affirms: "It seems to me that an artist who does not first please the eye, can never reach the soul." [27]

In the receptive experience, the senses of sight and hearing are of chief importance. Emerson's philosophical belief in the correspondence existing between man and external nature is here borne out by the natural affinity which he finds between the human senses and the stimulating qualities in nature and art. The naturalness of this relation leads him to conclude that pleasurable mental reaction to the stimulus of beautiful objects within the senses has a normal and necessary place in the universe. Man in perceiving beauty is thus fulfilling an important, God-assigned function. Especially in the sense of sight, Emerson detects a natural connection between light and the structure of the eye: "As if to secure this end [pleasure] in the constitution of all men, the eye is so fitted to the face of nature or the face of nature to the eye that the perception of beauty is continually awakened in all places" (lecture on Natural History, 1833). Man's pleasure in nature and art is "partly owing to the eye itself":

> The eye is the best of artists. By the mutual action of its structure and of the laws of light, perspective is produced, which integrates every mass of objects, of what character soever, into a well rounded and shaded globe, so that where the particular objects are mean and unaffecting, the landscape which they compose is round and symmetrical. And as the eye is the best composer, so light is the first of painters. There is no object so foul that intense light will not make beautiful. (*Nature*)

Thus Emerson conceives of the physical law which governs light and the anatomical law which governs the eye as coinciding to produce the aesthetic principle of man's natural delight in beauty. Through the "organic" relation between light and the structure of the eye he shows the law of perspective operating to produce a pleasing sensation. Particularly impressed with the contrasts effected in landscapes through light and shade, he speaks of the satisfaction to the eye when familiar objects are revealed in new and surprising light. A man just recovered from illness, for example, may find fresh powers of vision to detect picturesque compositions never seen before.

In hearing also, Emerson discovers a close connection between the material stimulus of sound and the human ear, from which he concludes that one may enjoy musical sounds without training:

> The basis of music is the qualities of the air and the vibrations of sonorous bodies. The pulsation of a stretched string or wire gives the ear the pleasure of sweet sound, before yet the musician has enhanced this pleasure by concords and combinations. (Second essay on "Art")

Here Emerson recognizes a natural tendency in the physical structure of the ear which leads the mind to enjoy simple musical sounds, before they have become "sophisticated" into the developed harmonies of music. Willing to admit that his ears were less sensitive than his eyes, Emerson took delight in telling of the blind voice teacher who, on hearing several of the young lads sing, pointed toward Waldo and said, "Send that boy away; he has no ear." Certainly one who discovered the height of musical pleasure in the simple strains of an aeolian harp, or ice cracking on the pond, could not be said to possess high sensitivity to instrumental music. More alive to the sounds of poetry than to those of music, Emerson is awake to roughnesses of meter as well as to subtle rhymes. In his lecture on Art and Nature (1868) he relates the senses of sight and hearing to the principle of iteration or rhyme in nature: "In optics, no number of reflections of the same object displeases; and, in acoustics, no number of echoes displeases; rather, the more, the better." Just as the eye takes delight in the repetition of the same form throughout a long colonnade, so the ear finds a charm in the repeated echo of the voice from the mountain rock "the cry repeated three times, five times, seven times, each time on a new key, and as in a spiritual distance." Thus in seeking and hearing beautiful things, the observer fulfills a natural function in the world.

Emerson's treatment of receptive sense impression contains one element not emphasized in his discussion of the creative process — the importance of *point of view*, in looking at an aesthetic object. "Everything, to be appreciated," he says, "must be seen from the point where its rays converge to a focus." [28] The principle involves an application of the physical laws of light to aesthetic appreciation. Especially with the fine arts, he states the need of distance for a right view: "The eye, too near, turns the fairest proportions of architecture or of sculpture into deformity." [29] What he has observed of the phenomena of vision leads him to conclude in *Nature* that "the health of the eye seems to demand a horizon." Satisfied with the grandeur of Stonehenge, he wonders why modern architecture so rarely appeases "the hunger of the eye for length of line." Seeking the right point of view for the cast of the Laocoön group at the Athenaeum, Emerson writes:

> The main figure is great: the two youths work harmoniously on the eye, producing great admiration, so long as the eye is directed at the old man; but look at them, and they are slight and unaffecting statues . . . At the Athenaeum, you cannot see it unless the room is nearly empty. For you must stand at the distance of nearly the whole hall to see it, and interposing bystanders eclipse the statue. (*J.*, 1837)

The whole matter of getting perspective on natural and artistic forms is well summed up in a late lecture on "Art" (1861) where Emerson says: "The forms need to be seen at some distance, and in easy action, to express a grace which is in them deep and total."

Except for this emphasis upon point of view, Emerson's analysis of sense impression in the aesthetic experience closely parallels his account of it in the creation of art. Here, as in the creative process, simple sense impression has importance in itself, but a greater value in bringing about that deeper impression, the mental "sight" of an object in the observer's mind. "Sensibility" and "perception" have the same meaning for the observer as for the creative artist; not merely a transference of images from retina to brain, but the *interpretation* of those objects by the receptive mind. In this higher power of the observer's sensibility lies the true "realizing" of the artifact, by which the observer's enjoyment is no mere *addition* to created beauty, but the very means of bringing it to life. It is this kind of sense impression that Emerson has in mind when he says that a book may be everything or nothing, according to the human eye that sees it.[30]

The mystical interpretation which Emerson frequently makes of sense impression does not mean that he ignores the element of education in training the senses. Characteristically, he has more to say of training the eye than the ear. His own eyes may have been naturally weaker than some, but they possessed wonderful educability. Of his brother Charles, who first assisted him in catching the shades of natural beauty, he says: "His senses were those of a Greek. I owe to them a thousand observations. To live with him was like living with a great painter. I used to say that I had no leave to see things till he pointed them out, and afterwards I never ceased to see them" (J., 1836). Going out to walk with a painter, he sees for the first time "groups, colors, clouds and keepings . . . and the pleasure of discovering resources in a hitherto barren ground, of finding as good as a new sense in such skill to use an old one." [31] In Rome the painters Cranch and Alexander helped to open his eyes to the charm of sculpture and architecture; here, too, he read Goethe, whose keen perception of beauty in art so impressed Emerson that he ranked this German critic in his "Natural History of Intellect" as "a sample of an eye." [32] The beautiful statue of Endymion in the Capitoline Museum at Rome, he says, deserves to be examined "by instructed eyes." We have seen that Emerson's sensitivity to line and color in nature preceded his awareness of form in art. It is hard to say how much interaction existed between his experience of the beauty in nature and the loveliness of art, but certainly he was open to suggestion from his friends in surveying both worlds. Margaret Fuller and Samuel Gray Ward helped to turn his vision in the direction of painting, while Ellery Channing and Henry Thoreau pointed out to him new details in nature. After a walk with Henry Thoreau, Emerson says that the pine and hemlock stems "almost gleamed like steel upon the excited eye." Thus the stimulus of mind as well as emotion acts upon the eyes, so that they see new objects, in art or nature, with a deeper sense. A mind filled with a rich background sense of historical religion, Emerson says, assists the eye to perceive beauty in Egyptian pyramids or English cathedrals: "Our associations . . . persuade the eye to forget its mathematics, and reconcile it to angles and distortions." [33]

The senses of sight and hearing, then — especially sight — represent the beginning of the aesthetic experience. Assisted by others who see farther and wider, the sensitive observer awakes to new perceptions of artistic beauty. As in the creation of art, so in its reception, these "senses" can best perceive art's secrets when the "inner" eye of the mind is enlightened. The nature of this relation between the senses and the whole act of aesthetic enjoyment is well explained by what Emerson says of Bettine von Arnim's assertion: "The senses produce only in art as they do in nature." [34]

> Bettine's petulant claim for the senses [he says] I take to mean only this: that, when the soul is awake, or vital throughout, it inundates the body, doubles its sensibility, thinks to the nerves of the eye, of the ear, of the nostril, of the fingers, so that the organs obey, and are pure vehicles, so that color blazes, and form enchants, and sound rings, and odors yield their finer increase, and all the obstructions give way as mists in the sun, and the soul sees itself reflect in nature [or in art]. (Lecture on Art, 1861)

Thus Emerson turns Bettine's claim for the "primary" value of the senses into his typical assertion that sense impression acquires a "secondary" or higher power when the soul of the observer has been aroused.

Not only sight and hearing, but the kinesthetic sense has importance in Emerson's analysis of the aesthetic experience. This motor response to art forms, to which he gives little importance in the creative process, looms large in his account of the observer's reaction. Emerson's sensitivity to the kinesthetic appeal of art, and the richness of his comment upon it make a definite contribution to early American aesthetics. Motor reaction appears not only in his statements about art, but in those concerning nature and people.

Emerson's enjoyment of nature is frequently expressed in kinesthetic terms. Admiring a squirrel's "beautiful leaping" from one bough to another, for example, he regrets that man's slow creeping on the ground lacks "the floating, exhaling, evanescent beauty" which pertains to the motion of squirrels and birds.[35] Again, of his high perch on the mountain at Troy, New Hampshire, he writes: "Every glance below apprises you how you are projected out into stellar space, as a sailor on a ship's bowsprit out into the sea." [36] His excitement over ideas also finds expression in motor terms. After discussing the higher aims of life with Margaret Fuller, he writes: "All my thoughts are spacious; the chambers of the brain and the lobes of the heart are bigger." [37] A similar kinesthetic effect is described from the stimulus of foreign languages, "to gird the loins and make the muscles more tense." [38] After watching the people on the streets of the North End, Emerson reacts to them as a painter might:

> When I pass these groups, I instantly know whence all the fine pictures I have seen had their origin: I feel the painter in me; these are the traits that make us feel the force and eloquence of *form* and the sting of color. But the painter is only *in* me; it does not come to the fingers' ends. (*J.,* 1841)

Here Emerson has given, in kinesthetic terms, an excellent analysis of the keen appreciation for aesthetic qualities which is not quite strong enough to go over into creative production. Another arresting though brief expression of motor response is that which he records on visiting the tomb of Michelangelo, when his mind, filled with the remarkable works of the artist which he had just seen, was overcome by a strange mingling of emotions. "My flesh crept," he says, "as I read the inscription." [39]

Among Emerson's friends, Henry Thoreau, both by his personal influence and by his writing, had the strongest effect upon his kinesthetic sense. To Margaret Fuller Emerson wrote that he admired Henry's "perennial threatening attitude, just as we like to go under an overhanging precipice." [40] Although this sensation of mingled fear and pleasure decreased with time as Henry delayed to act, it always remained a part of his response to Henry's writing. Reading Thoreau's journals after the death of his friend, Emerson notes that their vigorous "oaken strength" affects his muscles as well as his mind:

> He has muscle, and ventures on and performs feats which I am forced to decline. In reading him, I find the same thought, the same spirit that is in me, but he takes a step beyond, and illustrates by excellent images that which I should have conveyed in a sleepy generality. 'Tis as if I went into a gymnasium, and saw youths leap, climb, and swing with a force unapproachable, — though their feats are only continuations of my initial grapplings and jumps. (J., 1863)

Here, through motor terms, Emerson catches the essence of the receptive experience: the sense of identity with the artist, combined with a realization of his superiority, the terms "leap, climb, and swing" being used to show his sense that Thoreau's imagination has surpassed his own "initial grapplings and jumps." The passage is eloquent of that "entering into" a book, which is more than sympathy. The image of the gymnasium is also employed in the essay "Uses of Great Men," where Emerson describes the imaginative power of great men as "summersaults" which awaken the reader's mind, and "multiply ten times or a thousand times his force."

To indicate his response to poetry, Emerson frequently uses motor terms. The effect of fanciful rather than imaginative writing he describes in "The Poet": "The winged man . . . whirls me into mists, then leaps and frisks about with me as it were from cloud to cloud." The reaction to an excellent poet goes deeper:

> Straightway I feel the presence of a new and yet old, a genial, a native element. I am like a Southerner, who, hav-

ing spent the winter in a polar climate, feels at last the south wind blow, the rigid fibres relax, and his whole frame expands [*sic*] to the welcome heats. In this bland, flowing atmosphere I regain, one by one, my faculties, my organs; life returns to a finger, a hand, a foot. A new nimbleness, — almost wings, unfolds at my side . . .

I . . . am a ship aground, and the bard directs a river to my shoals, relieves me of these perilous nubs and strains, and at last fairly uplifts me on the waters, and I put forth my sails, and turn my head to the sea. (*J.*, 1839)

So vivid is his own kinesthetic response to poetry that he readily understands the excitement which bardic lines are said to have on the Bedouin tribes, uplifting them more strongly than wine, and sending them into battle unafraid of death.

Especially in eloquence Emerson feels the importance of motor reaction. A good speech, he asserts, should affect the audience's nervous system. If the speaker's own nerves tingle, he probably can stimulate those of his audience. As a lecturer, he thinks of the lyceum platform as an opportunity "for painting in fire my thought, and being agitated to agitate" (second essay on "Eloquence"). He describes his active response to a speaker's movements:

The flashing eye, that fills up the chasms of language, the living brow, throwing meaning and intellect into every furrow and every frown; the stamping foot, the labouring limbs, the desperate gesture, these must all be seen in their strong exercise, before the vivid conception of their effect can be adequately felt. (*J.*, 1820)

The plastic arts also have an effect upon Emerson's kinesthetic sense, as when he terms painting and sculpture "gymnastics of the eye," and compares painting to dancing:

Painting seems to be to the eye what dancing is to the limbs. When that has educated the frame to self-possession, to nimbleness, to grace, the steps of the dancing-master are better forgotten; so painting teaches me the splendor of color and the expression of form . . . (First essay on "Art")

A close analogy to this kinesthetic reaction appears in Emerson's statements about music, where he describes the sound in terms of *motion*. Of the complex feelings which Handel and Mozart wish to express, he finds the simple air of a lute inadequate. "They must," he says, "ride on the singing whirlwinds and rivers and storms of sound of the great orchestra of organ, pipe, sackbut, dulcimer, and all kinds of music." In a similar way, a good voice in a mediocre choir seems to him "to inundate the house with spouts and jets and streams of sound, and to float the old hulk of the choir itself . . . and hurrying them all away, the spoils of its own stream." [41]

The relief to the whole personality from the enjoyment of art Emerson describes in motor terms:

As the body is rested and refreshed by riding in the saddle after walking, and by walking again after the saddle, or as new muscles are called into play in climbing a hill, and then in descending, or walking on the plain, an analogous joy and strength flows from this exercise. (*J.*, 1838)

Here Emerson uses physiological imagery to show the joy and strength contributed to the tired mind, in the same way that riding rests muscles weary from walking. Thus, by a motor image, Emerson shows the effortless way in which the mind gains refreshment from art. Books also, he says, can correct the gloomy view of the world which results from a "sprained mind."

By means of kinesthetic imagery, then, Emerson gives freshness to the description of his aesthetic reactions. Although he was most sensitive to the motor appeal of eloquence, since the essence of enjoyment in that art seemed to him to be an electric response of audience to speaker, he makes use of motor terms in analyzing all the arts: poetry, painting, sculpture, and music. The richness of his statements about kinesthetic reaction raises the question whether in any sense he anticipates the modern theory of "empathy" in response to art. If we accept the requirement of a modern critic, that empathy must include involuntary projection of self into the object, the sharp focus of former experience upon the object, and the attribution of one's inner experience to the thing perceived,[42] one must admit that Emerson's analysis of kinesthetic response does not constitute empathy. We may, however, say that his use of motor imagery denotes a sympathy with the creative artist so vigorous that it cannot be expressed merely in visual or auditory terms, but seeks the enlargement of another sense to convey its meaning to the reader. Nor may we minimize the importance of kinesthetic reaction in Emerson's account of the aesthetic experience, since it is the element which he considers particularly characteristic of the observer, as contrasted with the creator of art. If the observer must bow to the creative artist, as Emerson does to Thoreau, he must realize that his particular kinesthetic response is a new means of completing the creative cycle begun by the "maker" of art.

Memory. Without recognizing the part played by memory, that "store of power and peace," we cannot give a true estimate of Emerson's theory of aesthetic experience. The simplest work which the memory does is to retain an echo of sensory impressions. From observation of nature, Emerson

describes the way in which the memory keeps the patterns
brought to it by sense:

> If you gather apples in the sunshine, or make hay or hoe
> corn, and then retire within doors and shut your eyes and
> press them with your hand, you shall still see apples hanging
> in the bright light with boughs and leaves thereto, or the
> tasseled grass, or the corn-flags, and this for five or six
> hours afterwards. There lie the impressions on the reten-
> tive organ, though you knew it not. (Essay on "Intellect")

Thus Emerson explains the way in which images caught by
the sensitive retina remain etched on the "remembering eye"
for hours. This might be called random recollections of observed objects, in which the eye exercises its native powers.
In a similar way, the mind carries over into nature patterns
previously observed, both auditory and visual designs:

> When we study architecture, everything seems archi-
> tectural, the forms of animals, the building of the world,
> clouds, crystals, flowers, trees, skeletons. When we treat of
> poetry, all these things begin to sing. When of music,
> Lichfield Cathedral is a tune. The world is picturesque to
> Allston, dramatic to Garrick, symbolical to Swedenborg.
> (*J.*, 1837)

Emerson writes to Margaret Fuller that one should be able to
carry over into the rest of life what he observes in art: "A
genuine hint furnished out of a picture ought to serve us
not in pictures only but also in seeing the lights of the landscape or the shadows on my study-wall. Yes and to an infinity
of applications beside" (*L.*, II, 143, 1838). Again, in the first
essay on "Art," he says that painting has opened his eye "to
the external picture which Nature paints in the street, with
moving men and children capped and based by heaven, earth
and sea." If his memory of painting helps him to see the pic-

turesqueness of landscape and street, sculpture has a similar effect on his view of the human form: "As picture teaches the coloring, so sculpture the anatomy of form. When I have seen fine statues and afterwards enter a public assembly, I understand well what he meant who said, 'When I have been reading Homer, all men look like giants.' " [43] Thus Emerson has vividly expressed a phenomenon familiar to all sensitive observers of art: the way in which the memory retains the shapes and sounds caught by the senses, so that afterwards the eye sees art figures in clouds and on buildings; the ear hears musical patterns in speech. In this respect memory helps the observer to carry into the world what his senses have revealed to him of the "mystery of form."

Memory also serves to correct erring first impressions. If Emerson was sometimes suspicious of the "sophistications of second thought," he still recognized the value of memory in clearing the eye from a false first impression.

> Inestimable [he says] is the criticism of memory as a correction to first impressions. We are dazzled at first by new words and brilliancy of color, which occupy the fancy and deceive the judgment. But all this is easily forgotten. Later, the thought, the happy image which expressed it, and which was a true experience of the poet, recurs to mind and sends me back in search of the book. (Essay on "Poetry and Imagination")

Here sense impression is shown to be deceptive, by the very force of its effect; while memory performs the service of clearing the mind, so that the good lines of a poem stand out. Just as he expresses faith in the beneficent necessity which brings appreciative observers to art, so does he extend that faith by asserting that the best works will survive, through memory's power to retain them.

Memory of an overexuberant first impression is of course subject to the check of a second reading of a book, a second (or third) view of a work of art, a later hearing of an eloquent speaker. Thus Scott's dialogue, delightful at first acquaintance, seems to Emerson on rereading to have lost its warmth. Comparing the effect of poetry with that of fine art, Emerson asserts that fine art more quickly takes hold of the mind than does poetry, but that the pleasure derived from a poem lingers longer in the memory. To Ward, for example, he writes: "The eye is a speedier student than the ear. By a grand or lovely form it is astonished and delighted once for all." [44] On the other hand, he bears witness both by theory and experience to the value of re-viewing the plastic arts. While in Rome he lost no opportunity to see St. Peter's, his "favorite church," under as many different conditions as possible; he made frequent visits to the Allston and Athenaeum galleries in Boston; and in his lecture on England (1849) he says: "People go to the Elgin chambers many times, and, at last, the beauty of the whole comes to them at once, like music." [45]

Nowhere more than in listening to speakers does Emerson show the importance of correcting an enthusiastic first reception. Perhaps because his requirements for eloquence were high, he sensed more dwindling of the great among speakers than among poets or artists. The supreme example of this loss of admiration Emerson experienced with Everett, who caused young Emerson to burn after the *aliquid immensum infinitumque,* but whose size decreased as his source of power was perceived to be technique rather than idea. Hearing Everett on the same day (March 5, 1832) with the Cherokee Indian Ridge, Emerson asserts the superiority of Ridge's plain Indian eloquence over Everett's, adding ironically that Everett sat down "as if one would say The mind of man can scarcely contemplate the grandeur of my effort." [46] A young preacher shows similar degeneration; delighted at first with "the pleasing efflux of the man through his sentences and gesture," Emerson later discovers a fixedness in his manner, "the finest graces of youthful eloquence, hardened by the habit of haranguing, into a grimace." [47] Nor was he so convinced of Dr. Channing's power that he could fail to rejoice in an occasion when Channing heard the spellbinder Father Taylor at the Bethel Mission: "Glad was I to have the Doctor hear somebody as good as himself do what he could not." [48] Impressed as Emerson was by Webster's oratorical strength, which he termed a new phenomenon in nature, his disappointment over the Seventh of March (1850) speech approaches as close as Emerson ever came to bitterness. Here the element of character, always more important in Emerson's judgment of eloquence than of the other arts, loomed large in his denunciation; like Whittier, Emerson felt that Webster's stand for conciliation was not merely wrongheaded, but immoral. Meeting Sampson Reed the next September, and deploring to him "the downfall of our great man," he was shocked by Reed's response. Recalling his long admiration for Reed, from the oration on Genius, delivered at Emerson's graduation from Harvard (1821), and at that time impressing only John Quincy Adams and Emerson (Abel Adams said it was spoken "in a meeching way"), his delight in *The Growth of the Mind*, and his long acquaintance with Reed, Emerson was shocked by Reed's reply to his lament over Webster: " 'He thought it his best speech, and the greatest action of his life.' So there were my two greatest men both down in the pit together" (Ms. J. NY, 1868).

Memory's first importance, then, in Emerson's theory of aesthetic experience, is as corroborator of the delight which the observer takes in art. Retaining the patterns of art forms, memory assists man in carrying over these designs to nature and other art. Secondly, memory aids the reason when a second impression of a work is less gratifying than a first view. Sorting and arranging his experiences with the help of memory, man can give the right place to the painting, poetry, and music he has enjoyed. Whereas Emerson treats the creative memory in its mystical as well as its psychological aspect, he considers the receptive memory only on the matter-of-fact level, as a photographic plate from which art forms can be reproduced, or as a clarifier of the understanding after the first enthusiasm of aesthetic enjoyment has passed.

The subconscious. Emerson's satirical comment on the experiments in animal magnetism, spiritualism, and hypnotism conducted in New England in the thirties and forties appears in the essay on "Demonology," where he terms this class of facts "merely physiological, semi-medical, related to the machinery of man, opening to our curiosity of *how* we live, and no aid in the superior problems why we live and what we do." [49] That this scorn is mingled with a kind of fascination should not surprise us if we consider that the experiments in animal magnetism represented a practical application of certain ideas closely resembling tenets of Emersonian thought. The casting of a hypnotic spell, for example, by fixing the eye on the subject to be mesmerized shows an attempt to make use of that strange power of human vision on which Emerson often comments.[50] The subject's submission to his hypnotizer might be termed a heightening of the passivity which Emerson demands of the observer in the aesthetic experience. Even the convulsions of subjects in the mesmerized trance may be considered merely a more nervous and violent manifestation of Emerson's kinesthetic reaction to aesthetic experience. If one regards these quaking, fortune-telling experiences as a kind of Under-soul forming the counterpart to Emerson's Over-soul, one easily grasps the combination of interest and repulsion with which Emerson regarded them.

One element from this "limbo and dust-hole" of thought throws light on Emerson's theory of aesthetic experience — the speculation about dreams. Interested in this phenomenon and recording in his journal dreams which he sought to interpret, Emerson has made provocative suggestions about the relation between sleeping and waking knowledge. "The text of life," he says in the lecture on Demonology (1839), "is accompanied by the gloss or commentary of dreams." The consciousness of power often felt in dreams, and lost with regret on waking, Emerson compares to the prescience of "mesmerized patients who are clairvoyant at night and in the day know nothing of which they are told." [51]

In dreams Emerson finds some explanation of the perplexing matter of the human will. In the essay "Demonology" he speaks of man's feeling that he is free in dreams as he is not in real life, to execute his desires: "Sleep takes off the costume of circumstance, arms us with terrible freedom, so that every will rushes to a deed." On the other hand, sleep also reveals the higher aspect of will: "Without the phenomenon of sleep, we should be atheists; because, if we had no experience of the interruption of the activity of the will, we could never be brought to a sense of its dependence on the Divine Will" (lecture on the Moral Sense, 1860). From this combination of freedom and submission which he experiences in dreams, the observer may better understand the related state of active passivity which is a precondition of enjoying art.

Through his experience in dream, the observer may learn to interpret the mystery of the creative mind. In dreams, Emerson says, the two aspects of consciousness, active and receptive, become united:

I have often experienced, and again last night, in my
dreams, the surprise and curiosity of a stranger or indifferent observer to the trait or the motive and information
communicated. . . The fact that I, who must be the author
of both parts of the dialogue, am thus remote and inquisi-
tive in regard to one part, is ever wonderful. (*J.*, 1867) [52]

Here the strange combination in the dreaming mind of creation with observation helps the observer to understand what
happens in art.

Again, Emerson mentions the fact that dream creations
sometimes escape the will: "Their double consciousness,
their sub- [*sic*] and objectiveness is the wonder. I call the
phantoms that rise the creation of my fancy, but they act like
volunteers, and counteract my inclination." [53] Of the dream,
he asks, "Was I not artist as well as the spectator, — actor and
audience?" [54] "The *I* partial makes the dream," he explains,
"the *I* total, the interpretation." [55] What the ordinary man
knows of the creative process, he suggests, is derived largely
from dreams, during which he gets the "feel" of the creative
consciousness, at the same time that he remains an observer.
By sharing in these two natures at the same time, he can better
appreciate the two-ness melted into unity which is the foundation of aesthetic experience.

Dreams also illuminate that surprised delight by which
man recognizes himself in the work of art. Emerson compares
this kind of aesthetic enjoyment to Prince Le Boo's pleasure
on seeing himself for the first time in a mirror: "A poem, a
sentence, causes us to see ourselves. I be, and I see my being at
the same time." [56] Through dreams every man obtains an insight into his own mind which helps to explain this combination of "being" and "understanding" in aesthetic pleasure.

Without in any real sense anticipating Freud's concept of
the subconscious, Emerson reveals a keen awareness of sup-

pressed ideas rising to the surface in dream. His nightmare, for example, of a company debating the institution of marriage, when a man stopped the debate by turning a hose of water on each of the company in turn (finally on Emerson), shows some recognition of subliminal sexual desire. From the experience of a friend who was a gentleman by day but always a servile drudge in his dreams, he draws the conclusion: "Civil war in our atoms, mutiny of the sub-daemons not yet subdued." [57] In the same way, the essay on "Demonology" speaks of dreams as man's key to understanding animal consciousness, since in dreams man is more like a beast than a human being. He also recognizes the fun and humor, the "arch satirical" quality of dreams — as in his vision of the horse always rearing on its hind legs, as if to win a race, but never running at all. "I hope," he adds, "they did not mean anything personal." This whimsical aspect of dreams Emerson finds illuminating to man's self-knowledge, not in a divine sense so much as on the level of "a Franklin-like sagacity."

Since Emerson's daytime view of life and literature is dominantly optimistic, one might conjecture that he has suppressed his sense of the terrible in that "Chimborazo under the line" of the conscious mind. The modern psychological critic, therefore, will not be surprised to see Emerson turning to dreams for an explanation of the terrible in literature. In such widely differing creators as Blake, Michelangelo, Shakespeare (in *Macbeth* and *Lear*), Milton, Aeschylus, and Dante, he finds the terrible vividly expressed. In his lecture on Demonology (1871) he seeks to define this element: "Is the *dire* the act of the imagination when groping for its symbols in those parts or functions of nature which nature conceals because painful to the observer?" In this view, the creative artist is conceived as dredging up from the subconscious those frightening images which are suppressed in the ordinary course of life. From the terror of dreams, then, Emerson affirms that the average man derives a sense of the terrible, which helps him to understand that element in literature or art. Man's awareness of evil outside himself, as of good, he explains as merely a reflection of his own hidden nature: "On the Alps the traveller sometimes beholds his own shadow magnified to a giant, so that every gesture of his hand is terrific. . . The good, compared to the evil which he sees, is as his own good to his own evil" (essay on "Spiritual Laws").

Thus in dreams the element of the terrible, freed from the will's domination, is clearly observed by the dreamer. If he has perception, he can apply this experience of terrifying shadows to art as well as to life. Emerson's description of his sensations on awaking from a nightmare suggests that the dream itself may become an aesthetic experience: "After I woke and recalled the impressions, my brain tingled with repeated vibrations of terror; and yet was the sensation pleasing, as it was a sort of rehearsal of a tragedy" (*J.*, 1842).

Through his experience in dreams, then, the observer gets an insight into the creative consciousness; by his own creation of dialogue and action while asleep, he comes to understand the curious paradox of the active-passive will; he learns more about himself, especially his animal or subhuman nature, so that he can more readily comprehend the lower elements in literature and art; and he gains a heightened awareness of the terrible, which introduces him to the tragic element as treated by Michelangelo, Shakespeare, and Dante.

The suggestiveness of what Emerson says of the subconscious in relation to aesthetic experience should not lead us to give this element undue importance in his general theory. He does not go so far as a modern philosopher, De Witt H. Parker, who defines art's relation to the dream as "a free creation of the imagination under the domination of a wish." [58] One remembers that in Emerson's thought this element of the subego always exists in subservience to the super-ego, or Over-soul. Distrustful of the dangerous extent to which a theorist like Goethe values "the daemonic" in creative power, Emerson has made little analysis of the subconscious as an element in creation, but has considered it chiefly as related to the receptive experience of art. With this reservation of not claiming too much importance for Emerson's statements about the desires suppressed in dream, it is clear that he has studied the subego more carefully than any other contemporary critic, and that he has made definite use of it in relation to aesthetics.

THE CORE OF THE EXPERIENCE

The awakened imagination. In actual contact with the work of art, the observer is first conscious of its power to focus his attention. Other concerns shut out, the poem or painting takes possession of his mind. "Every work of art," Emerson says, "excludes the world, concentrates attention on itself. For the time it is the only thing worth doing, to do just that; be it a sonnet, a statue, a landscape, an outline head of Caesar, or an oration" (*J.*, 1839). Art's special virtue is defined in the first essay on "Art" as its "detachment," its capacity to separate one object from a bewildering variety so that man can give it real thought. The work seeps its way into the mind, focusing all man's mental activity upon itself. An idea derived from literature possesses all the mental powers:

> It had no analogy to any notion I ever remembered to have formed, it surpassed all others in the energy and purity with which it clothed itself; it put by all others by the novelty it bore, and the grasp it laid upon every fibre; for the time, it absorbed all other thoughts; — all the faculties

— each in his cell, bowed down and worshipped before this new Star. (*J.*, 1822)

The physiological imagery in this passage indicates that Emerson thinks of the mind as undergoing an easy expansion during the experience, as if the chambers of the intellect grew larger to absorb the new work.

Concentration of attention is usually followed by a shock of surprise. In his lecture on Genius (1839) Emerson speaks of the paradox that creative power, itself unsurprised, always has the effect of astonishment upon its observers. There is a complexity in this feeling of surprise, as Emerson describes it: "This ambiguity which touches the springs of wonder in the soul at the contemplation of beauty; this feeling of relationship to that which is at the same time new and strange; this confusion which at the same time says It is my own and It is not my own . . ." [59]

Because surprise plays so important a part in his aesthetic enjoyment, Emerson places special value on the stimulus of a mind quite different from his own. He finds his indolence dissipated by the novelty of a writer like Sturlason, born nearer the pole, or like Averroës, whom Emerson associates with the Sahara. Thus a reader immersed in the streams of English poetry will be excited by reading poetry of a different tradition — French, Italian, Welsh, Persian.

From the concentration of attention and the arousing of astonishment, it is only a step to awakening the observer's imagination. As with the creative artist, so with the observer of art, the distinctive quality of the enlivened imagination is its sense of freedom. The poet's excitement in discovering a symbol is reflected by a similar uplift in the reader:

If the imagination intoxicates the poet, it is not inactive in other men. The metamorphosis excites in the beholder

an emotion of joy. The use of symbols has a certain power
of *emancipation* and *exhilaration* for all men. We seem to
be touched by a wand which makes us dance and run
about happily, like children . . . Poets are thus *liberating*
gods. Men have really got a new sense, and found within
their world another world . . . (Essay on "The Poet";
italics mine)

Not only the poet, but the singer, orator, and painter can
convert the spirit to "nimbleness and buoyancy." Under this
influence, Emerson says: "We tread on air; the world begins
to dislimn." [60] Though some writers who "freed" Emerson's
imagination later failed to charm, he never read the Neo-
Platonists without a sense of liberation. The effect of Proclus
he compares to opium:

It excites my imagination to let sail before me the pleasing and grand figures of gods and daemons and demonical
men. . . By all these and so many rare and brave words I
am filled with hilarity and spring, my heart dances, my sight
is quickened. (*J.*, 1843)

Like the creative artist, the observer thus finds his material
senses aroused when the imagination's "inner eye" has been
opened. The exhilaration is not produced only by literature,
but by varied stimuli. Made aware of new possibilities in the
style of building by studying plates of architectural remains
in Mexico, Emerson feels "emancipation of the spirit." From
the eye's glance or from graceful manners, as well as from
poetry, he gets the effect of wings to the spirit: "As if the
Divinity, in his approaches, lifts away mountains of obstruc-
tion, and deigns to draw a truer line." [61] Through poetry,
philosophy, painting, and architecture — even through the
"poetry" of human nature — the observer's imagination becomes so free that his burdens are cast off and his whole personality lifted up.

In the observer's response to "largeness" of expression in the work of art, this liberation is often accomplished. One recalls Emerson's statement concerning the *expression* of creative intuitions, that "imagination is not good for anything unless there be enough." [62] The observer's reaction to *quantity* of expression Emerson denotes as a recognition of *mass*. In Chaucer, Shakespeare, and Milton he finds the source of his pleasure not only in the excellence of single passages, but also in the broad scope of these writers: their ability to produce large narratives, epics, and plays, which excels the writing of single lyrics as a cathedral triumphs over a single chapel. [63] In a lesser poet like Thoreau, Emerson considers that quantity makes up for lack of finish:

> Mass here, as in other instances, is some compensation for superior quality, for I find myself stimulated and rejoiced like one who should see a cargo of sea-shells discharged on the wharf, whole boxes and crates of conchs [*sic*] . . . though there should be no pearl-oyster nor one shell of great rarity and value among them. (*J.*, 1842)

In architecture also Emerson's imagination is stimulated by size, as in the great Italian cathedrals where he experiences a sense of exhilaration at their tremendous plan.

The observer's imagination most closely approaches that of the creative artist when it perceives the *fluidity* which Emerson considers the heart of beauty. Explaining his own reaction to beauty, Emerson says:

> The statue is then beautiful when it begins to be incomprehensible, when it is passing out of criticism and can no longer be defined by compass and measuring-wand, but demands an active imagination to go with it and to say what it is in the act of doing. The god or hero of the sculptor is always represented in a transition *from* that

which is representable to the senses, *to* that which is not. Then first it ceases to be a stone. (Essay on "Love") [64]

Here Emerson thinks of the receptive imagination as *going with* the statue, just as he conceives of the creative imagination as "sharing the path" of spirit through nature's forms.[65] The fact that the observer's response actually completes the original creative act appears in the statement that he not only *goes with* the marble figure, but is able to *say* "what it is in the act of doing."

The fluid motion which Emerson here describes as an important part of the observer's reaction bears a vital connection to his theory of "the flowing," the dominant philosophical strain in his aesthetic theory. In this view, the work of art is considered as a moment of transition from *matter* to *essence*. When the creative imagination works, as we have seen, it first perceives the *flowing* beneath the apparently *fixed* quality of things, and then reproduces that quality in a finished work. The very essence of imagination, according to Emerson, lies in this ability to see the rigid outlines of matter passing into the flowing curves of beauty. Thus in "Poetry and Imagination" Emerson explains "the shudder of joy with which in each clear moment we recognize the metamorphosis" by means of the sympathy felt by the "free spirit" not only "with the actual form, but with the power of possible forms." In this passage concerning the "moving form" of the statue, Emerson asserts that the receptive imagination, by perceiving in the work of art the *flowing* which was implicit in the creative act, has brought the work to true completion. Not only, then, does the receptive imagination show an expansion similar to the creative, but in its turn it also creates, since it discovers in the work of art that fluidity which for Emerson constitutes the essence of beauty.

This emphasis upon the fluidity characteristic of aesthetic enjoyment strikingly resembles the view of Pater. Since Emerson did not read Pater until late in life, the similarity is one of interesting coincidence rather than of influence. Like Emerson, Pater places value on equilibrium of the mind as a precondition of aesthetic enjoyment; on the exhilaration felt by the observer in the presence of art, which Pater calls "blitheness"; and also on the *abundance* of spiritual insight, of "getting as many pulsations as possible into the given time." Pater's analysis of the aesthetic moment, like Emerson's, is governed by a conviction that the mind's impressions are "in perpetual flight," but Pater asserts, as Emerson does not, that in the aesthetic moment the flux of life is arrested, briefly but beautifully, and that the observer thereby experiences an awareness of perfect union between matter and spirit. Pater values Greek sculpture, for example, for its keeping passion "always below that degree of intensity at which it must always be transitory." [66] Pater's grasp of the sensuous values of art is firmer than Emerson's, since he conceives of the observer's enjoyment as a balanced apprehension of matter and form. Emerson's is less valid aesthetically, since he thinks of form itself as fluid and the observer's perception of beauty as therefore most keen when he sees the statue before him "moving," or in transition. By this very emphasis on fluidity, however, Emerson confirms the imaginative power of the observer, who "goes with" the art form in the same plastic fashion with which the creative artist's mind "flows through" natural objects.

Recreative escape. Emerson's most fruitful account of aesthetic experience shows the observer completing the artist's creation by a vivid perception of his intent and a sense of identity with the artist. On occasion, however, Emerson regards the work of art solely as a means of providing delightful freedom from worldly cares. Consider, for example, this observation of a painting:

> I can see freely the forms, and dream pleasantly of what they would say; — I carry the picture out far and wide on every side, and I highly enjoy the unity of the hour . . . I conspire with the painter, lend myself willingly to him, see more than he has done, see what he meant to do. (*J.*, 1839)

Although this comment shows concentration on the subject and sympathy with the artist, it falls short of true aesthetic appreciation, for Emerson is dreaming "of what the forms *would* say," without thinking of what they really *do* say; he sees *more* than the painter has done, but makes no definite reference to actual achievement. Instead of looking at the painting itself, he "carries it out far and wide on every side." The observation has clearly gone over to the land of faëry.

Although Professor Foerster has maintained that Emerson sees no value in art or literature unless he can make some application of that art to the whole of life,[67] an emphasis upon the value of art simply as escape exists throughout Emerson's writing. Nor is this view of art as escape an immature attitude which Emerson later cast off. It occurs, of course, as early as 1823, when young Waldo writes ecstatically to his aunt Mary Moody Emerson, of poetry "that soul of all that pleases." In 1836 *Electra*, which he read with his brother Charles, is considered as a means of escape: "It is as if you had left the noisy fuming world of mortal men and taken passage with 'that grim ferryman whom poets speak of,' and the slow *Styx*, *novies interfusa*, lay between you and all earthly interests" (*J.*, 1836). Two years later literature is classed with natural science as an "asylum of the mind," both nature and reading termed "Bowers of joy that beguile us of our woes, catch us up

into short heavens and drown all remembrance, and that too
without a death-tramp of Eumenides being heard close behind, as behind other revels" (*J.*, 1838).

Again, through the beauty of art and poetry he finds himself "above the region of fear, and unassailable like a god at
the Olympian tables." [68] In later life he expresses relief at
leaving contemplation for his books: "When visions of my
books come over me, as I sit writing, when the remembrance
of some poet comes, I accept it with pure joy, and quit my
thinking, as sad lumbering work; and hasten to my little
heaven . . . as angels might" (*J.*, 1867). Of the delightful
escape offered by his favorite art of eloquence, Emerson
writes: "It draws the children from their play, the old from
their arm-chairs, the invalid from his warm chamber; it holds
the hearer fast; steals away his feet, that he shall not depart;
his memory, that he shall not remember the most pressing
affairs." [69]

The art which for Emerson most patently represents
escape is that of music. Totally unacquainted with musical
technique, Emerson enjoyed music — when he got anything
from it at all — with almost pure instinct, and little mind. Of
music's "asylum" he says:

> It takes us out of the actual and whispers to us dim
> secrets that startle our wonder as to who we are. . . All the
> great interrogatories, like questioning angels, float in on its
> waves of sound. "Away, away," said Richter to it. "Thou
> speakest to me of things which in all my endless being I
> have found not and shall not find." (*J.*, 1838)

Of two or three "delicious voices" in the church choir, he
says: "There in music is the world idealized, in poor men's
parlors, in the work room and in the kitchen. Every strain of

a rich voice does instantly imparadise the ear. I cannot wonder that it is the popular heaven."

Opportunities for hearing music in Boston were few in the forties and fifties. Aside from church music, there was little beyond an occasional quartet,[70] and the rare visits of such European artists as Jenny Lind or Ole Bull. From London in 1848 Emerson writes to his wife that Chopin has sent him a ticket for his *matinée musicale*, and adds: "Could he only lend me ears!"

Such musical theory as Emerson had he derived from Platonic and Pythagorean statements concerning music's power to mold character,[71] and from a few contemporary critics. Perhaps he learned more than he realized from his friend John Dwight's lectures on music, which he says he read as "a mute reads of eloquence." Certainly the technical aspect of Dwight's discussion did not interest him, nor did the importance placed by Dwight and Margaret Fuller on music as a katharsis of emotion loom large in Emerson's theory. The escape which music gives to Emerson is rather of the intellect and the fancy than of human passion. William Gardiner's *Music of Nature* attracted him as an illustration of organic form in music, drawing parallels between musical sounds and natural phenomena.[72]

Very appealing to Emerson was the stress placed by Bettine von Arnim on the religious and spiritual qualities of music. From a wide experience in hearing music and a native sensitivity to its charm, Bettine expresses the current romantic conception that music depends less on intellect than on emotion, that it is the most "inward" of the arts, that it can be felt but not taught:

> Music [she says] is the medium of spirit, through which the sensual becomes spiritual — and as redemption extends itself to all, who, embraced by the living spirit of the God-

head, long after eternal life, so the flat seventh by its solution leads all tones, which pray to it for delivery, in a
thousand different ways, to their source — divine spirit.
(Goethe, *Correspondence with a Child*, I, 283)

Bettine compares the effect of music on man to Christian
redemption:

> As it is with Christians, so it is with sounds: every
> Christian feels the Redeemer within himself, each tone
> can elevate itself to Mediator, or seventh, and thus perfect
> the eternal work of redemption from the sensual to the
> heavenly . . . (*ibid.*)

Bettine cites a statement of Beethoven, the high god of romantic music, on the exhilarating effect which he desires his
compositions to have upon mankind.[73] While Bettine, like
Dwight, gives some place to music as expression of passion,
Emerson is attracted not by that element in her criticism so
much as by her use of religious parallels.

Emerson's comments on music's delights include little
effort to connect man's enjoyment with the technical aspects
of music. An early journal passage (1825) mentions the value
of what he calls *keeping* in music, that is, avoiding sudden
transition from loud to soft volume; and his journal of 1841
mentions the violent effect upon the nerves of country or-
chestras in their first stages of practicing — chiefly, he says,
because of their loud volume; afterwards "they learn to be
still and to sing underparts." Emerson's denotation of adjusted volume rather than concord as the key to success in
music shows that he had little awareness of harmonic principles.[74] Characteristic of the nontechnical enjoyment which
he takes in music are the program notes which he records for
some "admirable music" heard in Boston:

It seemed, as I groped for the meaning, as if I were hearing a history of the adventures of fairy knights, as some
Wace . . . was telling, in a language which I very imper-
fectly understood, the most minute and laughable particulars of the tournaments and loves and quarrels and religion
and tears and fate of airy adventurers, small as moths, fine
as light, swifter than shadows — and these anecdotes were
illustrated with all sorts of mimicry and scene-painting, all
fun and humor and grief, and now and then, the very persons described broke in and answered and danced and
fought and sung for themselves. (*J.*, 1841)

These notes show an appreciation of musical imagination,
with some awareness of development in theme. They are an
excellent example of Emerson's enjoyment of music, un-
trammeled by the sophistication of technical knowledge, and
thus the chief instance among the arts of an aesthetic experience that represents pure escape.

A different, but no less characteristic escape from the
seriousness of life Emerson found in humor. His essay on
"The Comic" defines humor as "an honest and well-intended
halfness," "the intellect's perception of discrepancy" between
the ideal of right and "the yawning delinquencies of practice." By getting distance on life's pain, Emerson says, the
intellect can see the comedy which is obscured to the reason
or the conscience. His special interest is in jokes which concern religion, since in religious faith, theoretically the soul's
highest expression, divergence of idea from actuality is most
clearly perceived.

Among the numerous religious jokes which Emerson has
recorded, there is his comment on the efficacy of prayer, as
shown by Dr. Ripley's earnest appeal for rain, at the morning
service, "Lord, thou knowest me, thy servant, Ezra Ripley,"
and the parishioners' demonstration of faith in Dr. Ripley's

power, evidenced by their bringing umbrellas to the afternoon service; and the Cape Cod minister's practical advice to the farmer who wanted a prayer for the crop: "No, this land doesn't want praying, it wants manure."

Some of these religious anecdotes reveal a sharp discrepancy between theory and practice. Emerson thinks that Choate receives meet punishment for his "hypocritical church deaconing" by having "this poor dunce of a Dr. Adams braying over his grave — that Jesus Christ is getting on, for Mr. Choate has signified his good opinion." Emerson got his revenge for having to listen to dull sermons by aiming satirical shafts at them: as in his comparison of the "one orthodox sermon" to the "standard English novel," repeated every Sunday with slight variation from many English pulpits; or his comment on the Massachusetts version, "the prevailing Boston beverage of Channing and water." Perhaps Emerson's own experience never afforded a more poignant example of the discrepancy between the demands of matter and those of spirit than the occasion when he interrupted a philosophical discussion with a friend to attend to a delivery of wood, saying apologetically, "We must attend to these matters as if they were real." He is tenderly amused at the enthusiasm of some seventeenth-century Puritans, who, in the words of the old lady's recollection, were so pious that "they had to hold hard to the huckleberry bushes to hinder themselves from being translated."

But Emerson's enjoyment of humor is not limited to religious jokes. As an orator, he prized the concentrated shaft of wit in an epigram — such a comment as Mirabeau's on the corpulent bishop of Autun, who "had been created and placed upon this earth merely to show to what extent the human skin might be stretched."

In distinguishing between wit and humor, Emerson says

that true wit "keen as a sword and polished as the scabbard," never makes us laugh — that is, it appeals to the intellect rather than to the feelings. Humor of the lower sort (sometimes termed by Emerson "cheap wit") constitutes "the stale game" of each man calling the other a donkey, or telling him that he is going to hell.[75] Emerson's own use of amusing illustrations in his lectures impressed his hearers as being witty rather than humorous, intellectual rather than emotional. After hearing the lecture on Comedy, Alcott stated that Emerson excelled in wit, "the contribution of the intellect," but lacked "the humor of the heart." In the audience's laughter Alcott missed any "reverent, kindly feeling." [76] That Emerson's impression on modern readers is serious rather than amusing is not, as has been conjectured, because all the wit was excised from the lectures before they were printed as essays, though some contemporary references were omitted. Some of his entertaining effect doubtless sprang from his manner of delivery — as in the testimonies which appear of his use of surprise; some of it arose from associations known to his audience, but since evaporated from the printed page.

Emerson's wit could turn to satire, as in his calling spiritualism "the Rat-revelation, the Gospel that comes by taps in the wall and thumps in the table-drawer," practiced in Concord by Miss Bridge, who forsook the respectable trade of dressmaking for this new occupation, charging "a pistareen for a spasm, and nine dollars for a fit." Sometimes his wit touches the bitter side of irony, as in his remark that Horace Greeley does the thinking for the "solid farmers" of the West, at a dollar a head. The gentler side of wit is, however, more characteristic of Emerson.

If his dominant interest is in wit's intellectual appeal, he nevertheless shows hospitality to other types of humor. Not only in his own essay on "The Comic," but in his recording of other critics' definitions, he reveals a fascination with the theory of comedy. He notes Steffens' statement, that speed is a necessary element in wit,[77] Ruskin's, that wit is "the power of playing with the lights on the many sides of truth," [78] and Hobbes' definition of humor as "the passion of sudden glory," by which men are pleased either by their own actions or by deformities in another, with the exhortation that men rise above the weakness of excessive laughter at others' imperfections.[79]

Emerson's journals reveal a pleasure in the sort of native wit that might be called country humor, sometimes sharp, sometimes foolish, often depending for its substance upon colloquial language. Of this type is Dr. Ripley's remark to Mrs. Foster, "Well hove, but you are not the one to heave it." Nor was he — despite his disapproval of low and "bastard" jokes — above enjoying the pun. His own most brilliant play on words was provoked by the question whether he approved Platonic friendship between men and women. "Yes," he replied, "but hands off!" And he possessed that saving grace of all humorists, the ability to laugh at himself. He was amused rather than offended by Mrs. Helen Bell Choate's answer to the riddle of what the Sphinx said to Mr. Emerson: "You're another!"

For Emerson the only pain in humor was the extreme physiological reaction which he experienced from violent amusement, because of an infirmity in his facial muscles which made it hard for him to compose his face again afterwards. Margaret Fuller had this effect on him, particularly on her first visits, of causing him to laugh too violently for comfort. His enjoyment of humor thus varies from his general aesthetic experience, in which physiological reaction was pleasurable.

The fact that Emerson thought the most amusing jokes

religious ones shows the connection he makes between the sublime, which is the fit expression of the ideal, and the ridiculous, which points out the incongruity between actual and ideal. Emerson finds in ridicule the natural complement of the deep awe which characterizes the sublime. Lloyd has well symbolized the connection which Emerson makes between the ridiculous and the sublime when he compares Emerson's thought to a spectrum which ranges from the shady end of wit to the brightness of wisdom, so that he "surprises the truth in front and rear." [80]

But we have seen that Emerson's enjoyment of humor covers a wider range than his theory of the "ideally amusing." It includes satire, especially of the gentler sort, irony, plays on words, epigrams, "country humor," and that quality which endears a humorist to others, the ability to appreciate a joke at his own expense.

If music for Emerson is a "heaven" of escape from life's harshness, humor may be termed a sort of "fiddlers' green" between heaven and hell, which keeps a balance between the realms and narrows the distance between them by its healthy laughter.

Although Emerson offers abundant evidence that he values art and literature as pure escape, he does sometimes show that escape may have a good aftereffect upon the personality. He distinguishes the pleasures of art from "mere luxury and the drunkard's bowl," and he suggests that the delightful sway which poetry has over the mind sometimes directs the observer to fresh activity: "Although so long as the spell endures, little or nothing is accomplished, nevertheless, I believe it operates to divest the mind of old and worn-out contemplations and bestows new freshness upon life" (*J.*, 1820). In this instance the enjoyment of poetry, which looks like useless escape, has actually given the mind a good workout.

It is the lesson of passivity again, this time with emphasis upon the mental refreshment which follows submission.

One may conclude that Emerson sometimes withdraws into the "paradise" provided by art and literature, forgetting about the real world; but that he is always aware of the avenue by which he can return.

The climax: mystical ecstasy. The element of recreative escape, when raised to a higher power, becomes mystical ecstasy. For Emerson, the culmination of the aesthetic, as of the creative experience, consists in the fusion of the observer's soul with that of the Divine. As with the creative artist, ecstasy comes to the observer through subordination of the will; it is characterized by brief moments of vivid illumination; and it comes to the intuition, or to the emotions, rather than to the ratiocinative intellect. Emerson's account of aesthetic enjoyment differs from that of the creative process, in giving a fuller analysis of psychological conditions; but he shows clearly that the receptive experience, in its culmination, shares the mystical quality of creation.

The direction of Emerson's thought concerning the climax of aesthetic experience is indicated in the second (*Dial*) essay on "Art," where he says: "The contemplation of a work of great art draws us into a state of mind which may be called religious." The art object thus acts as a means of bringing the observer in touch with that "absolute mind" from which the creative artist drew his intuition. Recalling Emerson's theory of the symbol as an embodiment of spiritual form,[81] one is not surprised to find that works of symbolic character have special power to exalt his mind. From art which holds the great within the small, Emerson experiences a feeling similar to that aroused by natural beauty, becoming assured of the "identity at the fountainhead" of the great works of art and nature. Here the artist's success in catching the spirit of nature in his symbol is attested by the observer's reaction, since his delight in the work of art resembles his joy in nature. The pleasure is based upon resemblance: not of the work of art to nature, but of the observer's *emotion* in the presence of art, kindred to the emotion aroused by nature.

The sympathetic union between observer and creator, as a necessary condition of aesthetic experience, has already been observed. For Emerson, the question "What is Art?" leads inevitably to a second question "Who is the Artist?" Instead of identifying ourselves with the work, we must, he says, feel "the soul of the workman" streaming through us. The next step must be a progress away from the individual artist to the larger nature which he represents. In fact, union with the artist's soul (if a great one) is inevitably to reach "the All":

> The great man, even whilst he relates a private fact personal to him, is really leading us away from him to an universal experience. His own affection is in Nature, in *what is*, and, of course, all his communication leads outward to it. Starting from whatsoever point . . . the more they draw us to them, the farther from them or more independent of them we are, because they have brought us to the knowledge of somewhat deeper than both them and us. (Essay on "Modern Literature")

In a sense, following the artist's guidance will lead one to the Over-soul, since the artist's intention is precisely that — to lead the observer away from persons to a more comprehensive nature.

The kind of "nature" indicated is definitely a supersensible reality, or *Over*-soul; not the outdoors, nor human nature, but that essence of nature behind all its manifestations which is revealed only through mystical experience.

The great [Emerson says] lead us to Nature, and in our age to metaphysical nature, to the invisible awful facts, to moral abstractions, which are not less nature than is a river, or a coal-mine, — nay, they are far more nature, — but its essence and soul. (Essay on "Modern Literature")

The state preceding ecstasy may be called a balance of the mind, similar to the equilibrium required as a condition of enjoying art, but raised to a higher power:

The mind pauses, and without any conscious reviewing of the details of experience, looks with quiet eye into its present state, which is the result of all before. This state of lofty contemplation, of deepening knowledge of oneself and the universe, is the end for which feeling warms and action strengthens the intellect. ("Painting and Sculpture," *Dial*, II, 78–81)

Like the creative artist, the observer in a state of mystical illumination experiences a freedom from the conditions of time and space. In *Nature* Emerson suggests that time and space themselves, usually considered limitations, have "a sort of infinitude." The burden of the essay on "History" is the theme that all archaeological and historical study seeks not to gain a more accurate sense of each period, or each type of architecture, but to bring home to the modern mind the "higher" meaning of all these antiquities: "To do away with this wild, savage, and preposterous There or Then, and introduce in its place the Here and the Now." Thus, in reading the *Philoctetes*, Emerson feels "time passing away as an ebbing sea," "the eternity of Man, the identity of his Thought." His pleasure in reading Chaucer, Marvell, and Dryden he traces to a sense of "the abstraction of all *time* from their verses." Although this sense of escaping time and space usually comes without effort in the moment of mystical excitement,

Emerson indicates that the young reader can deliberately exercise his mind in that direction. He can, for example, strip from a writer like Dante "the whole mass of images, thoughts, and emotions" peculiar to "certain Florentine flesh and blood," and thus grasp "the eternal flower of the world" which is the heart of Dante's message.[82]

Such a subtraction of time and space from works of art leads of course to an equation among the arts. When Emerson regards the arts from this point of view, he favors the Romantic tendency to seek resemblances among different arts; such as terming architecture "frozen music," relating Gothic building to German printed type, likening Ben Jonson's poetry to the painting of old masters. Impatient though the modern critic may be with this attitude which makes an ode of Hafiz equal to the Parthenon, one must urge a point in its favor. The observer does not derive this sense of "timeless universality" from a work of art until it has first been brought home to his mind with a freshness and immediacy which testify to its inner life. If this were the only way of looking at art and literature, one might well abandon criticism; as a corrective, however, to the slow precision of historical scholarship, mystical reaction offers the proof that a modern mind has kindled *now* to the appeal of a work produced by a former age and a distant place.

The intensity of mystical illumination for the observer as for the creator is so brief as to be measured by moments. "This dangerous little minute," Emerson says, "revolutionizes a long life of plausibilities." [83] Emerson describes the uplift of the experience:

> The Intellect, fairly excited, overleaps all bounds with equal ease, and is as easily master of millions as master of one. With each divine impulse it rends the thin rinds of the

visible and finite and comes out into Eternity, inspires and
expires its air. (*J.*, 1834) [84]

Thus the receptive soul, freed from the technical measure of
the work of art and from association with the artist, has an
intense consciousness of power as well as of refined pleasure.
This mystical enjoyment for Emerson represents the climax
of aesthetic experience.

The kinesthetic imagery which we have found characteristic of Emerson's response to art is carried over into the
"mystical moment." Thus Emerson is impressed with the
physiological effect upon Newton of that moment of discovering the law of gravity: "His hands shook, the fingers
danced, and he was so agitated that he was forced to call in
an assistant to finish the computation." Though Newton's
illumination comes from science rather than art, the effect of
mental excitement on his body closely resembles art's effect
upon the observer. On one occasion, while reading, Emerson
records an intellectual perception of his own so vivid that it
spills over into the nerves and muscles.

> Am I not [he asks] one of these days, to write consecu-
> tively for the benefit of the intellect? It is too great for
> feeble souls, and they are over-excited. The wineglass
> shakes, and the wine is spilled. What then? The joy which
> will not let me sit in my chair, which brings me bolt upright
> to my feet, and sends me striding around my room, like a
> tiger in his cage, and I cannot have composure and concen-
> tration enough even to set down in English words the
> thought which thrills me — is not that joy a certificate of
> the elevation? What if I never write a book or a line? For
> a moment, the eyes of my eyes were opened. The affirma-
> tive experience remains, and consoles through all suffering.

For art, for music, overthrilled,
The wine glass shakes, the wine is spilled.

I admire those undescribable hints that power gives of itself. (*J.*, 1859)

This passage shows the effect of emotional uplift upon
the body as well as the mind; the sense that the experience is
sufficient in itself; and a recognition of creative power behind
the book Emerson has been reading. The absence of any
specific mention of the book marks it a magnificent failure in
the light of literary criticism. On the other hand, his feeling
that he lacks "composure and concentration" to set down his
thought in words does not cause him to despair; rather, he
states that his joy is sufficient "certificate of elevation." If the
lack of definite comment upon the book seems the height of
critical obscurity, it becomes clearer when related to mystical
experience.

Jacob Boehme, for example, a mystic whose work
Emerson studied during his formative years, speaks of the
combination in his experience of a certain "high seeing" with
a difficulty of putting the vision into words: "When the flash
rises up in the centre, one sees through and through but
cannot well apprehend or lay hold on it; for it happens to
such an one as when there is a tempest of lightning, when the
flash of fire opens itself and suddenly vanishes." [85]

Considered in mystic terms, Emerson's failure to note the
specific source of his "high elevation" is one testimony of its
genuineness. A modern mystic, Allen Brockington, who has
been influenced by Emerson's thought, further illuminates
this matter of remaining "dumb" about the cause of elevated
experience, when he contrasts the poet's *expression* with the
mystic's *silence*. In the created poem the poet's experience is
dissipated, while the mystic, by remaining silent, preserves the
ineffable quality of his intuition.[86] While Emerson's theory of
creative experience does not state that the poet's expression

dissipates his insight,[87] in the passage under consideration Emerson shows exactly the same kind of reluctance to name the cause of excitement, which Mr. Brockington notes as a general characteristic of mystical illumination.

The unifying and energizing effect of reading upon the personality, shown in Emerson's "wineglass" passage, is also typical of the mystical state, described by Evelyn Underhill as "a whole being welded into one, all its faculties, neglecting their normal universe, grouped about a new centre, serving a new life, and piercing like a single flame the barriers of the sensual world." [88] This energy of the ecstatic experience characterizes Emerson's aesthetic reaction, aroused to bodily excitement by the soul's perception.

Such moments of illumination, Emerson indicates, provide the mind with a new power which it carries over into other experience:

> It is the property of the human mind, when strongly aroused by any sentiment, by any passion, by the love of any science or art, to give its whole knowledge and powers the new force of an arrangement after that principle. And then it acts with as much more efficiency than before, as an organized army acts than a great mob. Whatever passion, whatever love, arrives at a certain heat in a mind, melts away all resistance, fuses all its knowledge, turns everything like fire to its own nature. (*J.*, 1831)

As in his analysis of the creative mind, so in this statement of aesthetic experience, Emerson uses a natural metaphor; here the figure of heat shows how the raw material of thought is shaped into new form by the fire of aesthetic perception.

This idea that the moment of excitement not only elevates but disciplines the mind is also indicated by William James, who was not a mystic but who took great interest in the psychology of mystical experience. James suggests that the shock of sudden illumination jolts the mind from its equilibrium and gives it a new center:

> A new perception, a sudden emotional shock, or an occasion which lays bare the organic alteration, will make the whole fabric fall together; and then the centre of gravity sinks into an attitude more stable, for the new ideas that reach the centre seem now to be locked there . . .[89]

Like Emerson, James asserts that a powerful mystical experience gives the mind a new method, though James' emphasis is on the state of repose which ensues, in contrast to Emerson's assertion, as in the "wineglass" passage, of high nervous excitement.

In stating the "ineffableness" of aesthetic experience and the energetic unifying which the whole personality derives therefrom, then, Emerson shows a close parallel to accounts of mystical experience. The late Rufus Jones, who claims Emerson as his aesthetic ancestor, points out the value placed by Emerson upon the "moment" of vision, and relates the aesthetic to the mystical "moment." [90]

To assert that Emerson's account of aesthetic experience on its highest level is mystical, however, implies some qualification of the term. The usual mystic view, for example, of the enjoyment derived from a single literary line or phrase is to regard that pleasure as the *inception* of a higher mystical experience. Thus Milton's line, "Nymphs and shepherds, dance no more" for Mr. Brockington *starts* the "psychological mechanism of prayer." [91] Clearly this differs from Emerson's interpretation, in which the "high seeing" of the aesthetic moment represents the whole experience. In that "perception" he has already left the object behind him and sensed the excitement of truth in body as well as in soul.

There is no need to go beyond that moment to a religious prayer.

And there are certain extremes to which Emerson's aesthetic mysticism does not extend. One of his attractions for Allen Brockington is that he is no "mush of concession." His appreciation of art never reaches the sensual quality, for example, which Leuba denotes as the Oriental experience of ecstasy: "A state of exquisite exhaustion in which every limb is in complete repose, in which thinking becomes brooding absorption, while the soul revels in melancholy sensuality or senselessness." [92] Emerson's analysis of emotional excitement never sinks into such an abyss, nor into the trembling agitation of Mme. Guyon, who regards union with the Divine as "marriage with a bridegroom." [93]

Avoiding these extremes, Emerson derives from art and literature the kind of "inner" experience which is found in the writings of the saner mystics. The very fact that works of art and literature have the power to bring Emerson into touch with the universal soul indicates that his mystical elevation is not the result of Christian or any other religious discipline. Although it implies a withdrawing from external demands and a yielding to the work before it, it is not considered in the ascetic terms of a "mystic way," nor does it imply an achievement of victory over sin. Emphasizing the operation of intuition rather than of ratiocinative intellect, it yet lacks the burning emotional thirst of an Augustine in his search for God. Its kinship with other accounts of mystical experience appears in the manifestation of bodily as well as mental excitement, in the conviction that the momentary illumination has pierced to the white of truth, in the resulting sense of unity throughout the whole personality, and in the difficulty felt by the subject in giving adequate expression to his experience.

Emerson's mystical aesthetic may be better understood through comparison with another contemporary theory, that of Hegel. Although Hegel's speculation about art reached Emerson too late to influence his thinking, the religious quality of Hegel's aesthetic renders it comparable with that of Emerson.

In what Hegel says of the effect upon the observer of romantic or Christian art,[94] there is a parallel to the union postulated by Emerson between the observer of art and the Over-soul. Considering the end of romantic art the attainment of union between the human soul and the Divine, Hegel states that art must transcend sensuous perception and appeal to the inner spirit.[95] Like Emerson, Hegel asserts the joyous freedom of the experience. The spiritual manifestations of art (for Hegel, as for Emerson, the most important ones) appear in art, painting, music, and poetry; music being denoted more "ideal" than painting, and poetry the highest art in the sense of being least dependent on material qualities.[96] In restricting the highest art to that which is Christian in inspiration, Hegel reveals a limitation which does not obtain in Emerson's discovery of the spirit in such un-Christian sources as Hafiz and the sayings of Confucius. With a philosopher's discernment, however, Hegel realizes, as Emerson does not, that this spiritual aim of art is paradoxical. From the high pinnacle of poetry, that most "spiritual" example of romantic art, Hegel looks back with something like longing to the classical art of sculpture which he has placed on a lower level, but which embodies physical medium perfectly fused with spiritual idea. This, Hegel says, is what happens when one refines art into pure spirit: "Just in this its highest phase art ends by transcending itself, inasmuch as it abandons the medium of a harmonious embodiment of mind in sensuous form, and passes from the poetry of imagination *into* the prose of thought." [97]

Sooner or later this criticism upon the "religious" or "spiritual" theory of art had to be made. Secure in his "sublime" conviction that inner ecstasy was the certificate of great art, Emerson for the most part ignored this suicidal element in the spiritual concept of art. It was, truly, the hole in the "religious-aesthetic" dyke; and even Hegel, who could point to it with unerring finger, could not stop the flood from coming through.

The sublime. That special power in art and literature which can awaken in the observer a mystical illumination Emerson denotes as *the sublime.* He considers it a certificate of a writer's power that he can inspire that feeling in a reader: "If I could tell you what you know not; could, by my knowledge of the divine being, put that within your grasp which now you dimly apprehend, and make you feel the *moral sublime*, you would never think of denying my inspiration" (*J.,* 1834).[98] The sublime also meets the test of memory, that arbiter over aesthetic experience. "When I have owed that pure feeling which we call the moral sublime to any writer," Emerson says, "I am not likely to forget his name or . . . genius." [99]

Aware of the speculations of Longinus, Burke, Alison, Blair, and Landor on the sublime,[100] Emerson made his own special interpretation of the term, chiefly to express the elevated emotion felt by man in the presence of art or nature. As early as 1835 he is asking where he can seek the analysis of the "elements and process" of the moral sublime. If Emerson's trumpet call in *The American Scholar* for "the near, the low, the common" led some readers to expect an ignoring of the sublime, they were undeceived by the next entreaty in which he asks writers to show "the sublime presence of the highest spiritual cause lurking . . . in the suburbs and extremities of nature." [101]

In its rhetorical aspect, Emerson frequently discovers sublimity in single lines or short passages.[102] He recognizes the power of repetition to evoke an emotional effect, as in Milton's

> though fallen on evil days,
> On evil days though fallen, and evil tongues,

and the "sublime" death of Sisera in *Judges*: "At her feet he bowed, he fell, he lay down; at her feet he bowed, he fell; where he bowed, there he fell down dead." Other lines which awakened in Emerson the feeling of *moral sublime* were Young's

> Forgive his crimes — forgive his virtues too,
> Those minor faults, half converts to the right,

Shakespeare's "The more angel she," and Homer's "One omen is ever good — to defend one's country." In all these expressions Emerson finds a sense of nobility deeply and eloquently expressed which inflames his mind. In contrast to these lucky hits, he senses a fault in Blair's "Like a disabled pitcher out of use," which he terms "a very great fall from sublimity."

Denoting Herbert a master in arousing the feeling of *moral sublime*, Emerson cites his verse:

> Ah, my dear God, though I am clean forgot,
> Let me not love thee, if I love thee not.

Terming this an example of the pathetic sublime, Emerson recognizes pathos as a legitimate element of the sublime, and does not, like Longinus, place it below the *moral*.[103] Johnson's preface to the *Dictionary* represents for Emerson a "shade of majestic pathos that seems to me more sublime than the passages . . . usually so called in books of rhetoric." [104] Burns' saw on the pathetic sublime seems to him eloquent:

> Weans and wife,
> That's the true pathos and sublime of human life.

The mechanical or material sublime Emerson does place on a lower level, as Brisbane's socialism, which he calls "the sublime of mechanics," or Luther's expression: "If the heavens should pour down Duke Georges for nine days," which he terms "mere sublimity of magnitude and number." Death can never arouse any feeling in Emerson's imagination but the material sublime. Emerson does, however, recognize that increase in the volume of an artistic or natural object may reach the point of inducing the wonder which accompanies the true sublime. "The greater the material apparatus," he says, "the more the material disappears, as in Alps and Niagara, in St. Peter's and Naples." [105]

In his observation of nature, Emerson finds that bright light, as from the direct rays of the sun, may induce the feeling of sublimity. His appreciation of art reveals a sensitivity both to light and darkness, as in his view of the Coliseum at night with the painter Cranch, which fills him with "dread." [106] In St. Peter's he enjoys the contrast of illumination with darkness, as in the service at Michelangelo's chapel, when the last candle is taken down and the chant *Miserere mei, Deus*, rises through the silent dark; in the view of a religious procession moving through the cathedral as night is settling down, giving him a sense of immensity in the structure; and in the night illumination on Easter Sunday of innumerable torches around the whole edifice. This alternation of darkness and light, as well as the cathedral's vastness, contributes to the high praise Emerson gives St. Peter's: "the sublime of the beautiful."

Like his eighteenth-century forbears, Emerson is aware of the power which mountains and sea possess to awaken the sense of sublime in man. After seasickness on board ship has dislocated his imagination, he says: "The whole music of the sea is desolate and monitory. The wave and the cloud and the wind suggest power more than beauty to the ear and eye. But the recovery is rapid, and the *terrible* soon subsides into the *sublime*" (*J.*, 1826; italics mine). This passage resembles Burke's idea that the sublime is a feeling just on the balanced side of terror.[107]

From the shore the sea's majesty can be enjoyed without fear; thus in July of 1841, Emerson writes to his wife of his satisfaction in the color, curve, and roar of the sea. To Margaret Fuller at the same time he writes that he can appreciate the sea as never before:

> Now a surfeit of acorns and whortleberry pastures has restored the equilibrium of my eyes and ears, and this beach and grand sea line receive me with a sort of paternal love. I quite comprehend how Greece should be Greece, lying in the arms of that sunny sea. Cut off its back woods from New England, and it would be more likely to repeat that history of happy genius. (*L.*, II, 422)

Here the emotional impression of the sea is so forceful that Emerson thinks it capable of changing the whole course of American literature. This appeal lies chiefly in its grandeur and majesty.

Mountains, another recognized source of the sublime, have varying effects upon Emerson. He feels the "proved moral efficiency" of the "queer ridge of matter," the Swiss Alps, and the healing effect of those "magnets to the eye," the

White Mountains, as well as the "thought" that made the mountains greater. But mountains do not always inspire in him the emotion of true sublimity: "The New Hampshire landscape though savage and stern does not reach the surprising and overwhelming grandeur that in some spots of the world draws a man as by the hair of his head into awe and poetry" (*L.*, II, 221, 1839).

The stars, however, never fail to lift Emerson off his feet. In the rude figures of the constellations he sees reminders to mankind throughout the ages of Nature's great stability. When he contemplates the stars, he frees himself from the worldly concerns pertaining to the understanding, and lifts himself to the plane of Reason. On a fine June night he says:

> The moon and Jupiter side by side last night stemmed the sea of clouds and plied their voyage in convoy through the sublime Deep as I walked the old and dusty road. The snow and the enchantment of the moonlight make all landscapes alike, and the road that is so tedious . . . by day, by night is Italy or Palmyra. In these divine pleasures permitted to me of walks in the June night under moon and stars, I can put my life as a fact before me and stand aloof from its honor and shame. (*J.*, 1838)

The importance of the majestic elements of mountain, sea, and heaven looms large in Emerson's analysis of the sublime. "In America the geography is sublime," he told the Williams College boys in 1854, "the men are not." It remains his conviction that however far man may wander from this source of strength, "Everybody is bedded and based on the sublime." [108] Much of Emerson's effort is directed toward the fulfillment in man's work of the outer world's deep inspiration. This purpose appears in his effort to bring about a happy marriage of the fine and useful arts; as he says of the boat at St.

Petersburg, plying along the Lena by magnetism, that it needs "little to make it sublime."

Whether the source of inspiration be nature or art, Emerson finds the height of the moral sublime in union between man and the Divine spirit. In "The Over-soul" he asserts that those "announcements of the soul" which constitute revelation "are always attended by the emotion of the sublime." The essence of these communications is the influx of the Divine into the human mind. Man's recognition of "the first philosophy of mind," as "the science of what *is*" (ideas of the Reason), distinguished from what *appears* (ideas of the understanding) will always be marked by the emotion of "the moral sublime." [109] In this awareness of kinship with the Divine, he discovers man's health of mind, using "mind" in the sense of a balance between intellect and soul. Like all mystical experience, the sublime vision is difficult to express. "I cannot," he says in "The Method of Nature," "nor can any man, — speak precisely of things so sublime, but it seems to me the wit of man . . . is the grace and the presence of God." But the excitement of the experience may lead man to an overstatement. Such an exaggeration is cited in *The Divinity School Address* as one explanation for the doctrine of Christ's divinity: that after such a mystical experience, "in this jubilee of sublime emotion," Christ said, "I am divine." In its quality of moral sublimity Emerson finds the chief appeal of Christianity.[110] Significantly, Emerson speaks of the exaltation of this highest aspect of sublimity, in mysticism, as an experience quite devoid of fear. His emphasis differs from that of Burke, who finds terror an indispensable part of contemplating the Deity, but strikingly resembles that of Longinus, who considers man exalted rather than lowered by his contact with the Divine.[111]

We shall not go far wrong if we term the emotion of the

sublime Emerson's trade-mark óf the highest phase of aesthetic experience. Not only by his rich and varied applications of the term, but by his own special interpretation of it, Emerson has contributed to critical understanding of "the sublime" in American aesthetics. Touching other theories at some points, such as Longinus' idea that the sublime may be found in single passages, or Burke's conception that the vast induces sublime emotion, Emerson has also made independent application of the term. Two original contributions are made by Emerson to the critical literature of the sublime: first, in his effort to urge art forward to a deeper inspiration, his use of the sublime as a touchstone to indicate how closely man's art catches the greatness of nature; second, the quality of emotion felt by him in mystical ecstasy, which we may denote the "Emersonian sublime": an erect submission, or a humble self-reliance, embodying the paradox of deep awe before the Divine spirit and clear recognition of the same depth in man himself.

Passive to active: the observer turns creator. The observer's realization through art of his own right in the greatness of Nature, like the "grace" experienced by the creative artist, carries with it the desire to express that favor in good works. The first and most obvious way in which the receiver of art may turn to activity is by criticism of the work enjoyed. Though Emerson considers himself rather in the light of an appreciator than of a critic, he recognizes that analysis as well as synthesis can be creative. "The poet is the lover loving," he says, "the critic is the lover advised." [112] Shakespeare, for example, owes a debt to the critics Goethe and Coleridge for the "wisdom" they have detected in his Hamlet and Antony. Through the "creative imitation" of a poem like

Philip Taylor's *Philip van Artevelde*, Emerson sees light on the problem of Shakespeare's creative genius.[113]

Not only by enlightened criticism, but by oral interpretation, an observer may give active life to a work. Since Emerson's was a "reading and speaking" as well as an "orating" age, this method of recitation has real importance for him. His brother Charles' recitation of Milton, for example, "which told, in the diamond sharpness of every articulation, that now first was such perception and enjoyment possible," [114] seems to him superior to all the criticisms of Dryden, Addison, and Johnson.

Quotation came to be known as the specially Emersonian method of interpretation, because of his ability to illuminate the author by well-chosen lines, at the same time that he adapted the quotation to his own purpose. The lines which he jotted down in his journal were later developed into the complex structure of his own thought. Thus such widely scattered authors as Aristotle, Herbert, Goethe, and Xenophanes contribute facets to that strange gem, Emerson's theory of the symbol. It is Emerson's belief that a creative writer must approve such quotation, which shows him off to better advantage in another book than he enjoys on his own. Thus in the nineteenth century Shakespeare, Milton, and Burke have first achieved their due fame through the keen perception of their quoters.

Through criticism, oral reading, and quotation, then, the observer may turn his enjoyment of art into activity, along the lines indicated by the writer or artist who has given him pleasure.

The observer may also turn creator in his own right. Proceeding directly from the "received" work as from a springboard into his own, he may create a work similar to that he has enjoyed. This sort of "new creation" is represented not as conscious imitation so much as immediate, direct influence. Thus he conceives that the very pencil in Raphael's hand is moved by Michelangelo's touch; and that his own writing is "immediately modified" by the reading of Goethe. Less direct, but parallel to this kind of inspiration, was Emerson's absorption of the great poets, "standing near" them, listening to them with joy, and proceeding to speak his own "lines and half stanzas." [115]

Not only in creating a work similar to that enjoyed, but in a different kind of activity, the observer may give expression to his appreciation of art. Often, following the ecstasy of aesthetic experience, Emerson expresses the conviction that he must leave the work and hasten to his own concerns — which are very likely to *differ* from what he has just enjoyed. In this light, Emerson's self-admonishment after seeing the great architecture of Italy — "Do your duty, *yours*" — is revealed as no bombastic egotism, but the proper reaction to aesthetic enjoyment. Thus, of Michelangelo's effort to pour his intoxication with beauty into the ceiling of the Vatican, Emerson asks: "Helps he not me?. . . Can I not polish my expressions sweeten my temper impart a moment's delight to those next me and thus express the divinity that haunts me?" [116] Of the soul finding its own path through the guidance of great art, Emerson says:

> There is, at this moment, there is for me an utterance undoubtedly bare and grand as that of the colossal chisel of Phidias, or trowel of the Egyptians, or pen of Moses or Dante, but different from all these. Not possibly will the soul deign to repeat itself, but if I can hear what these patriarchs say, surely I can reply to them in the same pitch of voice. (*J.*, 1839)

"The same pitch of voice" is a phrase that strikes the heart of this creation following enjoyment, showing the likeness of inspiration but the difference of expression. Byron has given this kind of response to the beauty of Rome, especially the statue of the Dying Gladiator, on which he has fixed "his pathetic thought"; to his poetic expression of Roman art, Emerson says, Italy will always be in debt. The whole matter of observer becoming creator in his own right is well expressed in the lecture on Greatness: "His admiration is sympathy . . . His sympathy leads him at first to imitation, but *imitation with a difference*, and, as his power of execution increases, that difference magnifies, and slowly his nature, his proper style emerges" (1868; italics mine).

Emerson takes an extreme position on the creative use of what one has enjoyed when he says: "I think I have done well if I have acquired a new word from a good author; and my business with him is to find my own, though it were only to melt him down into an epithet or an image for daily use" (essay on "Nominalist and Realist"). In this metaphor, originality triumphs over appreciation; by grinding down the book's structure to one small image, turned to new uses, the observer shows himself to be greater than the book which inspired him. Just after he has completed the essay on "The Preacher," with the recollections of great speakers like Channing, Everett, and Father Taylor fresh in his mind, Emerson describes the effect of eloquence in turning him into his own proper channels: "I am happy and enriched. I go away invigorated, assisted in my own work, however different from his, and shall not forget to come again for new impulses" (J., 1867).

The receptive experience of art thus terminates in "the active soul." The experience which began in passivity has touched the receiver's active impulse; the wheel has come full circle and we are back at the beginning of another creative process. In the Emersonian scheme, the process of creation does not end in the work of art; it comes to rest temporarily in the person who enjoys the work, but does not stop there, since the observer who truly responds to the spirit in art proceeds to some expression of his enjoyment. Allowing for a certain amount of waste in aesthetic as in natural energy, Emerson does not say that every receptive experience will start a creative act. Despite its admission of the pleasurable aesthetic experiences that fail to produce creation, and of the works which lie unappreciated for centuries, this view of art postulates a tremendous amount of spiritual energy in the world from the chain of action and reaction that follows the creative process. Of the varying kinds of active response — criticism, oral interpretation, and new creation — Emerson of course places greatest emphasis upon new creation, especially that which takes a different direction from the work enjoyed. A typical Emersonian method is to save the sparks from other writers, and fan them into a new flame. If we should assume, for example, that only three of a dozen creative cycles may set the receiver off on another creative cycle, we have a good imaginative picture of the spiritual force which is thereby let loose in the world. We must recall also that Emerson thought of the cycle as having an upward impulse in the direction of a spiral, which gives to the propagation of aesthetic energy the same kind of ascension which Emerson observed as the method of nature. It is as if

A subtle chain of countless rings
The next unto the farthest brings.

CONCLUSION

Although Emerson never organized into a system his fertile explorations of the mind's reactions to art, they readily admit of shaping into such a plan as this chapter has presented. Emerson's account of the aesthetic experience not only shows a central consistency with the creative process, but provides the rationale of art. His sense of the observer's importance in the aesthetic cycle bears out his conception that art is made for man, and his faith in the average man's capacity to enjoy art establishes the democratic basis of his aesthetic. Through the observer's reaction the aesthetic realm is proved to be governed by the same beneficent tendency which rules the world of nature. The laws of beauty do possess mystery, but a mystery closely linked to the laws of biology and physics. The observer's discovery of man-made beauty in art, furthermore, enables him to perceive more vividly the spirit in nature which bears an innate relation to his mind.

Though Emerson's aesthetic experience is subtly linked to the creative process through the ultimate value of mystical uplift, the fuller exploration of its more "human" psychological aspects gives substance to Emerson's whole view of art. One might compare the creative process to a region of blinding light covered for the most part with a dark curtain, through which brilliant flashes are occasionally seen, and the receptive experience to a daylight realm in which objects are more clearly, if less transcendently, discerned. To use a religious analogy, one may compare Emerson's theory of aesthetic creation to Moses' twelve tablets of the Law, which we believe in but cannot read; while one considers his account of response to art as a prayer book, which demands a similar act of faith, but is easily read. The emphasis upon point of view in surveying the fine arts, the concept of memory as an interpreter of first impressions, the use of the subconscious to illuminate the active-passive will and the element of terror in literature, the abundant evidence of kinesthetic reaction as the special physiological province of the observer — all these show a keen mind plumbing the depths as well as the surface of consciousness in its response to art.

Emerson's frank enjoyment of art on occasion as pure recreative escape shows that he was far from taking the moralistic view that art should always admit of application to life's problems. On the other hand, as we have noted that Emerson's description of the height of aesthetic enjoyment in mystical ecstasy is saved from certain extremes of drowsiness or sensuality, so his general conception of pleasure in art is saved from the ivory tower of a Swinburne, and from the psychopathic realm of death, disease, and sensual excitement which characterizes some phases of Poe's experience, by the strong rock of the moral, a faith in the good and true underlying the beautiful.

The dominant emphasis which we discover in Emerson's aesthetic experience is, however, enjoyment rather than judgment. We have seen his recognition of the power possessed by the work of art, which sometimes forces the observer into admiration, and his admission of a "classic" quality in works of art which exists independent of individual reaction. Thus his view of art, as of nature, stops short of extreme idealism. The observer is, however, conceived as enjoying rather than as ranking or differentiating artifacts from each other. And the important element in Emerson's aesthetic is the soul's discovery of the loveliness latent in art and literature, and its expression of that discovery, by criticism, comment, or new creation. In the effect of the sublime upon the observer we have Emerson's best expression of that enjoyment, the state which we have denoted as "erect submission" before the magnificent qualities in art and nature.

The abundant psychological reaction which appears in Emerson's personal response to literature and art shows an open mind, awake to many styles and varieties of aesthetic expression. Through art as well as through nature he achieved union with the Divine spirit; and art no less than nature sometimes gave answer to the often repeated question of his searching soul: "What benefit if a rule could be given whereby the mind, dreaming amid the gross fogs of matter, could at any moment EAST ITSELF AND FIND THE SUN!" (*J.*, 1833).

CONCLUSION

The Significance of Emerson's Aesthetic Theory

Emerson led American critical thinking of the nineteenth century in the direction of a more enlightened aesthetic, based on philosophical conceptions, enriched by varied experience, and elastic in its application to fresh discoveries in literature and art. Alive to the speculations of earlier thinkers and open to suggestion from friends like Alcott, Thoreau, and Ward, Emerson was recognized in his time as a leader rather than a follower, a thinker whose critical generalizations always bore the stamp of originality. Through *The Dial*, the lectures, and the *Essays*, he crystallized the inchoate intuitions of "the Newness" floating in the air of Concord, Cambridge, and Boston. His immediate successors as well as his contemporaries attested his power in freeing American art and literature from ecclesiastical bonds. To continental critics like Emile Montégut and Herman Grimm, Emerson seemed the archrebel against all crippling conservatism. Impressed with his iconoclasm, these critics ignored the fact that Emerson retained, at the heart of his aesthetic, convictions of the passive will and of reverence for Divine power which were religious in their origin. Emerson's importance, however, in the context of the nineteenth century is clearly that of a religious leader who turns his followers from the track of dogma into the open fields of literature and the fine arts. He entertains his hearers with reports of Italian and classic art; he comes to know such great Englishmen as Carlyle, Landor, and Tennyson, and in turn makes the English aware of American creative production; he gives attention to every project which can raise the level of American culture.

Emerson's high ideals for the fine arts reappear in the criticism of late nineteenth-century writers, who cite Emerson as authority for inspiring the technique of art with great ideas and beliefs. His enjoyment of the human body as portrayed in sculpture is not only in advance of his own time, but of a later day. Up to 1900 the battle of the nude was still being fought in the periodicals, with an occasional offer for compromise between the "completely naked and the completely clothed." From such prudery Emerson's concept of aesthetic form in sculpture was free. Critics of the useful arts continue to be aware of Emerson as a thinker interested in elevating the useful arts to beauty. It is not until our own time, however, that his application of the organic principle to architecture becomes crystallized in the practical functional theory of Frank Lloyd Wright.

It is beyond the purpose of this study to trace the influence of Emerson's theory, either of art or literature, through the years to the modern day. There is, however, no question that his speculation about poetic theory has impressed not only his immediate followers, but twentieth-century writers as well. Like Longfellow and Lowell, Emerson was recognized as a creator as well as a theorist in poetry; and he enriched the American poetic tradition, as they did, by introducing his readers to the poetry of other times and places: the early ballads, the odes of Hafiz, Dante's *Divine Comedy*. Emerson's theory of inspiration was embraced, ironically enough, by the rationalistic Dr. Holmes. If today the concept of inspiration seems to suffer a decline in authority, the idea of organic form retains a strong grip on the criticism of poetry. In the nineteenth century this principle finds its most vocal adherent in Walt Whitman, whose very title *Leaves of Grass* indicates his desire to give his poems the vitality of natural phenomena. Both the organic principle and the idea of the symbol in poetry, as Emerson defined them, have affected poets of such widely differing interests as Maeterlinck, George William Russell ("A.E."), and Robert Frost.

The Americanism which is insistently voiced by nineteenth-century critics finds its sanest and most cogent definition in Emerson. Over a long period, through varying exhortations, he urged his countrymen to a sound native production. We must, he reiterated, stand on our own feet. When his artistic friends departed for foreign shores, Emerson wished them Godspeed, but advised them to follow his example in bringing home the values gained from older cultures to enrich their native tradition. Critics who followed Emerson's definition of Americanism escaped both extremes: that of aping other cultures, and that of chauvinistic admiration for their own product. The very catholicity of Emerson's "Americanism" implied an awareness of other cultures; yet it held in deep respect the intuitions nourished by that district which the artist called home. Emerson's concept of "American" literature and art was broad enough to include Howells' realism with his own idealism; it admitted Sarah Clarke's miniatures as well as Allston's broad canvases; it could embrace Whitman's "barbaric yawp" together with the tender grace notes of Ellery Channing. It is this rare combination of breadth with intensity, of culture with originality, that makes Emerson's definition of Americanism in the arts still valuable in the twentieth century as it was in his own time.

What importance has Emerson's theory for us today? First, it is a better rationalized aesthetic than his critics have generally suspected. It requires no torturing of his thought — merely a study of its relations — to place it in the cycle framework of three phases: creative process, work of art, aesthetic experience, an organization inherently faithful to Emerson's "spiral form." The connection which appears between his ideas of literature and art and those of the Neo-Platonists, the seventeenth- and eighteenth-century thinkers, and the Romantics, shows that at no point was he soaring into a vague empyrean of irresponsible speculation, but was always sustained by the support of other thinkers, however disparate those thinkers may be from each other. Nor does this complex tissue of background thought behind his critical ideas indicate that he picked up all kinds of notions in a careless way; as with the net-like web of "organic form," whose varied and derivative strands yet make up a new fabric, so with the greater number of his critical ideas, the mark upon the finished work is indubitably Emersonian.

Not only with the reasonableness of Emerson's aesthetic speculation must the modern reader be impressed, but also with the number of points which it touches. The problem of the artist's relation to the world Emerson faced in his own life; the title *Society and Solitude* represents his statement of the paradox which confronts every writer: how to satisfy the human demands of family and friends, so necessary to thought as to life, and yet manage to get work done. The mystery of creative imagination Emerson has interpreted as a process that moves inexorably from the inflow of inspiration, to the image- or symbol-creating act, to expression. In stating that expression results as naturally from inspiration as exhaling from inhaling, Emerson has anticipated the kind of interpretation which is made by some modern psychological critics. If Emerson's statement that art exists as the complement to nature in a Divinely ordered universe seems to the modern reader to make too celestial claims, he must nevertheless admit that such high purpose produces a good effect on art. The psychological aspects which Emerson has differentiated in the aesthetic experience — such as memory, kinesthetic reaction, and the subconscious — make this phase of his aesthetic a forerunner of the theory of Herbert Read, who asserts that only in psychology can the true formula for artistic enjoyment be discovered. The energizing power of Emerson's mind appears in his ability to adapt contemporary scientific ideas to his concept of the symbol. In this greater hospitality to scientific thought, and more lively imagination about physical and biological discoveries, Emerson surpasses Matthew Arnold, with whose "high seriousness" his inspiration has much in common. Far from sharing Arnold's wish to separate science from poetry, Emerson was convinced of their mutual dependence. The modern thinker must be impressed with the versatility of this speculation, which pervades nearly all phases of aesthetic thought, giving even to problems which it does not solve a fresh, provocative statement.

Not only by its breadth, but by its democratic emphasis, Emerson's aesthetic has importance today. The very fact that he finds a work of art first coming into vital existence when it impinges on the observer's sensibility implies a faith in the importance of those who appreciate but cannot create art. The term "representative man" in contrast to Carlyle's "hero" involves recognition of the common man's place in the aesthetic world. Emerson's literary democracy is of course enlightened, seeking not to lower the great masterpieces, but to urge young scholars to grow up to them. A chief delight of his lyceum lecturing in Western towns was to discover young men inflamed with the torch of new ideas. Perhaps his friendliness to those still in an inchoate intellectual state was a counterpart of his belief in "becoming" as a key to aesthetic form. His whole effort in writing as in lecturing was to spread to an ever wider audience the perceptions of beauty which had already dawned upon his sensitive intelligence.

Stimulating in its psychological analysis and right in its democratic emphasis, Emerson's aesthetic theory presents least satisfaction to the modern reader in its treatment of evil. Today's critic does not easily see ugliness "melting into the All," nor does he readily believe that the conformation of his own life to the mind's "pure idea" will cause nature's filths to dry up in the sun. Deficient though this concept appears to the twentieth-century thinker, it may have the advantage of its defect, in pouring a stream of optimism into an age too frequently given over to gloom.

In a sense, the modern reader's feeling of discomfort in the presence of this optimistic view of evil is but a symptom of his difficulty in grasping the mystical basis which underlies Emerson's aesthetic. For Emerson, both the creative and the receptive experience, at their height, are characterized by a sense of union between the subject and a larger source of spirit outside himself. To some critics this explanation of aesthetic experience seems sacrilegious, in its attempt to derive from art an emotion which properly belongs to religion. Sensitive persons who have experienced a high delight in the presence of a beautiful painting may be aware of an intense, even exalted integration of mind and feeling, but may still deny that in such a moment they attain that "feeling of oneness with the Divine" which constitutes the height of Emersonian aesthetic experience. But these objectors may find in their more normal enjoyment of the beautiful a basis for understanding Emerson's mystical uplift, since their experience differs from his sense of "freedom from time and space" only in degree. Nor can the skeptics deny, even though they do not participate in it, the validity of that elevation which Emerson frequently describes as characterizing the enjoyment of art, so unmistakable in his reports are the marks of genuineness.

It is, of course, possible and valid to say that Emerson has given us much on the purely human level of aesthetic enjoyment. Actually this has been the essence of neohumanist interpretation of Emerson, and it has not been without justification. But Emerson could not remain the exclusive property of the American humanists. He has done much to enrich their tradition, but the "leaping lightning" of his spirit sprang from their grasp when they sought to confine him within the sharply-defined boundaries of their critical world. The bad effect of neohumanist criticism upon readers of Emerson has been to close their eyes to the existence of that element of mysticism in Emersonian thought, which, embarrassing though it may be, is the highest rationale Emerson has offered of art's value in the world of man. In the event of a new upsurge of faith, this element in Emerson's aesthetic may again take on the fresh colors which it wore for nineteenth-century seekers. Failing that, the modern scholar must at least be aware that for Emerson, art fulfilled its highest function when it lifted the spirit above material concerns, out of the world of time and space. If today's reader does not stand with longing eyes outside the gates, like Henry Adams before the Virgin at Chartres, he will avoid the blind skepticism which leaves this "super-ego" out of account.

The religious basis for that Emersonian doctrine much needed today, self-reliance, must also be kept in mind. "Whim" may appear on the door lintel; but once over the threshold, the scholar or artist finds his deepest intuitions through a power greater than himself. Thus confident in the validity of his inspiration, the artist can affirm his independence. A follower of Emerson may claim too much for the effect of this self-reliance when he says: "Even if a man says he has outgrown Emerson, it is Emerson who has helped him to do it." Yet, when and if men did thus react, they were applying, consciously or not, the principle of self-reliance in criticism — as Whitman attested when he practiced the theory of self-reliance by refusing to take Emerson's advice on revision of "The Children of Adam." Today in a world too much given to social values, this emphasis upon the individual can help to restore a better balance. When turned inward upon the creative mind, furthermore, this self-reliance must ever urge the artist to discard secondhand intuitions and produce only his best work.

However much modern speculation has surpassed Emerson's aesthetic in historical scholarship and philosophical analysis, it is still dealing with the same problems which Emerson treated. Not without its effect upon continental writers, his aesthetic seems most properly adapted to American soil. Some of his high demands for our culture still remain unfulfilled. This study has shown how intensely he shared in the life of the nineteenth century, how keen was his awareness of current problems and of the best literary production of his time. Yet the "solar eyes" of his spirit pierced beyond the 1800's to our day, and it is not only for his original interpretation of current literary ideas, but for his vision of the future, that Emerson's critical theory speaks to us now. If this study has done something to redeem Emerson's aesthetic thought from the charge of vain dreaming, by showing its inherent system; if it has helped to save his critical reputation from the opposite charges of Rousseauistic pantheism and arbitrary moralism, it has accomplished some service in the right reading of Emerson.

Emerson's aesthetic theory is the reflection of his mind: curious about the new in literature and art, often holding in delicate balance ideas antagonistic to each other, looking for inspiration to the future rather than the past; positive rather than negative, empirical more often than dogmatic, not fixed, but flowing, with the accent on becoming rather than being. Ranging far and wide through all periods and countries, seeking out the beautiful in statues, paintings, and poems, delighting in the ridiculous as well as the sublime, Emerson's creative appreciation touches into instant life the spirit of beauty implicit in art and literature. From its simple kinesthetic stage of a tingling in the fingers to the high ecstasy of union with the Divine, Emerson's enjoyment of art is inward, vital, and compelling. In the Emersonian universe, art takes its place with God-created nature as man's vision of loveliness, no less powerful than nature in its effect on human sensibilities. Through art man recovers his lost sense of unity with spirit, and art, no less than nature, is made for man. As Emerson sees the Divine essence in nature moving back upon itself, but ever upward, so in art he conceives the form as a spiral, driven on and forward by the creative impulse. His is a theory suggestive in its implications, broad in its scope, and deeply rooted in the heart of man.

NOTES

BIBLIOGRAPHY

INDEX

Notes

The following abbreviations are used in the Notes: *J. — Journals*; Ms. J. — Manuscript Journals; *L. — Letters*. References to the published *Journals* are given only to the year, except where more specific reference seems necessary; references to the Manuscript Journals are given with the initial or title which they bear in the Houghton Library Catalogue, as Ms. J. TU, with the year; references to the lectures are given by title, as lecture on the Eye and Ear, with date; references to the letters are given with volume, page, and year. References to primary works which represent sources of or parallels to Emerson's ideas are given to the editions used by Emerson, either to books in his own library or to contemporary editions, wherever possible. Otherwise an early or definitive edition of the writer is employed. Notations made by Emerson in his own volumes are mentioned where they seem significant. Following Emerson's practice, quotations from foreign works are given in English.

INTRODUCTION

1. Henry James, *Partial Portraits* (London, 1888), p. 30.

2. Lectures on Italy, I and II, 1834; lecture in Manchester, England, 1847; lecture on Beauty, 1859.

3. See, for example, Marie Dugard, *Ralph Waldo Emerson, Sa Vie, et Son Oeuvre* (Paris, 1930), p. 359, who cites James' passage.

4. Francis H. Underwood, "Ralph Waldo Emerson," *North American Review*, CXXX, 479–498 (May 1880).

5. Charles W. Eliot, "Emerson, Centenary Address," *Four American Leaders* (Boston, 1906), pp. 78–126.

6. Dwight says: "It is a fact of some significance that the interest here felt in Beethoven began at the same moment with the interest in Emerson" ("Music a Means of Culture," *Atlantic*, XXVI, 321–331, Sept. 1870).

Dwight's definition of musical composition strikingly resembles Emerson's "spiral form": "It is the most fluid, free expression of form, in the *becoming* . . . form developing according to intrinsic and divine necessity" (*Atlantic*, XXVI, 614–625, Nov. 1870).

7. Possibly Emerson's reluctance to take the leap over to complete idealism was based on his early reading in the Scotch metaphysicians — Reid, Brown, Stewart, and Mackintosh — whose "common sense" system affirmed the reality of both spirit and matter. Reid and Brown he studied as college texts, and Stewart and Mackintosh he was reading attentively in the years 1832–33.

8. Although this study was not published until after Emerson's death (*Works*, XII, 1–110), he was beginning to formulate some of the ideas for the London lectures in 1848, which he presented again at Cincinnati in 1857–58, and reworked for the Harvard lectures of 1870.

9. Coleridge, *The Friend* (London, 1837), 3 vols., I, 266–270. Cf. *Biographia Literaria* (Boston, 1834), p. 98.

10. Carlyle, "State of German Literature," *Works*, 30 vols. (New York, 1896–99), I, 81–83.

11. See, for example, his statements in Ms. J.B, 1835: "I should be glad of a Catalogue of Ideas; Objects of the Reason, as Conceptions are objects of the Understanding. Mr. Coleridge names a Point, a Line, a Circle, as Ideas in Mathematics. God, Free Will, Justice, Holiness, as Ideas in Morals." Cf. Emerson's comment on Kant's overemphasis of the categorical imperative, in an undated manuscript fragment on Goethe.

12. See, for example, *L.*, I, 412–413, 1834; "Plato," *Works*, IV, 61; *J.*, III, 340.

13. Cf. I Corinthians 15:42–44: "It is sown in corruption; it is raised in incorruption. It is sown in dishonour; it is raised in glory. . . It is sown a natural body; it is raised a spiritual body."

14. To the limited definition of a mystic as one who follows a definite religious regimen, proceeding through a recognized number of "steps" before reaching union with God, Emerson does not of course conform. Such a definition is the basis on which Professor Patrick Quinn concludes that Emerson cannot be called a mystic ("Emerson and Mysticism," *American Literature*, XXI, 397–414, Jan. 1950). Professor Quinn admits, however, that Rufus Jones, a recognized authority on the mystical experience, employed a broader definition of the term, and considered Emerson a mystic. Actually Emerson has given in the body of his writing more statements than Professor Quinn has discovered concerning his experiences of union with the Divine. Professor Quinn further ignores Emerson's close reading of such mystics as Jacob Boehme and of Neo-Platonic writers other than Plotinus — notably Proclus and Iamblichus. For further clarification of my

use of the terms "mystic" and "mysticism," see Introduction, pp. 9–13; Chapter I, pp. 17–21, 50–53, and Chapter III, pp. 198–208.

15. George Santayana, *Interpretations of Poetry and Religion* (New York, 1924), pp. 230–231.

16. Irving Babbitt, *The Masters of Modern French Criticism* (Boston, 1912), p. 392.

17. H. L. Mencken, "An Unheeded Law-Giver," *Prejudices, First Series* (New York, 1919), pp. 191–194.

18. For the relation to Platonism and Neo-Platonic thought, see John S. Harrison, *The Teachers of Emerson* (New York, 1910), and Frederic Ives Carpenter, *Emerson and Asia* (Cambridge, 1930). For the relation to Calvinism, see Perry Miller, "From Edwards to Emerson," *New England Quarterly*, XIII, 589–617 (Dec. 1940). For the relation to the Scotch school, see William Charvat, *Origins of American Critical Thought* (Philadelphia, 1936). For the relation to German idealism, see René Wellek, "Emerson and German Philosophy," *New England Quarterly*, XVI, 41–63 (March 1943).

CHAPTER ONE: THE CREATIVE PROCESS

1. Proclus, *Commentaries on the Timaeus*, tr. by Thomas Taylor, 2 vols. (London, 1820), II, 444. Passage marked by Emerson as "impassive soul in passive body."

2. Thus Iamblichus distinguished enthusiasm from intellect, in which the soul apprehends forms, and from dianoetic power, in which it understands science. Enthusiasm, he states, passes from the gods to the human soul, affecting it above the reflective powers, and so inspiring it that even the body is illuminated (*On the Mysteries of the Egyptians*, transl. by Thomas Taylor, Chiswick, 1821, pp. 350–351). This passage is a quotation from Proclus, *Commentaries on the Timaeus*.

3. *Ibid.*, p. 351.

4. Ms. J. IT, after 1868.

5. Ms. J. PH, 1869.

6. For an early passage showing Emerson's interest in this problem, with reference to Edwards, see *J.*, I, 286–287, 1823.

7. Jonathan Edwards, *Works*, 8 vols. (Worcester, Mass., 1808–09), V, 9–334.

8. *Ibid.*, IV, 9–416.

9. Plotinus, "A Discussion of Doubts Relative to the Soul," *Select Works*, tr. Taylor (London, 1817), p. 365.

10. Emerson's own longing for the mystical state is well expressed by his comment: "Do you think I am in such great terror of being shot, I who am only waiting to shuffle off my corporeal jacket to scud away into the

back stars, and put diameters of the solar system and millions of sidereal orbits between me and all souls, there to wear out ages in solitude, and forget memory itself, if it be possible?" (Ms. J. SO, 1856).

11. Proclus, *Six Books on the Theology of Plato*, tr. by Thomas Taylor, 2 vols. (London, 1816), I, 8–10. Passage marked by Emerson.

12. *J.*, 1838.

13. *L.*, II, 405–406, 1841.

14. Plato, *Works*, ed. Sydenham and Taylor, 5 vols. (London, 1804), V, 461–462.

15. Thomas Reid, *Works*, 4 vols. (Charlestown, 1813), I, 196.

16. *Ibid.*, I, 376–377.

17. The printed version in "Natural History of Intellect" contains the term *percipiency*; the ms. lecture on Instinct, Perception and Talent (1866), from which the printed version was taken, uses *recipiency*.

18. Plotinus, "A Discussion of Doubts Relative to the Soul," *Select Works*, p. 365. Cf. also the passage marked by Emerson in this work, as an extract by Plotinus from Synesius' treatise on *Providence*, on the two pairs of eyes, one for contemplation, one for action, one closed while the other is opened (*ibid.*, p. 531).

19. Plato, "Epistle VII," *Works*, ed. Bohn (London, 1855), IV, 524.

20. Reid, *Works*, I, 279.

21. Ms. J. IL, after 1868.

22. Ms. J. DO, 1852.

23. Plotinus, "A Discussion of Doubts Relative to the Soul," *Select Works*, pp. 380–381.

24. Emanuel Swedenborg, *Animal Kingdom*, tr. Augustus Clissold, 2 vols. (London, 1845), II, 354.

25. Carlyle, "Heroes and Hero-Worship," *Works*, V, 105.

26. Carlyle explains Fichte's "Divine Idea" (as explained in *Über das Wesen des Gelehrten*), as the reality which lies at the bottom of appearance, visible not to the mass of men, but only to the gifted writer (*ibid.*, V, 156).

27. Coleridge, *Biographia Literaria*, p. 90.

28. Ms. J. IL, after 1868.

29. Plotinus, "A Discussion of Doubts Relative to the Soul," *Select Works*, pp. 320–321.

30. Charles J. Woodbury, *Talks with Ralph Waldo Emerson* (New York, 1890).

31. Dugald Stewart, "Elements of the Philosophy of the Human Mind," *Works*, 7 vols. (Cambridge, 1829), I, 359.

32. Ms. J. PH, 1869.

33. For a fuller discussion of Emerson's criticism of Tennyson, see Chapter II, pp. 120–121.

34. Carl F. Strauch, "The Background for Emerson's 'Boston Hymn,'" *American Literature*, XIV, 36–47 (March 1942).

35. Benedetto Croce, *Aesthetic*, tr. Douglas Ainslie (London, 1922), pp. 1–15.

CHAPTER TWO: THE WORK OF ART

1. "Art," *Works*, VII, 38–39. With a few omissions, this second essay on "Art" is the same as that in the *Dial*, I, 367–378 (Jan. 1841).

2. For a fuller discussion of Emerson's adaptation of Cudworth's thought, see my article, "Plastic Nature and Transcendental Art," to appear in *American Literature*.

3. *J.*, V, 376. Cf. Plotinus' statement, translated by Emerson from Goethe's German: "Also [*sic*] was in art a far greater beauty, since not that form which resides in art came to the stone, but that remains where it was, and there went out into the stone another, inferior, which does not abide pure in itself, nor quite as the artist wishes, but only as far as the material world would obey Art" (quoted in *J.*, IV, 218, from Goethe, *Letters to Zelter*, pp. 38–39, tr. from Plotinus, *Ennead* V, lib. viii, c.l. p. 541, ed. Marsil. Ficinus, Basil., 1615).

4. Ms. J. AZ, 1850.

5. "The form is mechanic, when on any given material we impress a predetermined form, not necessarily arising out of the properties of the material; — as when to a mass of wet clay we give whatever shape we wish it to retain when hardened. The organic form on the other hand is innate; it shapes, as it develops itself from within, and the fulness of its development is one and the same with the perfection of its outward form. Such is the life, such is the form" (F. T. Raysor, ed., *Coleridge's Shakespearean Criticism*, 2 vols., Cambridge, 1930, I, 224).

6. Ms. J. B. Pt. II, 1836.

7. Ms. J. NO, 1855.

8. Ms. J. IO, 1854. Emerson remarks that, though Channing did not like the landscape, his dog did: "He strode gravely as a bear through all the sentimental parts, and fitted equally well with the grave and the gay scenes. He has a stroke of humor in his eye, as if he enjoyed his master's jokes" (Ms. J. VS, 1853).

9. Ms. J. BO, 1850.

10. Francis Bacon, "Advancement of Learning," Book II, *Works*, 10 vols. (London, 1824), I, 102–104; II, 152. Passage marked in Emerson's copy. Emerson remarks in his journal (1830) that Bacon's own investigation was confined within narrower limits than the universal principles of "prima philosophia," namely: "to the discovery of the 'form,' that is, the *essential*

nature of physical things, as the nature of whiteness, or heat . . . and secondly, the discovery of 'final Causes,' as why we have eyebrows, etc."

11. *Ibid.*, I, 187.

12. Emerson quotes Goethe: "We meet in Bacon's writings some such axioms which he with special stress harps upon; e.g., the doctrine of final causes is particularly odious to him" (*Werke*, 55 vols., Stuttgart and Tübingen, 1828–33, XIII, 157) in Ms. J. C, 1837. Emerson had of course known Bacon's theory before he read Goethe.

13. "Art," *Works*, VII, 52. Cf. Emerson's translation of Goethe: "The great Art-works are, like the highest works upon nature of Man, after true and natural laws executed. Everything arbitrary, fanciful perishes; where is necessity, there is God" (*Werke*, XXIX, 80; tr. in Ms. J. B, 1836).

14. Sampson Reed, *Observations on the Growth of the Mind* (London, 1827), p. 37.

15. Emanuel Swedenborg, *Principia*, 2 vols. (London, 1845), II, 531.

16. G. Oegger, *The True Messiah* . . . (Boston, 1842), pp. 5–6. This, Elizabeth Peabody's translation from the French, *Le Vrai Messie* . . . (Paris, 1829), was evidently in Emerson's hands in manuscript before it was published, since the phrasing of his extracts in the journal for 1835 is identical with that of her version (*J.*, III, 512–515, and Ms. J. B).

17. Ms. J. D, Pt. I, 1838. No doubt Emerson's theory of evil and of compensation derives something from Dr. Charles Bell's Bridgewater treatise, *The Hand* (London, 1833). Although Emerson's copy was not published until 1835 (Philadelphia), he must have read Bell in a periodical, since his Blotting Book IV (1830) cites a passage from the work on the composure and cheerfulness observed by Bell in incurable patients. Emerson used this passage in 1843 in his *Dial* essay on "The Tragic."

18. Plotinus, *Select Works*, tr. Taylor, p. 84. Passage marked by Emerson.

19. Though Wren had little opportunity to observe Greek art, he expresses respect for its principles, and Emerson frequently cites him as authority for such Greek ideas as symmetry and proportion (see, for example, *J.*, IV, 100–101). Emerson found most of his quotations from Wren in "Life of Sir Christopher Wren," *Lives of Eminent Persons*, Library of Useful Knowledge, vol. III (London, 1833). Emerson apparently read with some care the first two volumes of this series, concerning the Elgin and Phigaleian Marbles (London, 1833). Emerson notes Flaxman's comments on the Theseus as an embodiment of "anatomical" as well as ideal truth (II, 7) and of the care with which the sculptor finished the backs of Ceres and Proserpine, unnoticed by most observers (II, 9).

20. In our time Robinson Jeffers' recasting of Greek tragedy in modern mold has adjusted the focus somewhat by revealing the violence and bru-

tality which existed along with the *edle Einheit und stille Grösse* by which the romantics characterized Greek culture.

21. As these casts were made from the originals, a procedure no longer considered practical, they were unusually fine, and perhaps give a better sense of the originals than modern casts can do. Of those listed by Emerson from the original gift, only the Discobulus still remains in the Athenaeum.

22. Archibald Alison, *Essays on Taste* (Boston, 1812), pp. 276–291. Christopher Wren also expresses the idea of Greek beauty as derived from fitness (*Lives of Eminent Persons*, Library of Useful Knowledge, III, 4).

23. This description probably owes something to Goethe's lyrical passage on the Strasbourg Cathedral ("On German Architecture, 1773," J. E. Spingarn, *Goethe's Literary Essays*, London, 1921, p. 9). In Ms. J. D, Pt. I (1838), Emerson speaks of Goethe's "apostrophe" to Erwin of Steinbach and his minster. In his essay on "Modern Literature" Emerson remarks Goethe's conception of architecture as based on natural forms.

24. "The Problem" embodies the poetic expression of this idea:
Earth proudly wears the Parthenon,
As the best gem upon her zone,
And Morning opes with haste her lids
To gaze upon the Pyramids;
O'er England's abbeys bends the sky,
As on its friends with kindred eye.

25. See Ms. J. D, Pt. I, 1838, and J., V, 26, 68, for Emerson's transcriptions from Arnold Heeren, *Historical Researches into the Politics, Intercourse, and Trade of the Carthaginians, Ethiopians, and Egyptians*, 2 vols. (Oxford, 1832), II, 254, 369. Emerson was also interested in the comments made on Egyptian art by his friend Samuel G. Ward, who was in Egypt at the same time as Emerson, though the two parties did not meet. Emerson records in Ms. J. ST (1873), Ward's letter of Dec. 20, 1872, from Siout, Egypt, in which Ward describes the graceful dress of the Egyptians against the background of mosques and palms, compares the antiquity of the pyramids to that of the fixed stars, and adds: "My mind tries to seize it, but Homer and Moses remain obstinately my standard of antiquity, and the Egyptians as modern as the English."

26. Emerson speaks of the advance made in Renaissance mansions over the "fortresses" of the Middle Ages for more expansive, social living. Thus he praises the invention of the Marquise de Rambouillet in making doors and windows wide and high, and placing the staircase on one side, in order to have a suite of chambers in enfilade (Ms. J. HO, 1853–54).

This allowance for decoration in architecture is at variance with the often-heard modern dictum that form must admit no design unless it fulfills a necessary function.

27. For Emerson's visit to the Duchess of Sutherland at Stafford House in 1848, see *L.*, IV, 89–90.

28. Horatio Greenough, "Aesthetics at Washington," Tuckerman, *A Memorial of Horatio Greenough* (New York, 1853), p. 77. Emerson records in Ms. J. VS (1853), an interesting observation of Greenough on the "organic form" of the human body: "He saw a man starved to death and he crouched down precisely into the figure of a child in the womb."

29. In Ms. J. NY (1868) Emerson records a number of quotations from Greenough concerning architectural form, but, convinced of our "excessive native strength," he fails to share Greenough's concern over European importation.

30. Edward L. Garbett, *Rudimentary Treatise on the Principles of Design in Architecture* (London, 1850). Such a modern architect as Frank Lloyd Wright, for example, agrees with Emerson that architecture must satisfy human needs, but at no time shares the Ruskinian point of view (which prevails in Garbett's treatise) that specific human qualities, as sacrifice, truth, or power, can be detected in buildings (see, e.g., Wright, *Modern Architecture*, Princeton, 1931, pp. 27, 36, 39).

31. "Art," *Works*, II, 368.

32. Surely Professor Michaud over-extends Emerson's interest in the useful arts when he says: "He forecast modern industrial development and the triumph of mechanical arts in the United States. He outlines an aesthetic of the machine. . . His aesthetic . . . especially fits a people of pioneers and builders (*L'Esthétique d'Emerson*, pp. 21–22). One can hardly make Emerson's organic principle the nucleus of an "aesthetic of the machine" — unless by postulating a transcendental machine, to derive its power as well as its inspiration from the air.

33. Emerson's English journal for 1848 (Ms. J. LM) contains an interesting record of Coventry Patmore's ideas of architecture, which Patmore explained to him in conversation. Patmore's idea closely parallels Emerson's, with fuller illustration: in the Gothic he detects a combination of "growth and geometry," which he illustrates by such ornaments as the ball-flower; in the Egyptian he finds the key in the use of base, as with the pyramid; in the Greek, competence of support, the flutes of the Doric column representing the upward principle and the metopes, the descending.

34. Comparing Michelangelo with Raphael in respect to organic form, Emerson finds Michelangelo more "organic," since he would proceed from skeleton to flesh, while Raphael would work from nude to draped figure (Ms. J. E, Pt. I, 1839).

35. Bernard Berenson, *Aesthetics and History in the Visual Arts* (New York, 1948), p. 185.

36. Emerson's Blotting Book Y (1829–30) records the same term of reproach, "stone dolls," from Spence, as credited to Ramsay.

37. Ms. J. F, 1840.

38. *L.*, I, 347, 1832. Emerson takes note of similar good sense shown by Thomas Appleton, who managed the fund for the statue of Franklin in front of the City Hall, and who had $15,000 subscribed before Richard Greenough began work on it (*L.*, IV, 461, 1854).

39. *L.*, III, 114, 1843.

40. First lecture on Italy, 1834.

41. *J.*, 1833.

42. *J.*, 1834.

43. Giorgio Vasari, *Lives of the Most Eminent Painters, Sculptors, and Architects*, 2 vols. (London, 1851), II, 390, 393 (passages marked by Emerson in his copy). Ms. J. CO (1851) contains notes from Vasari on Raphael, Piero di Cosimo, and Correggio.

44. Ms. J. O, 1846. Emerson notes that the Danie was taken by Caroline Sturgis.

45. Emerson mentions his receiving a print of Correggio's Madonna from Ward's friend Haggerty (*L.*, III, 58, 1842).

46. *J.*, 1851. Emerson states that Allston violates the organic principle when he allows the beards on his "Polish Jews" to overwhelm the human characteristics so that the faces resemble satyrs or goats rather than men (*J.*, 1839).

47. Ms. J. AZ, 1850.

48. Ms. J. H, 1841.

49. *J.*, 1839.

50. Lecture on the Eye and Ear, 1837.

51. Ms. J. F, 1840.

52. Ms. fragment on Art and Nature, 1868.

53. Ms. fragment on Beauty, 1860.

54. Lecture on England, 1849. See Gustav F. Waagen, *Treasures of Art in Great Britain* (London, 1854).

55. This disappointment was alleviated by his meeting the American artists Cranch, Wall, Alexander, and Thorwaldsen at Rome, as well as the English sculptors Gibson and Wyatt, and Greenough at Florence.

56. Lecture on Art, 1861.

57. Emerson drew most of his material on the Anglo-Saxons from James Mackintosh, *History of England* (London, 1830), vol. I of the Cabinet Cyclopedia, in which he made extensive notes. Later he continued his reading about Alfred and Arthur in J. A. Giles, *Six Old English Chronicles* (London, 1848).

58. Besides the essay in *Representative Men*, Emerson gave two lectures on Shakespeare in 1835, readings in 1869, and scattered comments in the *Journals* and *Letters*. His reading covers the *Sonnets*, *Venus and Adonis*,

and some twenty plays, including a few that are still caviar to the general —
Coriolanus, Troilus and Cressida, Measure for Measure.

59. There are some exceptions to this general comment. Mention of
passion appears in Emerson's recording Alcott's comment after seeing
Midsummer Night's Dream played, that "it was a phallus to which fathers
could carry their daughters, and each had their own thoughts, without sus-
pecting that the other had the same" (Ms. J. SO, 1856). Emerson's comment
on hearing Mrs. Dallas Glyn read the dialogue between Antony and
Cleopatra shows a sense of the importance of real dramatic action. Though
Mrs. Glyn varied her voice to show the two parts, it seemed to Emerson
that she did not really feel the "great passages," and that "she ought to go
on the stage, where the interruption by the other actors would give her
the proper relief" (Ms. J. ST, 1870).

60. Emerson records in Ms. J. C, Pt. I (1837), Goethe's statement that all
advancing epochs are objective, while all receding periods (like his own)
are subjective (*Conversations with Eckermann*, 2 vols., Boston, 1839, I, 240).

61. Ms. J. E, 1839.

62. Ms. J. AZ, 1849.

63. Ms. fragment, The Sovereignty of Ethics, 1877.

64. Ms. J. C, 1837.

65. *L.*, IV, 179, 1850.

66. Ms. J. Y, 1845.

67. Ms. J. E, 1839.

68. Ms. fragment, The Fortune of the Republic, 1878.

69. Hugh Blair, *Lectures on Rhetoric* (Philadelphia, 1833), p. 150.

70. In Ms. J. B (1835), Emerson copies Oegger's statement on the idea:
"The passage from the language of nature to language of convention is
made by . . . insensible degrees . . . Primitively men could not name objects they must show them; not corporeally it is true but substantially and
by force of thought as those objects exist in God and as we still view them
in dreams" (*True Messiah*, p. 15). Emerson's addition of a note to Reed
here shows that he associates the two theories of language.

71. Ms. J. ZO, 1856.

72. Emerson may well have been attracted by the catalogue description
of the Venus de' Medici (#15 in the Athenaeum 1840 exhibit) where this
Anadyomene or Marine Venus is described as "formed from a mass of
white foam," "first seen floating on the sea," "afterwards driven by the
billows to the island of Cyprus, where the mass suddenly opened, and this
beautiful Goddess issued from it."

73. Cf. the "Ode to Beauty":

Thee gliding through the sea of form,
Like the lightning through the storm,
Somewhat not to be possessed,

Somewhat not to be caressed.
Thou eternal fugitive.
Hovering over all that live.

74. For a good survey of this question, see Harry Hayden Clark, "Emerson and Science," *Phil. Quarterly*, X, 225–260 (July 1931).

75. G. Cuvier, *A Discourse on the Revolutions of the Surface of the Globe*, tr. from the French (Philadelphia, 1835), p. 184.

76. John Herschel, *Astronomy* (London, 1833), p. 22.

77. Peter Roget, *Animal and Vegetable Physiology*, Treatise V of the Bridgewater Treatises, 2 vols. (Philadelphia, 1836), I, 52.

78. "Swedenborg," *Works*, IV, 112–116. For passages marked by Emerson in his copy, see Augustus Clissold, "Introduction," Swedenborg, *Animal Kingdom*, II, lxxvii–lxxviii.

79. The protest from Swedenborgians concerning *Representative Men* (which still appears in modern criticism) was mildly expressed by Emerson's friend J. J. G. Wilkinson, who wrote from Hampstead, England, in 1850, that Emerson's statement of Swedenborg would require "some tough work" to reverse, that Swedenborg apart from his mystic dreams knew more of the spiritual world than Emerson gave him credit for, but that he wholly agrees with Emerson "that the spiritual world is not absolute but fluxional" (Emerson, *L.*, IV, 175).

80. In a late manuscript fragment, Notes on Thoreau, Emerson records Thoreau's own statement from his journal, 1840, on "the hound": "A good book will not be dropped by its author but thrown up. It will be so long a promise that he will not overtake it soon. He will have slipped the leash of a fleet hound." Emerson adds: "The bay horse might be such command of property as he desired, and the turtle dove might be the wife of his dream."

81. Ms. J. Z, Pt. II, 1842–43.

82. Ms. J. DL, 1866. Ellen's objection appears in "Poetry and Imagination" as that of "a young student," who "does not wish to know what the leopard, the wolf, or Lucia signify in Dante's Inferno, but prefers to keep their veils on."

83. Ms. J. B, Pt. II, 1836.

84. Ms. J. TU, 1849.

85. Ms. J. HO, 1848.

86. William Blake, "On the Bard," *Descriptive Catalogue*, Works, eds. Ellis and Yeats, 3 vols. (London, 1893), II, 373.

87. Emerson G. Sutcliffe, "Emerson's Theories of Literary Expression," *U. Illinois Studies in Language and Literature*, VIII, 17–20 (Feb. 1923).

88. Hugh Blair, *Lectures on Rhetoric*, pp. 158–169.

89. *J.*, 1833. For a fuller explanation of Goethe's effect, see my article, "The Influence of Goethe on Emerson's Aesthetic Theory," *Phil. Quarterly*, XXVII, 325–344 (Oct. 1948).

90. Although Emerson apparently studied Aristotle very little at first hand, he was familiar with Bacon's statement of the distinction between poetry and history, which he marked both in his Latin copy, *De Augmentis Scientiarum*, and in the English, "Advancement of Learning," *Works*, I, 90. He frequently cites Bacon's phrase that poetry submits "the shows of things to the desires of the mind."

91. Ms. J. FOR, 1863.

92. This sentence was printed in "Thoughts on Modern Literature," *Dial*, I, 137–158 (Oct. 1840).

93. Donald A. Stauffer, *The Intent of the Critic* (Princeton, 1941), p. 3. Compare Margaret Fuller's formula in "A Short Essay for Critics," *Dial*, I, 5–11 (July 1840).

94. Norman Foerster, *American Criticism*, p. 56.

95. This "high selection" sinks in importance when compared with the number of lists of great names which Emerson reads off, as if he took a satisfaction in their recital similar to a Catholic's recital of the rosary. The significant fact is that so many different names occur. Shakespeare, Homer, Herder are cited as examples of nonegotistic writers (*J.*, II, 233–234); Shakespeare, Milton, Bacon, as the only writers whose works he would save (*Works*, VII, 193–194); Homer and Aeschylus, Horace, Ovid and Plutarch; Erasmus, Scaliger, and Montaigne; Ben Jonson and Izaak Walton; Dryden and Pope, as ideal writers (*Works*, XII, 341); such disparate elements as *Laodamia*, James Naylor's dying words, an extract from Coleridge's *Friend*, and Sampson Reed's oration on *Genius*, as "the undying words of great men" (*J.*, V, 112).

96. Some of this material appears in "Europe and European Books," *Dial*, III, 511–521 (April 1843).

CHAPTER THREE: THE AESTHETIC EXPERIENCE

1. Professor Michaud recognizes but does not explore the element of response to art (*L'Esthétique d'Emerson*, p. 24). It is also mentioned by Donald MacRae, "Emerson and the Fine Arts," *Art Bulletin*, XX, 93 (March 1938).

2. *J.*, 1823.

3. *J.*, 1834.

4. *J.*, 1842.

5. *J.*, 1854.

6. *L.*, I, 379–380, 1833.

7. Coleridge, *The Friend*, I, 205–206.

8. Lecture on American Nationality, 1861.

9. *J.*, 1838.

10. *J.*, 1833.

a recognition long overdue to the importance of Allston's theory of

J., 1833. Cf. Chapter II, p. 93.

J., 1834.

J., 1831.

0. J., 1835.

31. J., 1837.

32. Ms. J. AZ, 1850.

33. J., 1861.

34. Goethe, *Correspondence with a Child* (Bettine von Arnim), 3 vols. London, 1839), II, 134.

35. J., 1838.

36. J., 1866.

37. J., 1843.

38. J., 1834.

39. J., 1833.

40. L., III, 75, 1842.

41. J., 1839.

42. C. D. Thorpe, "Empathy," *Dictionary of World Literature*, Joseph Shipley, ed. (New York, 1943), pp. 186–187.

43. Emerson may have picked up this reference to Homer from Joshua Reynolds' comment: "The effect of the capital works of Michael Angelo perfectly correspond [*sic*] to what Bouchardon said he felt from reading Homer; his whole frame appeared to himself to be enlarged, and all nature which surrounded him, diminished to atoms" ("Fifth Discourse," *Seven Discourses Delivered in the Royal Academy*, London, 1778, p. 169).

44. J., 1839.

45. In a lecture on Metres of Mind (1870) Emerson says: "We ought to come to a picture twenty times, in the light of twenty new views of man and nature." He quotes Winckelmann on the same point in a lecture on Johnson, Gibbon and Burke (1869): "The first sight of beautiful statues is to him who has feeling, like the first view of an open sea, in which the eye is dazzled by its infinity, but, by repeated contemplation, the mind grows calmer, and the eye more steady, and we pass from the whole to the detail." Apparently Emerson translated this passage from Winckelmann's German. Cf. Johann Winckelmann, *The History of Ancient Art*, tr. G. Henry Lodge, 4 vols. (Boston, 1872; 1st ed. 2 vols., 1856), III, 236.

46. L., I, 346, 1832.

47. J., 1841.

48. L., I, 344–345, 1832.

49. The craze for animal magnetism began with Mesmer's experiments in Paris in 1779, using a combination of hypnosis, magnets, and music to cure the sick. Although the Royal Commission reported unfavorably on

11. *Ibid.*

12. *J.,* 1868.

13. Emerson and others, *Memoirs of M*
1852), I, 267, 263.

14. In reading Alcott's *Conversations,* how
the compliment of that receptive attention whi
others. "I listen with joy," Emerson says, "I feel
hear and receive than to speak or do" (*J.,* 1836).

15. G. Battista Belzoni, *Egypt: Operations and .*
(London, 1820).

16. *J.,* 1833.

17. *J.,* 1836.

18. These statements appear in three lectures on the .
1875), parts of which are reproduced in the essays on ".
1875), and in specific references in the *Journals* and *Letter*
ers of his day.

19. Hugh Blair, *Lectures on Rhetoric,* pp. 341–387.

20. Samuel Pepys, *Memoirs,* 2 vols. (London, 1825), I, 469
1875 lecture on Eloquence.

21. Ms. J. AZ, 1850.

22. Hermes Trismegistus, *Works,* Bk. IV, tr. Everard (Lond
p. 53.

23. Ms. J. CO, 1851.

24. This comment was quoted by Emerson in his 1867 lect
Eloquence (without attribution to himself). A pencil notation perh:
Edward Emerson explains that Father Taylor made the statement abo
father.

25. Emerson has altered Mackintosh's phrasing: "Every poem, ev
history, every oration, every picture, every statue, is an experiment (
human feeling" (James Mackintosh, *A General View of the Progress o,*
Ethical Philosophy, Philadelphia, 1832, pp. 42–43). This was an article in
the first introductory volume of the seventh edition of *Encyclopaedia*
Britannica. Emerson has changed Mackintosh's "feeling" to "mind" and
has omitted the rest of the sentence, "the grand object of investigation by
the moralist," as irrelevant to the matter of mental reaction which he considers here.

26. A contemporary of Emerson, Washington Allston, also emphasizes
the importance of the observer's reaction in his theory of art, in *Lectures on*
Art . . . (Boston, 1850), pp. 70–73. Though Emerson knew Allston person-
ally and enjoyed his art, he gives no indication of acquaintance with his
theory, which Allston was formulating in the 1830's, at the time of
Emerson's early speculation about art. Edgar P. Richardson, in *Washington*
Allston, A Study of the Romantic Artist in America (Chicago, 1948), has

his activity in 1784, experiments in that line spread to England, to Scotland (see John Hughes Bennett, *The Mesmeric Mania of 1851*, Edinburgh, 1851), and to America. The use of table rapping in spiritualistic séances was especially popular in New England in the forties. For a favorable report on animal magnetism, see John C. Colquhoun, *Isis Revelata, an Inquiry into the Origin, Progress, and Present State of Animal Magnetism*, 2 vols. (Edinburgh, 1833, 2nd ed., 1836).

50. See, for example, this comment in Ms. J. D, Pt. I, 1838: "Eyes are bold as lions roving running leaping here and there . . . they . . . intrude and pierce and come and go through you in a moment of time. The eyes of an insane person seem to diminish the distance betwixt you and him. The power of eyes to charm down insanity or ferocity in beasts is a power behind the eye it must be a victory first achieved in the will before it can be signified in the eye."

51. Undated ms. fragment, Philosophy.

52. Compare Emerson's statement in the lecture on Poetry and Criticism (1860) where he likens the poet's putting speeches into his characters' mouths to man's similar act with the creatures of dream.

53. *J.*, 1838.

54. Lecture on Memory, 1871.

55. Lecture on Demonology, 1871.

56. *J.*, 1837.

57. Ms. J. RS, 1848.

58. DeWitt H. Parker, *The Analysis of Art* (New Haven, 1926), p. 33.

59. In this lecture on Genius Emerson quotes Michelangelo's Seventh Sonnet as an explanation of the complexity in beauty's effect: "I know not if it be the reflected light of its author which the soul perceives, or if from the memory, or from the mind, any other beauty shines through into the heart . . ."

60. *J.*, 1836.

61. Essay on "Beauty."

62. See Chapter I, p. 40.

63. *J.*, 1842.

64. Emerson explains in this passage that the same experience holds true of painting and poetry.

65. See Chapter I, pp. 33–34.

66. Walter Pater, "Winckelmann," *Studies in the Renaissance, Works*, 10 vols. (London, 1922–28), IX, 228.

67. Norman Foerster, *American Criticism*, pp. 107–109. The term "recreative escape" is used to denote the admission of the human spirit, through art, into a delightful aesthetic world where the observer is free from the responsibility demanded of him in actual life. It should be dis-

tinguished from the modern term "escapism" whose sociological connotations do not obtain in Emerson's thought.

68. *J.*, 1839.

69. Emerson was adapting here a passage he had recorded from Alcott's journal (1835), in his Ms. J. B, Pt. II: "The eloquence that bringeth the old men from their corners, and taketh the children, by surprise, from the delights of play, doth at the same time impress and commend itself to the man in the full glory of his powers . . ." (Alcott borrowed a phrase here from Sidney's *Defence of Poesie* on the poet's power).

70. John S. Dwight in the *Dial*, I, 124–134 (July 1840), mentions the pianists Rackemann and Kossowski, the singer Knight, and several small chamber-music concerts where Handel, Haydn, Mozart, and Beethoven have been played. Recognizing that Boston music is still in a pioneer state, he proposes frequent public performances of the best music, a constant audience, and some lectures on music — an interesting foreshadowing of what was accomplished forty years later in the founding of the Boston Symphony.

71. In his copy of Iamblichus Emerson marks the statements about Pythagorean use of music before sleeping and waking. (*On the Mysteries*, pp. 133–134), and says in his journal (1844): "Pythagoras was right, who used music as a medicine." Compare Emerson's statement in Ms. J. U (1843): "Every act of man has the ground tone and the high treble. Nothing but is dual, or goes through the gamut," echoing Plato's statement in the *Republic*, Bk. IV, about the attainment of justice by a good man: "Well establishing his own proper affairs, and holding the government of himself, adorning himself, and becoming his own friend, and attuning these three principles . . . as three musical strings, base, tenor, and treble (Taylor, *Works of Plato*, I, 285).

72. William Gardiner, *Music of Nature* (Boston, 1840).

73. "It is the wine which inspires new creations, and I am the Bacchus that crushes out this noble piece for mankind, and makes their spirits drunk; and when they are sobered, then you see what a world of things they have fished up to bring back with them to dry land again" (*Correspondence with a Child*, II, 207. Copied by Emerson in Ms. J. T, 1834).

74. An exception is this comment in the essay on "Beauty": "It is necessary in music, when you strike a discord, to let down the ear by an intermediate note or two to accord again."

75. Ms. J. BO, 1850. Despite his disapproval of them, Emerson has recorded some of these "going to hell" jokes, as, for example, the compliments bandied between Dr. Barrow and the Earl of Rochester, "I am yours to the shoe-tie," "to the antipodes," and so on, until the Earl says, "I am yours to the lowest pit of hell," and the Doctor replies, "And there, my Lord, I leave you."

76. Bronson Alcott, *Journals*, ed. Odell Shepard (Boston, 1938), p. 114.

77. Henry Steffens, *Story of My Career* (Boston, 1863), p. 104.

78. John Ruskin, *The Two Paths* (London, 1859), p. 152.

79. Thomas Hobbes, *Leviathan, Works*, 11 vols. (London, 1839–45), III, 46.

80. Henry D. Lloyd, "Emerson's Wit and Humor," *Forum*, XXII, 346–357 (Nov. 1896). Lloyd has preserved much of the oral tradition about Emerson's humor in this article.

81. See Chapter II, pp. 121–134.

82. *J.*, 1839.

83. Emerson was familiar with Schelling's and Goethe's high evaluation of the aesthetic "moment." In ms. lecture fragments, 1869, he transcribes this quotation from Goethe: "I have this year . . . found, that all efficient intelligent men, more or less fine or coarse, hereto come and remain, — that the moment is everything; and that the privilege of an intelligent man consists therein, — so to bear himself, that his life as far as in him lies, shall contain the greatest possible number of reasonable happy moments" (*Werke*, XXIX, 120).

84. A similar passage occurs in "The Over-soul."

85. W. Scott Palmer, ed., *The Confessions of Jacob Boehme* (London, 1920), p. 11.

86. A. Allen Brockington, *Mysticism and Poetry* . . . (London, 1934), pp. 135–136.

87. See Chapter I, pp. 40–60.

88. Evelyn Underhill, *Mysticism* (New York, 1911), p. 437.

89. William James, *Varieties of Religious Experience* (London, 1902), p. 197. For the relation between Emerson's and James' thought, see F. I. Carpenter, *New England Quarterly*, II, 458–474 (July 1929).

90. Rufus M. Jones, *New Studies in Mystical Religion* (New York, 1928), p. 187.

91. Brockington, *Mysticism and Poetry*, p. 131.

92. James H. Leuba, *The Psychology of Religious Mysticism* (London, 1925), p. 19.

93. *Ibid.*, p. 76.

94. Bosanquet, ed., *Introduction to Hegel's Philosophy of Fine Art* (London, 1905), pp. 181–186. For Hegel, romantic or Christian art is deemed superior to Egyptian or classical art in passing beyond sensuous medium to pure spirit. Samuel Gray Ward, with whose theory Emerson was familiar, divides the history of art into three periods which roughly resemble those outlined by Hegel ("Notes on Art and Architecture," *Dial*, III, 107–115, July, 1843). Ward differs from Hegel in his preference for "those early works, where art is only just able to shadow forth dimly the thought the master was burdened with."

95. Hegel, *op. cit.*, pp. 190–191.

96. *Ibid.*, pp. 203–206. Perhaps Hegel's ranking of poetry as most "spiritual" proceeds from the same source as Emerson's similar classification of music — both conclusions resulting from a "deafness" to the auditory appeal of the art that is judged dominantly "ideal."

97. *Ibid.*, p. 209.

98. Lecture on Correct Taste in English Literature, 1835.

99. The immediate power of the sublime over the human mind is attested by Longinus when he says: "Sublimity flashing forth at the right moment scatters everything before it like a thunderbolt" (*On the Sublime*, sect. I, tr. and ed. by W. Rhys Roberts, Cambridge, 1907, p. 53).

100. Emerson's discussion of the sublime has more relationship to the theories of Longinus and of Burke than to those of Alison or Hugh Blair. His analysis shows no likeness to Alison's location of the sublime in the principle of association (*Essays on Taste*, pp. 96–115), and very little likeness to Blair's analysis of the sublime through metaphor (*Lectures on Rhetoric*).

101. Emerson's fondness for the term "sublime" leads him to use it frequently not in an aesthetic sense, but merely to mean "lofty," as when he mentions man's "sublime hope," or the "sublime Destiny guiding the human race"; or in the sense of "hidden" as in those "sublimest laws" obscured from vulgar daylight but playing "through atoms and galaxies," or "the sublime silent desert" or the "inexhaustible sublimity" of Nature, which eludes the grasp of science.

102. Though this predilection is especially Emersonian, it has authority from Longinus, who says, "Sublimity is often comprised in a single thought" (*On the Sublime*, sect. XII, p. 77).

103. Longinus says: "Some passions are found which are far removed from sublimity and are of a low order, such as pity, grief and fear" (*ibid.*, sect. VIII, p. 59). On this point Emerson cites Landor with approval: "Where the heart is not moved, the gods stride and thunder in vain. The pathetic is the true sublime" (*J.*, 1834).

104. Lecture on Ethical Writers, 1835.

105. *J.*, 1836.

106. Emerson's interest here certainly differs from Burke's, since Emerson on the whole sees light as more inducive to the feeling of the sublime, while Burke states that darkness can more effectively arouse deep feelings than light can ("On the Sublime and the Beautiful," *Works*, 4 vols., Boston, 1806, I, sect. XIV, 125–126). Emerson does give an uncharacteristic (almost decadent) comment on the "dark" appeal of Kenilworth (*J.*, 1833).

107. Compare Burke: "Whatever is . . . terrible . . . is a source of the sublime" (*ibid.*, I, 88–89). "The passions which belong to self-preservation turn on pain and danger . . . they are delightful when we have an idea of

pain and danger, without being actually in such circumstances . . ." (*ibid.*, p. 100).

108. Ms. fragment on America, 1865.

109. *J.*, 1833.

110. *J.*, 1826, 1833.

111. Longinus writes: "When [Nature] ushers us into life and into the vast universe as into some great assembly, to be as it were spectators of the mighty whole and the keenest aspirants for honour, forthwith she implants in our souls the unconquerable love of whatever is elevated and more divine than we" (*On the Sublime*, sect. XXXV, pp. 133–134). "As if instinctively, our soul is uplifted by the true sublime; it takes a proud flight, and is filled with joy and vaunting, as though it had itself produced what it has heard" (*ibid.*, sect. VII, p. 55).

112. *J.*, 1851.

113. *J.*, 1835.

114. Essay on "Milton."

115. *J.*, 1863.

116. Lecture on Tests of Great Men, 1835.

Bibliography

This bibliography, which is intended to be selective, includes only the most important books and a brief analysis of the vital manuscript materials. The notes include references to secondary works and to various sources for Emerson's ideas which are not reprinted here.

PRINTED WORKS

I. *Primary*

A Correspondence between John Sterling and Ralph Waldo Emerson, Boston and New York, 1897.

Correspondence between Ralph Waldo Emerson and Herman Grimm, ed. by Frederick W. Holls, Boston and New York, 1903.

Letters from Ralph Waldo Emerson to a Friend [Samuel Gray Ward], ed. by Charles E. Norton, Boston and New York, 1899.

Memoirs of Margaret Fuller Ossoli, ed. by Emerson and others, Boston, 1852.

Parnassus, ed. by Ralph Waldo Emerson, Boston, 1875.

The Complete Works of Ralph Waldo Emerson, Centenary ed., Introduction and Notes by Edward W. Emerson, 12 vols., Boston, 1903–1904.

The Correspondence of Thomas Carlyle and Ralph Waldo Emerson, 2 vols., Boston, 1883.

The Dial: a Magazine for Literature, Philosophy, and Religion, 4 vols., Boston, 1841–1844.

The Journals of Ralph Waldo Emerson, ed. by Edward W. Emerson and Waldo E. Forbes, 10 vols., Boston, 1909–1914.

The Letters of Ralph Waldo Emerson, ed. by Ralph L. Rusk, 6 vols., New York, 1939.

Uncollected Lectures, ed. by Clarence Gohdes, New York, 1932.

II. *Secondary*

James Elliot Cabot, *A Memoir of Ralph Waldo Emerson*, 2 vols., Boston and New York, 1887.

Kenneth W. Cameron, *Ralph Waldo Emerson's Reading, a Guide*, Raleigh, 1941.

———, *Emerson the Essayist*, Raleigh, 1945.

George W. Cooke, *A Bibliography of Ralph Waldo Emerson*, Boston and New York, 1908.

Ralph L. Rusk, *The Life of Ralph Waldo Emerson*, New York, 1949.

MANUSCRIPTS

I. *Lectures*

Although Cabot's *Memoir* indicates the chronological order of the Lectures, and the sections which have been printed in the *Journals* or *Essays*, this early work does not reveal the extent of the unpublished material. Those lectures, for the most part unprinted, which have some bearing on aesthetics are here enumerated, with a brief description of their content, and reference to the published works in which sections have been printed.

Italy, I and II, 1834. Statements on Italian art.
Literature, 1835–36.

On the Best Mode of Inspiring a Correct Taste in English Literature, Aug., 1835.

Ten Lectures on English Literature (series developed historically).

I. Introductory, Nov. 5, 1835.
II. Permanent Traits of English National Genius, Nov. 12.
III. The Age of Fable, Nov. 19.
IV. Chaucer, Nov. 26.

V and VI. Shakespeare, Dec. 3 and 12.

VII. Lord Bacon, no date.

VIII. Ben Jonson, Herbert, Herrick, Wotton, no date.

IX. Ethical Writers, no date.

X. Byron, Scott, no date. Although the last four were not dated, VII and VIII were probably given in late December, IX and X in early January, 1836, according to Emerson's custom of giving series lectures about a week apart.

Philosophy of History (series), 1836–37.

III. Art. Human creation compared to divine. Partially printed in *Works*, II, 349–369, and VII, 35–57.

IV. Literature. Literature defined; contrasted with art. Partially printed in *Works*, II, 323–347, and *J.*, IV, 170–171.

Progress of Man (series), 1837.

I. Introduction. Art shown as a bridge between Ideal and Real, Past and Present.

IV. Eye and Ear. Sense impression as basis of beauty; the importance of art.

Human Life (series), 1838–39.

I. Doctrine of the Soul. Historical analysis of the nineteenth century.

X. Demonology, 1839. Material on dreams. Partially printed in *Works*, X, 3–28.

The Present Age (series), 1839.

III. Literature, II. Literature in relation to history and science.

New England (series), 1843.

IV. Literature and Spiritual Influences. Modern writing considered against earlier background.

Middlebury College, 1845. Problems of the creative artist. Partially printed in *Works*, X, 259–289.

Eloquence, 1847. Theory and practice. Repeated with some additions in 1867 and 1875. Partially printed in *Works*, VII, 59–100, and VIII, 109–133.

England, 1849. Elgin Marbles; art history.

Poetry and English Poetry, 1854. Parallels with science; metaphor.

Williamstown, 1854. Idealism in letters.

Mind and Manners in the Nineteenth Century (series), London, 1848. Psychological analysis; repeated with some expansion in 1857–58 and 1866 courses, and in Harvard Lectures, 1870. Partially printed in *Works*, XII, 1–110.

Freeman Place Chapel Series, 1859.
> IV. Art and Criticism. Sculpture; value of selection in art and literature. Partially printed in *Works*, XII, 281–305.

Beauty in Art, 1859, including Miscellany of Beauty (1860) and Greek Art (no date). Elgin Marbles, quotations from Winckelmann.

Life and Literature (series), 1861.
> I. Genius and Temperament. Fullest analysis of genius in contrast to talent.
> II. Art. Need to maintain artistic creation in spite of war's havoc. Partially printed in *Works*, III, 223–248, and *J.*, V, 27–28.
> IV. Some Good Books. The Neo-Platonists.
> V. Poetry and Criticism in England and America. Distinction of levels in creation and reception of poetry. Importance both of poetry and criticism. Examples from Tennyson.
> VI. Boston. Her literary achievement and advantages of her environment. Partially printed in *Works*, XII, 181–211.

Father Taylor, 1866. Example of pure inspiration in eloquence.

Meionaon Series, 1868.
> I. Nature and Art (not listed by Cabot). Organic form, architecture, art criticism, quotation from Lessing.
> IV. Leasts and Mosts. The microcosm.

Readings in English Literature (series), 1869. Shakespeare and the seventeenth-century religious writers.

II. *Journals*

Unprinted material occurs here in a less concentrated form than in the Lectures, for the most part as sentences or paragraphs between printed sections. Only a few manuscript journals which are particularly rich are therefore indicated.

Ms. J. T, 1834. Statements of humor, comments on national characteristics, quotations from Coleridge and the Neo-Platonists.

Ms. J. RO, 1835. Laws of "first philosophy."

Ms. J. B, 1835–36. Comments on aesthetic form, art and science, philosophy, quotations from Goethe.

Ms. J. C, 1837. Comments on the age, inspiration, music.

Ms. J. Z, 1837. Quotations from the Neo-Platonists.

Ms. J. F, 1840. Art as creation.

Ms. J. AZ, 1850. Comments on art, eloquence, and the age; quotations from Stallo.

Ms. J. ZO, 1856. Material on poetry and imagination.

Ms. J. WAR, 1862. Impact of war upon letters.

Ms. J. NY, 1868. Statements on organic form; quotations from Greenough.

Ms. J. PH, 1869. Quotations and statements on philosophy and imagination.

Index

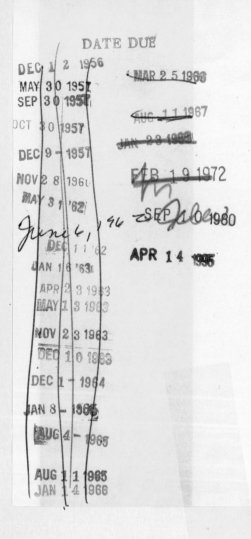

DATE DUE

DEC 1 2 1956	MAR 2 5 1966
MAY 30 1957	
SEP 30 1957	AUG 1 1 1967
OCT 30 1957	JAN 2 3 1968
DEC 9 - 1957	
NOV 2 8 1960	FEB 1 9 1972
MAY 3 1 '62	
June 6, '96	SEP 10 1980
DEC 1 1 '62	APR 14 1995
JAN 1 6 '63	
APR 2 3 1963	
MAY 1 3 1963	
NOV 2 3 1963	
DEC 1 0 1983	
DEC 1 - 1964	
JAN 8 - 1965	
AUG 4 - 1965	
AUG 1 1 1965	
JAN 1 4 1966	